**Books are to be returned on or before
the last date below.**

Loan Receipt
Liverpool John Moores University
Library Services

Borrower Name: Wong,Joanne
Borrower ID: **********8112

Adventure, mystery and romance :
31111013849714
Due Date: 27/09/2013 23:59

Romancing the postmodern /
31111006325821
Due Date: 27/09/2013 23:59

Total Items: 2
15/07/2013 13:56

Please keep your receipt in case of
dispute.

ROMANCING THE POSTMODERN

How has postmodernism encountered the figure of woman? Have the seductions of theory obscured the theoretical implications of romance? By exposing the theory of romance to the romance of theory, Diane Elam explores literature's most uncertain, least easily definable and most tenacious genre, assessing its implications for both feminism and the understanding of history.

Arguing for a parallel between postmodernism's divided relation to modernism and romance's difficult stance towards realism, *Romancing the Postmodern* not only highlights how postmodernism questions our assumptions about historical time, it also reintroduces the figure of woman to the theory of both history and literature.

Beginning with an analysis of how both romance and postmodernity disrupt the received categories of philosophy and literary theory, the book moves on to develop a theoretical stance of its own that weaves together feminism and deconstruction to argue for a postmodern feminism. Elam reaches back into the legacies of literature's greatest romance novelists – from Sir Walter Scott, George Eliot, and Joseph Conrad through to the postmodern "romances" of Italo Calvino, Kathy Acker, and Jacques Derrida – to illuminate the unorthodox function of romance from widely differing points of view.

Bringing together feminist analyses of genre, culture, and history, *Romancing the Postmodern* also highlights the philosophical responsibility imposed by postmodernism: the call to displace received meanings and re-read history through the agency of gender.

Diane Elam is Assistant Professor of English at Indiana University.

ROMANCING THE POSTMODERN

Diane Elam

London and New York

First published 1992
by Routledge
11 New Fetter Lane, London EC4P 4EE

Simultaneously published in the USA and Canada
by Routledge
a division of Routledge, Chapman and Hall, Inc.
29 West 35th Street, New York, NY 10001

Typeset in 10 on 12 point Bembo by
Falcon Typographic Art Ltd, Edinburgh
Printed in Great Britain by
Clays Ltd, St Ives plc

British Library Cataloguing in Publication Data
A catalogue record for this book is available
from the British Library.

Library of Congress Cataloging in Publication Data
Elam, Diane
Romancing the postmodern / Diane Elam.
p. cm.
Includes bibliographical references and index.
1. English fiction – 19th century – History and criticism.
2. Italian fiction – 20th century – History and criticism.
3. Love stories – History and criticism. 4. Postmodernism
(Literature). 5. Feminism and literature. 6. Romances –
Appreciation. 7. Women and literature. 8. Romanticism. I.
Title. II. Title: Romancing the postmodern.
PR868.L69E4   1992
809.3′91 – dc20   91–33915

ISBN 0–415–05732–9
ISBN 0–415–07987–X (pbk)

For Roger Henkle
December 15, 1935 – October 5, 1991

CONTENTS

CONTENTS

ACKNOWLEDGMENTS

I owe thanks to those who read all or parts of the manuscript in its various stages: Roger Henkle, Stephen Melville, Sue Roe, Sabina Sawhney, Bennet Schaber, Kaja Silverman, and Hayden White. Robyn Wiegman unselfishly read and commented on this project at length. Virginia Blum, Steven Cohan, Martin Jay, Veronica Kelly, and Robert Robertson have also engaged me in discussions over the years that have informed and directed my work. I also owe thanks to Bill Readings, without whom this book would not have been.

My students at Bryn Mawr College provided me with a constant source of intellectual challenge and inspiration and always made me reconsider my own romance with the postmodern. A summer research grant in 1990 from Bryn Mawr College provided the financial inspiration to complete the manuscript.

My greatest debt for direction and guidance is to Roger Henkle who taught me the necessity of taking risks. It is my deepest sorrow that he did not live to see this particular wager paid off.

Grateful acknowledgment is made to the University of Chicago Press for permission to quote from Jacques Derrida, *The Post Card: from Socrates to Freud and Beyond*, copyright © 1987; to Grove Weidenfeld for permission to quote from Kathy Acker, *Don Quixote*, copyright © 1986, *My Death, My Life by Pier Paolo Pasolini/Literal Madness*, copyright © 1989, and *In Memoriam to Identity*, copyright © 1990; to Harcourt Brace Jovanovich, Inc. for permission to quote from Umberto Eco, *The Postscript to The Name of the Rose*, copyright © 1984, *The Name of the Rose*, copyright © 1983. Portions of chapter 1 appear in an altered form as "Postmodern Romance" in *Postmodernism Across the Ages*, ed. Bill Readings and Bennet Schaber (Syracuse, NY: Syracuse University Press, 1992). A section of chapter 5 appears in "Is Feminism the Saving Grace of Hermeneutics?", *Social Epistemology*, 5, no. 4 (1991).

INTRODUCTION: A PREFACE WHICH SHOULD HAVE BEEN A POSTSCRIPT

An excessive relationship: romance and postmodernism

"You can never have too much romance." Or at least so it says on the covers of many Harlequin romances. Harlequin would like us to believe that romance is by definition a genre incapable of being exhausted. There will always be room for another romance, since a reader can never read, an author never write, too many. I will be arguing in this book that the excess characteristic of romance extends beyond the dreams of marketing agents to surface within the "literary" novels of high culture as a signature of postmodernism. Romance, by virtue of its complex relation to both history and novelistic realism, will have been the genre to address the problematic of postmodernity in narrative fiction.

This seems all the more the case, given the uncanny persistence with which the term "romance" crops up in the works of postmodern novelists. When Umberto Eco, for example, alludes to *The Romance of the Rose* in the title of his novel *The Name of the Rose*, we may be inclined to set this down to a generic debt to the magical realism of Borges. Yet, alongside the labyrinthine structure of the library at the Abbey, we find an explicit deployment of the clichés and conventions of popular romance in Adso's affair, or the putative editor's difficulties with the manuscript. "Trashy" romance invades literary modernism; we recognize that this might not be accidental when Barbara Cartland's confessions of a popular novelist share their title with radical-feminist artist Barbara Kruger's leap onto the coffee table – *Love For Sale*.[1] In postmodernism, as in romance, the division between high and low culture, the study and the boudoir, becomes blurred.

Before going any further with this line of thought, it is worth

1

pointing out a possible readerly anxiety at the very onset of such a project as this. To suggest that romance is a signature of postmodernism may seem to be just the kind of marketing move which I claim not to be making. That is to say, to some my argument may seem like just another application of the postmodern retrofit kit: if you have a stodgy topic and wish to dress it up for contemporary theoretical consumption, simply add the word "postmodern" and you're guaranteed to find an audience of theory-goers. Just as a certain "pomo look" is guaranteed to sell staplers and coffee cups that perform virtually the same function as their less stylish predecessors, the suggestion that an idea or area of academic consideration is "postmodern" has become a way to fix the gaze of the theoretical consumer.

However, in putting the terms "romance" and "postmodernism" side by side, I want to suggest instead that both romance and postmodernism share a common concern with the persistence of excess, a concern that leads to a rethinking of history and culture. By calling attention to the excessive relationship between romance and postmodernism, this book works out two crucial questions side by side. It asks what the historical and cultural stakes are in the privileging of realism over romance in the tradition of the novel. And at the same time, it interrogates notions of temporality and writing to show how postmodernism can serve as a viable tool for feminist cultural analysis.

In the academic study of the novel, romance has traditionally been relegated to the condition of "women's writing," to the position of poorer step-sister; in contrast, postmodernism attempts to revalue romance in the name of female desire and discourse. If romance becomes the genre in which the problematic of postmodernism is situated, then the "figure of woman" enters into a complex relationship with the creation of cultural and critical discourse. To put it another way, postmodernism allows a re-evaluation of the relationship between romance and realism that helps us to think our way through the difficulties of contemporary feminism. Recent publishing history indicates that feminism has begun to consider its relation to postmodernity, and this book attempts to shift the site of its debate beyond questions of antagonism or blissful matrimony.[2]

My assumption is that the identification of romance as a woman's genre, the site of female fantasy, is not coincidental. By revaluing the romance of women's desires as "postmodern" rather than simply "unrealistic" or "foolish," I want to link feminism to

2

postmodernism's calling into question of the established rules of historical and cultural representation. If realism can only deal with woman by relegating her to romance, if real history belongs to men, and women's history is merely the fantasy of historical romance, postmodern cultural analysis of history and the "real" offers a way of revaluing female discourse.

This is a particularly pressing point for the contemporary academy, which should have more on its mind than postmodern retrofit kits. By contrast, a turn toward a consideration of the ways in which aesthetic concerns are also political and historical ones is in order. The problem, however, is that there is no simple formula for calculating the relationship among the aesthetic, the political, and the historical. Yet by examining postmodernism and romance in a way that works both along and behind historical "lines," we are able to understand the complexity of the relation among these three terms: aesthetics, politics, history. I want to suggest that romance and postmodernism come together in a claim that dislocates the problem of postmodernity from any simple historical period. If contemporary writers turn to the romance genre in order to make themselves "postmodern," this has less to do with fashion than with the fact that romance, by virtue of its troubled relation to both history and novelistic realism, has in a sense been postmodern all along. That is to say, this book is concerned with postmodernism as a way of thinking about history and representation more than with postmodernism as a name for contemporary movements in the arts.

It is in this context that romance, as a signature of the possibility of postmodernism, is always present to *modernist* discourse. Postmodernism, that is, does not simply come after modernism but is a counter-discourse on history and the real which modernism must repress in order to establish itself as the statement of the real. History is always a consideration, but what it might mean to be historical is a point of contestation. Thus, the relationship between postmodernism and romance does not allow for any straightforward historical narrative. Postmodernism is not a perspectival view on history; it is the rethinking of history as an ironic coexistence of temporalities, which is why this book cannot be structured as a chronological survey. Accordingly, this book is not, in the traditional sense, an orderly arrangement of literary history. It looks at Umberto Eco's work before Walter Scott's, considers Joseph Conrad's novels before George Eliot's, and it "frames" its discussion of romance and postmodernism with the contemporary – Eco on one side, Jacques Derrida and Kathy Acker on the other. And just as this account of romance is not historically continuous, nor is it by any means exhaustive. This study limits itself to texts that seem more than usually troubled by the nature of romance, be it in distinction to their own professed realism (Eliot), or as a problem in historiography (Conrad), or as a disruption of the distance that guarantees interpretation (Eco or Derrida), or as a dispersion of any female identity (Acker), or as a troubling of simple faith in historical and political representation (Scott). This cast of characters is not what one might "realistically" call "representative" of a tradition. It is, perhaps lamentably, eurocentric, but it is so in the interests of decentering the European tradition of representation.[3] Within that tradition, differing historical rhythms coexist and, in a sense, agitate romance sometimes in spite of itself – returning us each time to a consideration of the political and the historical alongside the aesthetic.

What romance is not

With this said, I would now like to slow down for a moment to consider more carefully the terms of this discussion. I want to spend some time looking at how "romance" and "postmodernism" have been defined in the past and how I am going to deploy these definitions within the context of this project. It's tempting to try to find an easy definition of "romance," a quick fix, the stuff of guides to literary terminology. Why not, the ambitious student of literature might ask, go along with M. H. Abrams's glossary definition of romance as a narrative which represents "a courtly and chivalric age"?[4] The problem with this approach is not so much that it's "wrong," that Abrams or the hypothetical student have missed the boat. Rather, the generic function of romance is a complexity that belies such singular definition.

Romance, as an aesthetic term, uses and abuses conventional categories of genre. By this I mean that if we were to collect together the various conceptions of what the romance genre would form, we find that they cover a wide range of often widely divergent materials which simply do not seem to fit one generic category very comfortably. From high to low culture, from Emily Brontë to Barbara Cartland, from concerns with periodicity to concerns for thematic content, romance roams the range of aesthetic considerations.

It is more useful to begin by taking common ways of understanding romance and inverting them so as to come to an understanding of what romance is *not*. Romance is not just the kind of love story found next to the candy bars in supermarket checkout lanes: titles like *Always Love* or *Pagan Adversary* do not tell us all we need to know about romance. Similarly, romance is not restricted to medieval tales of brave and handsome knights or to novels opening on dark and stormy nights: romances do not need to begin, as does Chrétien de Troyes's tale of Lancelot, at the behest of "my lady of Champagne," nor do they need to have elements, in the way of Bulwer Lytton's *Paul Clifford*, which give rise to things which go bump in the night.

What is more important for us to recognize is that "romance" exists as a contradictory term from the start – that there is a problem with defining what a romance *must* do.[5] The examples I have just given go a long way in illustrating this point – Harlequin authors do not write the same kind of texts to which Chrétien de Troyes or Bulwer Lytton laid claim (for better or for worse).

I would like to make this point of contradiction even clearer by taking another example. On the one hand, romance *can* define a narrative that, according to one *OED* entry, documents events "very remote from ordinary life." The simple conclusion is that "romance" equals "a narrative which deals with the extraordinary." Yet if we turn back to the common experience of the supermarket, in the spirit of an advertisement for "Loveswept Romances," we find that, on the other hand, Loveswept claims to narrate events that are "so believable you'll feel you're actually living them." Romance becomes ordinary, or at least that which is made to seem ordinary, to seem like a part of everyday life. Although it could be argued that the common thread, from Chrétien to Harlequin, is the focus on love or love-making (a claim which would be harder to make about Walter Scott or even Bulwer Lytton), the shape which this thematic similarity takes is, in each case, quite different. So different, in fact, that the claim for similarity would be about the same as saying that *Hamlet* and *Ghostbusters* share the genre of the ghost story. The comparison seems to hide more than it reveals (like many ghost stories).

In laying out these contradictions as I do, I want to suggest that romance is neither merely "an alterable set of generic conventions," nor "a natural and immutable organic form."[6] Because of this, romance resists both the formalist and the organicist analyses

5

which have traditionally dominated genre studies. Instead, romance invokes what Jacques Derrida calls "the law of the law of genre": "a principle of contamination, a law of impurity, a parasitical economy," a "law of abounding, of *excess*, the law of participation without membership."[7] Romance always "(re)marks" itself, is always different from itself. What I will call a postmodern account of romance is a notion of theory which does not attempt to supply a formula for the generic identification of romance, for to do so would merely be to write another modernist account of genre. Although later on I will consider in more detail what I mean by the term "postmodern romance," let me make the point now that just as there can be no post-office box number to which we can send off for full instructions, detailing how to write a best-selling postmodern romance, there also can be no critical study which will delineate the aesthetic characteristics by which we can recognize all the romances of postmodernity.[8] Unlike the prescriptions of literary realism, it has no correct images or forms *per se*. Thus, romance does not form a *tradition* in simple opposition to that of realism, as Richard Chase has argued.[9]

In his preface to *The American*, Henry James calls attention to this generic uncertainty of romance, which critics like Chase have chosen to ignore. James explains that romance is essentially inessential, its only law the law of excess over itself. As such it cannot be the guardian of an originary identity whether national (as Chase claims) or gendered (as Radway argues). In James's words:

> The only *general* attribute of projected romance that I can see, the only one that fits all its cases, is the fact of the kind of experience with which it deals – experience liberated, so to speak; experience disengaged, disembroiled, disencumbered, exempt from the conditions that we usually know to attach to it and, if we wish so to put the matter, drag upon it, and operating in a medium which relieves it, in a particular interest, of the inconvenience of a *related*, a measurable state, a state subject to all our vulgar communities.[10]

Although one can hardly blame Richard Chase for having lost patience with James's syntax, it seems a little strange that Chase should want to claim this very same passage as an example of how the romance provides a medium for a specifically "American fiction . . . of the 'largest responding imagination.'"[11] James seems concerned precisely to insist that romance is the genre which liberates the representation of experience from known conditions and measurable states, including United ones, with all their "vulgar communities."

Picking up the threads of James's syntax, I want to argue that exactly what the genre of romance is remains an uncertainty: each text must in some way redefine what it means by "romance," must in the process of this redefinition create a meaning for the genre of romance to which it addresses itself, at the same time as it loses older, perhaps more established, meanings.[12] If a genre is most often understood as the contextual structure for the production of literary forms or meanings, the condition of postmodernism draws attention to the fact that texts work upon as well as within genres. Inevitably thematized within textuality, the romance genre transgresses the distinction of form and content which has traditionally governed genre studies. Romance makes us, in a word, uncomfortable because we are never quite sure what romance may mean or how it may mean. Romance seems in excess of itself, stepping beyond the lines which have always limited its definition. For example, Eliot's *Daniel Deronda*, the focus for chapter 4, seems to split into two sections: one half is the story of Gwendolen Harleth, the other that of Daniel Deronda. And it would seem that one half is romance, the other realism. Eliot's own prose describes her heroine in the terms of romance, while the Zionist section of her novel has recourse to realist conventions. However, F. R. Leavis rests his defense of George Eliot's consummate literary realism on the Harleth section. Although Eliot may mark her text with the conventional terms of romance, Leavis's own romance with Gwendolen Harleth leads him to claim this portion of the narrative for "realism." Yet for all of his praise of *Gwendolen Harleth* as the novel of Eliot's "maturest . . . clear and disinterested . . . vision," romance returns. That is to say, romance returns when Leavis's very defense of realism is at its most realistic. The defense against the excessive romance of the Deronda plot is itself an essentially romantic attachment, driven by the desire to "cut away" the rival Deronda at the point where Gwendolen learns the truth of "Deronda's intentions."[13] If, however, romance-writing appears as an excess to be cut out, this excess simply cannot be regulated. Excess is in the nature of the genre: romance returns even at the point where it is most violently excluded in the name of realism, making even a clear distinction between realism and romance impossible.

7

A significant implication of this self-excess, which (re)marks a generic departure from purely realistic representation, is that romance troubles the simple reference of novels to a political and historical "reality." That is to say, romance's ability to go beyond itself is also a capacity to go beyond realism. Thus, for instance Meredith's "Heroine of Reality," Diana of the Crossways, has to define herself as a romance writer. If literary realism considers reality as its ontological ground, romance threatens to expose "reality" as a constructed referent rather than as a "natural" state of existence to which we all naturally, textually, refer. Scott, for example, does not so much romanticize the history of Scotland as render that history "unreal," writable only as romance.[14] Yet before we can develop this point, we need to discuss in more detail the meaning of the term "postmodernism" and examine the ways in which it is linked to the transgression of historical periodicity. For it is through the overstepping of boundaries, both generic and temporal, that postmodernism opens a politics that questions the assured conceptual thresholds of referentiality or historical periodicity.

The discontinuous period of postmodernism

To discuss what is meant by the term "postmodernism" is to begin a conversation which is as vexed as the one that attempts to define romance. Turning to a list of recent academic book titles – *The Postmodern Turn*, *Postmodern Culture*, *A Poetics of Postmodernism*, *The Postmodern Condition: A Report on Knowledge*, *The Cultural Politics of "Postmodernism"*, *Postmodernist Fiction*, *Postmodernism and Its Discontents*, even *Milton and the Postmodern* – we can remark with some confidence that they do not, on the surface of things, tell us much more about postmodernism than that it is a popular topic of discussion.[15] This is a point whose validity also extends beyond the parameters of academic bookshelves; "postmodernism" has captured the popular imagination in all senses of the word. From "postmodern fashion" advertised on the walls of department stores to "Postmodern MTV" on late-night television, consumer culture has embraced the term with the greatest of enthusiasm, even if it hasn't spent much time defining what it is that it is embracing.

Where, then, do we look for a definition of "postmodernism"? Do the programmers at MTV define "postmodernism" in the same way as the author of *Milton and the Postmodern*? Not necessarily. To understand how this is the case, it is useful to repeat the warning that postmodernism is *not* simply that which comes after modernism. Although postmodernism does involve a consideration of what modernism might be, it cannot be seen as defining itself in simple opposition to modernism. That is to say, postmodernism is not simply "a set of plural departures from Modernism" that began in about 1960, as Charles Jencks claims.[16]

Although postmodernism may construct itself against modernism to some extent, the relation is not entirely negative. There is something of the postmodern in the way in which modernism is driven to turn against itself, to open the space for a new modernity. This is the point Jean-François Lyotard makes when he questions the status of postmodernism:

> What then is postmodern? What place does it or does it not occupy in the vertiginous work of the questions hurled at the rules of image and narration? It is undoubtedly a part of the modern. All that has been received, if only yesterday (*modo, modo*, Petronius used to say), must be suspected. What space does Cézanne challenge? The Impressionists'. What object do Picasso and Braque attack? Cézanne's. What presupposition does Duchamp break with in 1912? That which says one must make a painting, be it cubist. And Buren questions that other presentation of the work. In an amazing acceleration, the generations precipitate themselves. A work can become modern only if it is first postmodern. Postmodernism thus understood is not modernism at its end but in the nascent state, and this state is constant.[17]

Postmodernism does not simply happen after modernism but is a series of problems present to modernism in its continuing infancy. For Lyotard, to be concerned with the question of postmodernity is to be concerned with questions of temporality and sequence. It is to be concerned with questions of cause and effect, originality and derivation. In the relation of postmodernism to modernism, cause and effect do not keep their temporal sequence; the original is not located as the "source" that precedes the derivation. Lyotard sketches out how a theory of postmodernism accounts for such matters when he explains that "postmodernity is not a new age"; it's not the latest sequence of historical events. Instead, postmodernity is a rewriting of modernity, which has already been active *within* modernity for a long time.[18] The "post" (the effect) is already part of that to which it is "post," is already contained within the supposed moment of historical cause (modernity).

It is perhaps this point that most directly distinguishes the way in which "postmodernism" is used to sell fashion design or music videos from the way in which academic discourse has considered the term. Paradoxically, modernism's insistent division of high from low culture appears in a warped form here in that most – although certainly not all, as romance testifies – popular uses of the term are actually modernist. From the point of view of marketing, one might even be tempted to identify postmodernism as a modernism made available to the very masses that modernist aesthetics scorned. What this adds up to is that what passes as "postmodernism" might more usefully be understood as popular modernism. To imply that we live in a cultural moment that is even newer – more the "cutting edge" – than modernism, as the popular media often imply, is in its own way a very modernist statement. On the other hand, to think postmodernism as Lyotard does is to reconsider the validity of historical periodicity and historical thought *tout court*.

Yet by calling history into question, by forcing a radical revision of what historical periodicity might mean, "postmodernism" is not an ahistorical or antihistorical project, which would be a more appropriate criticism of supposedly "postmodern" popular songs like Billy Joel's "We Didn't Start the Fire." Joel's popular modernism reduces history to a mere procession of names – be they proper or brand names, Hitler or Hula-Hoops. Postmodernism, however, is a *way of thinking* about history and representation that claims there can be no final understanding. And as such it is concerned with practically nothing but the problem of trying to think historically, of trying to understand history.

To some, a historical claim for postmodernism may seem more than a bit strange, in light of recent critical attacks on postmodernism. To take one example among many, Griselda Pollock argues that "specific historical knowledge is a vital defense against postmodernist suspension of history."[19] For Pollock, post-modernism's relationship to history is one which virtually kills the partner. Postmodernism suspends history, places it out of sight, and only vaccinations of "specific historical knowledge" can fight off this deadly disease. I would like to suggest that postmodernism's relationship to history is closer and less pernicious than Pollock claims. Although postmodernism questions the construction of history, interrogates what it would mean to have "specific historical knowledge," it neither dismisses (nor suspends) history, nor does it ignore the impact of historical knowledge. Postmodernism responds to the pressures of the past, the force of historical thinking, but it does so in a way that does not necessarily legitimate conventional historical narratives or conventional ways of thinking about history.

In denying postmodernism its historical position (i.e. following modernism – the "post" is, after all, a prefix to modernism) while at the same time insisting upon its historicity as I have just done, I could be provoking a response once again from my hypothetical student of literature. "What is the point," he or she invariably asks, "of calling it *post*modernism if it doesn't follow modernism?" The point, I would like to argue, is that the re-evaluation of the "post" in postmodernism is performed in the name of a new way of thinking about historical periodicity. History is not merely a grand narrative that tells the sequence in which events happened; nor is it the perspective from which we are able to judge the meanings of events. The pre-eminence of chronology in modernist master narratives of history is thus called into question by postmodernism. Postmodernism, in contrast, insists on its own excess – an excess that defies the boundaries imposed by the continuous, chronological ordering of historical periodicity. This excess or defiance of historical boundaries also makes impossible the taking hold of what Lyotard calls the "now" or "the present from which we can claim to have a right view over the successive periods of our history."[20] Although a concept of a "now" is necessary to determine a distinction between what follows and what has come before (what is post and what is pre) at the same moment such a "now" is always vanishing. It is always "both too late and too soon for grasping something like an identifiable "now." "Too late" designates an excess in the vanishing ("going off"), "too soon" refers to an excess in the coming."[21] Temporality as presence is always deferred (as either coming or going) by the excesses of temporality itself.

Postmodernism, then, is the (never fully present) time in which there is a loss of credulity in master narratives. It marks the time when narrative knowledge, as Lyotard points out, no longer legitimates historical knowledge, no longer provides an authoritative way of understanding past events.[22] Instead, within postmodernism grand or master narratives lose their explanatory power, and we are forced to reconsider, re-remember the historical event – no longer in the form of realism but through the genre of generic uncertainty, through romance. The relationship between postmodernism and romance becomes a way in which to rethink narrative and its relationship to the legitimation of historical knowledge. Thus, while periodicity attempts to make the past representable as "past," romance and postmodernism attempt to be flagrantly anachronistic, upsetting our ability to recognize the past as past, challenging the way we "know" history.

Postmodern romance: an anachronistic story

At this point, I would like to introduce another term into the discussion: "postmodern romance." I don't want to suggest that the goal of this book will be to find even purer definitions of romance or postmodernity. Rather, the "quest" of this discussion will be for the implications of the intersection of romance and postmodernism in the term "postmodern romance."

In using this neologism, I want to suggest two things: 1) romance should be considered *as* a postmodern genre; 2) postmodernism *is* romance. First, let me focus on romance as a postmodern genre. This has to do, above all, with a common excess shared by romance and postmodernism. Romance's excess over itself, its capacity to appear where least expected, is analogous to postmodernism's paradoxical ability both to precede and to come after itself, to come both before and after modernism. In the case of postmodernism, temporal boundaries are exceeded; in the case of romance, generic boundaries are exceeded. Boundaries, whether temporal or generic, fail to maintain control over that which they are intended to delineate. Phrased another way, we could say that the relationship between romance and postmodernism comes about as the result of a common excess – the inability to stay within historical and aesthetic boundaries. If postmodernism is characterized by a definitive dispute about its location (at which "historical" point is it introduced?) then romance is characterized by a similar dispute about aesthetics: what kind of texts should be called romances? What, for instance, is romance doing in the quintessentially "realistic" novels of George Eliot?

This common problem of excess, of an inability to stay within boundaries (be they historical or aesthetic) leads us to the second implication of the term "postmodern romance." Flagrant anachronisms appear as the common effect of the disruption of

12

historical boundaries by postmodern romance. Not merely slips or errors, these anachronisms challenge conventional modernist understandings of history.

The particular role that anachronism plays can best be understood if we first recognize that postmodern romance *retains* a concern for temporality and historical periods by virtue of the very fact that it is concerned with what happens when periodicity is disturbed, when what we usually recognize as separate periods or genres come together in a way that is neither commensurate nor even dialectical.[23] This anachronistic disruption produces an anxiety not dissimilar to that which a museum director would experience if s/he were to discover that fourteenth-century religious art was inexplicably mixed up in an exhibit with Dutch realist painting. Something has gone decidedly "wrong" with the arrangement, something which requires an explanation, but how one would go about constructing the explanation is not self-evident. There is an anachronistic failure of narrative sequence, but there is no one narrative that can adequately narrate the failure of narrative sequence. The postmodern does not supervene as the accurate recognition of prior errors, a new Enlightenment as to the darkness of history.

The juxtaposition of differing historical periods is not simple contradiction; postmodernism does not simply reaffirm traditional narratives against modernism, does not just return to the past in order to separate the medieval or the mythic from the modern. Thus we find Scott facing the *coexistence* of the tribal and the modern; Eco anachronistically struggling with medievalism and modernism; Conrad attempting to account for the primitive and mythic alongside western imperialism; Eliot's female readers of romance articulating desires at odds with the standards of bourgeois Victorian culture; Derrida and Acker working through the implications of false citations and plagiarism. What we are dealing with here is the breakdown of an overarching historical sequence, of the possibility of "metahistory" itself, in Hayden White's terms. Postmodernism is not a new, more depressing, narrative but rather the coexistence of multiple and mutually exclusive narrative possibilities without a point of abstraction from which we might survey them. Postmodern romance offers no perspectival view; it is an *ironic coexistence* of temporalities.

From realism to postmodern romance

In its failure to legitimate conventional historical narratives and in its insistence on ironic temporality, postmodern romance's anachronistic quality challenges realism, in its historical as well as its aesthetic implications. This raises a difficulty in both the treatment of historical material and the understanding of what a sense of history might be. The romance narratives of postmodernity, including those available on airport bookstalls, challenge historical narrative's tendency toward realist representation. Postmodernism displaces realism, shifting the site of the representation of historical events to romance. Realism, as far as postmodern romance is concerned, ceases to be the privileged form of representation for the "real," for historical reality. To recall the discussion of excess, we could say that within postmodernism's literary genre of romance there can never be too much romance because there is always too much history. Again, this is really another way of saying that romance is never "pure" in the generic sense. As a supposedly literary genre, it always becomes contaminated with historical discourse. Likewise, within postmodernity, history becomes contaminated with the excesses of romance.

To suggest that history can be read in terms of literary genres like romance is, in itself, nothing new, as readers of Hayden White know.[24] But the point I would like to stress is the fact that, by displacing realism, postmodern romance is able to call into question the place of the referent of history. Postmodern romance calls our attention to the problematic nature of the historical event itself. We are thus led to ask: What constitutes a historical event? How can we represent it? And why, if the event is indeed historic, does it keep becoming a matter for romance? According to postmodern romance, we can no longer claim with certainty that we know to what history refers. Any attempt at creating a meaning for the past involves a loss of meaning, a loss in its representability. If the aim of realism is to construct a (historical) narrative of the past which seems to make the past intelligible and graspable, then the object of postmodern romance is to question whether we really can know the past, whether we can ever adequately re-member the event.[25] To put this another way, if the task of realism is "to preserve various consciousnesses from doubt," then the task of postmodern romance is to create doubt about what it is we know and how it is we know it.[26] Thus in *Nostromo* Conrad questions the validity of

14

"historical" knowledge by confronting historical narrative with its own "literary" tendency, its tendency to become indistinguishable from the very romance from which it attempts to distance itself.

If a postmodern understanding may allow us to trace in this self-divided movement the lines of a potential resistance, a reading of history as an ethical burden, realist representation can only forget this burden either by excluding it or by representing it within a historical reality. Within the terms of this "realism," affective disturbance is merely the effect of excessive feminine sentiment, of sentimentality. The sense of history may become the site of resistance to the way things are, precisely in that it *exceeds* a reactionary nostalgia for the way things were. An affective relationship to history, such as the one postmodern romance evokes, therefore exceeds realism's nostalgic project of recovering the past through purportedly accurate representations of it; postmodern romance reveals the constructedness of realism and resists a nostalgic "coming to terms with the past" – a nostalgia that would conveniently also be a dismissal of the past through the very "accuracy" of the representation. That is to say, if realism makes us believe that we can be done with the past because we have accurately represented it, postmodern romance insists upon the injustice of any such representation, especially that of realism, because we can never fully come to terms with the past, we can never justly represent it. As Adorno reminds us:

> "Coming to terms with the past" [*Aufarbeitung*] does not imply a serious working through of the past, the breaking of its spell through the act of clear consciousness. It suggests, rather, wishing to turn the page and, if possible, wiping it from memory.[27]

In light of these remarks, the difference between realism and postmodern romance can be seen in terms of remembering and forgetting: while realism remembers the past so as to forget it, the postmodern romance re-members the past, re-situates its temporality, in order to make the past impossible to forget. To render the past in this sense unforgettable is to point out that it is impossible fully to remember, fully to come to terms with the past. It is this sense of the past as an excess over consciousness that is shared by postmodernism and romance.

15

The figure of woman

Such a concern with the past brings us to the importance of the figure of woman; for within postmodern romance the figure of woman is what allows the work of re-membering to be performed. Postmodernity's re-membering of the past is performed through a re-engendering of the historical past as romance. That is to say, the figure of woman is what allows the past to be represented (via the en-gendering of romance), but she is also the figure whose very inscription reveals, through the play of gender, the impossibility of accurate and complete representation.

A realist discourse on romance as "women's literature" runs in the opposite direction on similar tracks. If romance evokes an unrepresentable other side to history, realism displaces the problem of unrepresentability from history onto gender. Romance, in this account, says less about history than about women's inability to come to terms with it. Romance is just "female fantasy," "wish-fulfillment," the recourse of bored and entrapped matrons. The flaw in this argument is that the very texts which claim to purify and separate "real history" from "romantic fantasy," as alternately male and female, are themselves unable to "come to terms" with the figure of the (presumptively real) female except by erasing her. History is preserved from fantasy and its anachronisms only by the becoming-fantastic of the female. The fantastic returns as the gendered complement of the real historical male that sought to exclude it. Woman, that is, may permit the past to be represented as romance, but the price of this is that she herself cannot be adequately represented. As we shall see in chapter 1 with Eco's *The Name of the Rose* and in chapter 4 with Scott's *Waverley* novels, the past is brought back within the ambit of representation only at the price of woman's expulsion from it. Thus, romance may be understood in realist terms as "just female fantasy," as it were, only by virtue of the misunderstanding of woman.

In effect, a realist understanding of postmodern romance needs woman but cannot finally come to terms with her: the figure of woman is drawn to excess – within the terms of the decorum of realistic discrimination and mediation of experience – and hence becomes disruptingly uncertain as the historical sign of uncertainty. For example, within Scott's novels, the female characters are always drawn with an excess of gender that results first in androgyny and then in narrative anxiety about that androgyny. Similarly, in

Meredith's *Diana of the Crossways*, the figure of woman bears within herself two temporalities (that of writer and wife) which prove historically incommensurable, leaving the problem of representing female subjectivity confined to the realm of the excessive and the uncertain. In its refusal to confirm the decidability of gender, the text ends up refusing to create an image of woman at all. It is not for nothing, then, that the character of Diana must find that "metaphors were her refuge," because the figure of woman vanishes within the metaphoric dissemination of Meredith's text.[28]

In the case of both Meredith's and Scott's novels, the figure of woman appears in literature as something other than accessible or legitimate historical record. This is woman as she arises as the figure of the self-excess of romance. Woman, in a sense, phrases history and its uncertainty in her simultaneous status as excluded from history and yet most fiercely historical. There is, as it were, a community between Scott's Flora Mac-Ivor (unable to act herself and yet more aware of the ethical burden of history than her own brother to whom that burden is bequeathed) and the female consumer of the Harlequin historical romance, for whom "history has never been so much fun" precisely because its burden has never been so felt and yet so irrelevant. It's typical of the anachronism of Scott's postmodernism that his first historical romance should have as one of its characters a figure (Flora Mac-Ivor) who is already the first reader of historical romances. History is both felt and irrelevant: whether in the attempt, over which women watch in Scott's novels, to produce history in the present, or in the attempt (equally impossible) to exchange history for the present that situates women's consumption of the mass-culture romance.

Repeatedly, the figure of woman remains a problem for the postmodern. One could, for instance, accuse Eco of not being postmodern enough in that woman appears as the irresolvable resolution of postmodernity's difficulty with historical knowledge. Gender boundaries remain untouched however gleefully historical and aesthetic boundaries are exceeded in *The Name of the Rose* and attendant texts. For Umberto Eco, the knowledge of the postmodern condition is bought only at the expense of a modernist inscription of gender: the postmodern is a romance encoded as heterosexist and classist. As we shall later see, Eco himself even points out that the condition of postmodernism is the relationship between a very cultivated woman and the man who tries to tell her that he loves her. In a similar fashion, while Calvino's *If on a winter's*

17

night a traveler confronts gendered versions of reading (the male reader and the female other reader) it then attempts to reunite the reader with the other reader in the most conventional of ways – they come together in the conjugal bed at the novel's end.[29] Likewise, Conrad's challenge of modernist history in *Nostromo* occurs at the expense of the marginalization of female characters, and, as a final example, Acker's *Great Expectations* is the beginning of a romance that never ends happily for the woman.

In bringing together this list of examples, I do not want to suggest, however, that postmodernism or romance is inevitably sexist. On the contrary, I want to argue that the persistence of gender boundaries as a site of either impasse or perfect resolution marks a failure on our behalf to make one last effort, if we were to become postmodern. Thus, situating the figure of woman within the postmodern romance, I want to disagree with the suggestion of critics like Meaghan Morris who insist that there is no "relationship" between postmodernism and feminist theory. Morris makes the terms of this position clear when she states that her book, *The Pirate's Fiancée: Feminism, Reading, Postmodernism*

> does not propose to present – or to "effectively situate" – feminist theory *as* "postmodernist," and it does not propose to salvage feminism *for* postmodernism. It does presuppose that since feminism has acted as one of the enabling conditions of discourse *about* postmodernism, it is therefore appropriate to use feminist work to frame discussions of postmodernism, and not the other way around.[30]

For her, feminism and postmodernism are in fact incommensurable. Feminism is not a part of postmodernism and vice versa. Rather, what feminism does, as far as Morris is concerned, is offer a critique of postmodernism, reminding postmodernism that it was feminism that, in many respects, made postmodernism possible. In short, the work of feminism from a perspective such as Morris's would be to write postmodernism's acknowledgment page.

My project differs significantly from this approach in suggesting that feminism and postmodernism are implicated in one another: that the figure of woman offers up a feminism within postmodernity, and that likewise romance offers a postmodernity within feminism. The issue, then, is not simply one of feminism resisting "incorporation into postmodernism" by means of revolutionary force, as Linda Hutcheon suggests; feminism should not be seen as merely a supporter of modernity and Enlightenment reason.[31] The persistent neglect of questions of gender characteristic of theorists of modernity is not merely an incidental blindness which should be corrected so as to allow modernity its full development by including women. As I shall show in my last chapter, feminism has more to lose than to gain from thinking itself as another modernist grand narrative, this time of the liberation of female identity, of a unified female subject. Postmodernism may well be the name feminism can give to its escape from identity politics.

The politics of postmodernism/The politics of romance

If feminism is the most obvious political question posed by romance or postmodernity, this is the mark of the extent to which each problematizes traditional conceptions of the political. Feminism's politics has been an exceeding of boundaries, a refusal to contain the political within the public sphere of discussions between men. As a political enterprise, this book revalues romance and insists upon postmodernity in ways that do not leave our notions of political calculation untouched. As I have remarked, a common feature of romance and postmodernity is a constant difficulty in calculating their politics. Is romance the radical reinvention of a freer world? Is postmodernism the subversion of existing cultural orthodoxy? *Or* is romance merely escapist fantasy, postmodernism merely ineffectual playfulness?

In response to traditional dismissals of romance and post-modernity as politically ineffective or suspect because of this uncertainty, I want to suggest that both may be operative in forcing us to rethink the political. The problem of the political has been our tendency to demand rational and precise calculation as the distinguishing feature which leads us to characterize an act as political. To rethink the political as uncertain may be something more than merely relinquishing the possibility of action. It may just be a way of inventing new modes of political calculation that can resist the growing certainties of nuclear annihilation, multinationalist capital expansion, and the rule of heterosexist patriarchy and other cultural orthodoxies.

As a symptom of the politics of romance, consider the different political values critics as diverse as Fredric Jameson and Northrop Frye place on "high culture" romance. Jameson argues that romance narratives pose a resistance to "oppressive representation," that

19

there is a transformative potential inherent in the very generic structure of romance.[32] That is to say that romance contains a transformative potential which allows the articulation of marginalized desire (usually of women or oppressed peoples). In effect, for Jameson romance is politically progressive in the face of realism's conservatism. Jameson's argument is quite tempting, but it is strangely at odds with Northrop Frye's position. Frye, on the contrary, believes that romance has been "kidnapped" and absorbed into "the ideology of an ascendant class."[33] Romance, in this view, legitimates dominant hegemonic groups through its capacity to act as a narrative veil that hides "the language of ideology," to use Pierre Macherey's phrase.[34] Thus for Frye, romance would be the genre of choice for magnificent tales of imperialism and colonization. So much for the progressive politics of romance, if we are to believe this portion of Frye's argument.

However, Frye's argument is not as opposed to Jameson's as it appears. Significantly, Frye also cites the "revolutionary" *potential* of romance, which is precisely what makes it "kidnapped" rather than merely oppressive in its service of dominant classes. Although romance, judging from the prevailing nature of his examples, seems to be by its very nature kidnapped, Frye also cites the "liberating" quality of romance in contrast to "conservative" realism. As Frye sees it, even though romance narratives may be put to reactionary political uses, there still remains within the genre a potentially radical political use of which Jameson would approve.[35]

A similar disagreement arises over the romances of popular culture. We find Rosalind Coward arguing that popular romances of the Harlequin variety are an oppressive form of mass culture which inevitably lead women into accepting the submissive roles prescribed by patriarchy. Romance, for Coward as for Frye, is politically conservative.[36] But the debate does not stop here. For example, looking at popular-culture materials similar to the ones that Coward examines, Janice Radway concludes that popular romance in fact leads women to find a voice with which to express their dissatisfaction and change their material conditions. In short, romance turns politically progressive again.[37]

If Frye makes the case for the progressive potential of reactionary romance, Radway turns the formula around and argues that progressive romance also inevitably contains a reactionary element. According to Radway, although popular romances ultimately support a progressive feminist agenda, they always in some way support the dominant hegemony. That is to say, in representing women in positions of power (as corporate executives, independent businesswomen) and showing their capacity to make decisions and assume control, popular romances provide women readers with a sense of self and with a potentiality for resisting the dominant hegemony's value system. Yet at the same time, these new positions of power and independence are not, in the long run, resistant, because they are positions of power that support the capitalist model. The only difference is that now women, and not men, assume the helm of the capitalist ship.[38]

The wide disagreement over the political valency of the romance genre echoes the theoretical debate concerning the political agenda and effects of postmodernity. Once again, we have some critics who claim that postmodernism is reactionary, others who insist upon its progressive potential. Ihab Hassan believes that postmodernism "is essentially subversive in form and anarchic in its cultural spirit."[39] But lest we rest assured of the politics of postmodernism, in quite a different spirit Bruno Zevi goes so far as to say that postmodernism is as repressive as fascism, while Fredric Jameson in a comparatively moderate position claims that postmodernism "replicates or reproduces – reinforces – the logic of consumer capitalism."[40] Finally, as a way around the difficulty of defining a single politics of postmodernism, Hal Foster suggests that there are indeed two different types of postmodernism, one which is aligned with neoconservative politics, and another which is related to poststructuralist theory; the former is profoundly humanist in its claim to "return to history," the latter profoundly antihumanist in its critique of representation. Or to be more reductive, there is "bad" (neoconservative) postmodernism and "good" (poststructuralist) postmodernism.[41]

What is striking about these divergent positions is their ability to argue convincingly that the romance genre and postmodernism are used for political purposes – be it progressive or conservative, or a little of both at the same time. One way or another, romance and postmodernism are not seen as ideologically neutral. In fact, what seems to characterize them are their inevitably *political* contents and their necessary ideological reversibility.[42]

The question of what politics might be in the last quarter of the twentieth century is no longer an issue that one can address with certainty. It is also necessary to make absolutely clear that this is not a call for a return to the indecisiveness of liberal pluralism. On the contrary, what I'm arguing is not that it's difficult to decide between competing certainties but that what happens in the political sphere may hold an importance inversely proportional to the degree of certainty with which we can predict it. For example, we are no longer sure what a revolution might be. A certain left-wing imperialism has been accustomed to retreat from the complexity of western politics to the exemplary, decisive, and sanguine qualities of "Third World" liberation struggles. In Angola, in Zimbabwe, in Algeria, it was clear which side one should be on. Roughly speaking, western leftists extolled national liberation struggles right up until the point where they were successful, when corruption would set in, leaving one more lost opportunity to lament. Developments in the eastern block have reminded us of just how much these politics simply inverted the struggles of superpower imperialism, how mortgaged they were to assumptions of political stagnation in the west and in the east. At the same time, the rise of Islamic fundamentalism is an uncomfortable reminder of the extent to which the "universal" ideals of social justice foisted on revolutionary struggles in the "Third World" were themselves specifically western notions. The implications that I am trying to draw from this do not suggest despair or hope; rather it's perhaps necessary that we recognize the extent to which our criteria for political judgment rely upon narratives of progress or decline that have their roots in cultural paradigms of which we have learnt to be suspicious.

A politics of uncertainty, then, would not necessarily be a politics of indecision. On the contrary, it would be a politics flexible enough to remain open to new modes of political calculation: a politics that would not judge events on the basis of a set of pre-existing criteria. This would require nothing less than that we admit that there is a politics to our definition of the political. Feminism is perhaps the clearest instance of a force that has retained its political drive precisely through a refusal to be pinned down to certainties. In the academy, a recurrent strategy of opposition to feminism, even when it masquerades as sympathy, is to demand that a clear definition be given. Feminists must categorize themselves as either campaigners for equal rights or as separatists. Similarly, in the "higher" reaches of the academy, feminists have been asked to categorize themselves as either essentialists or as constructionists. It is important to recognize that these issues are *not feminist*; they presuppose a desexualized ground on which we form our philosophical assumptions (that the female gender is or is not a cultural construct) or our political aims (that women should be equal to men or separate from them). Feminism has always been at its strongest when it has simply refused to answer such questions and insisted that the question of women cannot be answered in isolation from a personal, institutional, and political practice. To put it another way, what characterizes feminism is a refusal to go away. Feminism at its best refuses to pose its utopia of equality or isolation. It recognizes oppression but does not sell itself back to its oppressors as a definable program that can be satisfied once and for all. Feminism is a politics of uncertainty because it insists that we do not yet know what women can be, and that it is always men who have wanted to have the question of woman decisively answered once and for all, as Tiresias found to his cost.[43]

Not for nothing have the examples that I've chosen, of "Third World" liberation struggles and of the question of women, evoked the two dominant plot modes of the romance: heroic struggle and sexual intrigue. The condition of our politics is to recognize that there is a politics of sexuality and that there is a politics of representation – a politics to the way in which we understand the political. The ideological reversibility of romance is a product of the fact that it has dealt with issues that have not seemed political, issues whose political effect has always been decided elsewhere, realistically. Romance narratives – affairs of the heart or adventures – have been considered political only in their underlying repercussions elsewhere. And the nature of those repercussions is various. The same plot may trace imperialist aggression or anti-imperialist struggle. What I want to argue is that postmodernism's rethinking of the political permits us to revalue romance as political. It moves us away from an understanding of politics as a matter of drawing up balance sheets of real effects, of deciding on the "real" political meaning of romance. The political force of romance is to dislocate politics from the hegemony of the real, which is always the hegemony of the status quo, even when the utopian imagination of alternative reality functions negatively. If postmodernity is neither historical nor ahistorical, romance is neither realistic nor fantastic. Each evokes a practice of reading analogous to that of feminism at its strongest: a practice that refuses to be pinned down, that persistently opens up a space of transformation within the materiality of culture.

The function of this revisionary rereading is to open a sense of alternative spaces that are not simply utopian negations of the real, or the discovery of the hidden truth of the real. Romance and postmodernism evoke a difference that cannot be pinned down into simple opposition (realist/fantastic, historical/ahistorical). Their politics are thus as inexhaustible and disruptive as those of feminism, which has consistently refused to allow sexual difference to be controlled and kept in check as a decidable opposition of genders (female/male).

Thus, I want to argue that the concerns of this book are political, but that those politics cannot be decided in advance of the readings which put them at risk. To investigate the political stakes in the terms "postmodern romance" and "history" is to pressure aesthetic formalism toward historical and political concerns, to pressure historicism toward a consideration of its aesthetics. It suggests that genre and historical period are not merely a question of external labels applied to texts by critics or authors, but the site of a struggle over the ways in which cultural meaning is to be constructed, understood, and given value. The parallels between the ways in which gender and genre are at work in representation form the site in which this concern is played out. And it is in terms of the persistence of gender in the postmodern romance that I want to begin reading the scandalous success of Umberto Eco's *The Name of the Rose*.

As we shall see in the following chapter, postmodernism turns to romance in order to displace notions of historical propriety and authenticity. However, the radical force of this displacement is tamed and brought to narrative closure in Eco's novel by virtue of the persistence of rather less ironic and more modern tropes of gender. It is by considering the mass of documentation and incidental narrative with which Eco surrounds his novel that we can understand its postmodernity; the postmodernity of *The Name of the Rose* is above all an issue of a certain kind of framing: historical, documentary, political, literary. The text presents itself as available for multiple readings (detective story, treatise, political allegory, etc.), depending on the frame that is selected. However, not for the first time or the last, gender occupies an anomalous place in the workshop of *parerga*: rather than being another frame for reading the novel, woman

24

is "framed." I think that the framing of woman can be set up most clearly if we open our reading in the next chapter with a consideration of the place of the tropes of historical romance not merely in Eco's novel itself but also in the apparatus describing its genesis.

1

P. S. "I LOVE YOU": UMBERTO ECO AND THE ROMANCE OF THE READER

The manuscript of romance

I love you.

A statement that is pre-eminently pragmatic, "I love you" falls as prologue or epilogue to a story with which we are all familiar, as prefatory exhortation to, or concluding description of, intimacy. Yet here we are not intimate, and we don't know where we are in the story. And "I love you" will only have appeared in quotation marks, marked as taking place in a world of textual apparatus. Thinking romance is a questioning of how it is that one may say "I love you," a statement undecidably descriptive or performative, whose whole drama is bound up in whether it belongs to a rhetoric of persuasion or a system of tropes. Reading Eco's *The Name of the Rose* becomes interesting because of the way in which it stages the textuality and intertextuality of the apparently vacuous "I love you," a phrase which comes to stand as characteristic of the entire problematic of postmodernity for Eco. For the textual juggernaut that forms *The Name of the Rose* and its various outriggers (postscripts, prefaces, editorials, etc.) constantly links epistemological difficulties about the determination of the meaning of texts (for editors as for detectives) to the social (or, as we academics prefer, cultural) embarrassments attendant upon the declaration of love.

The Name of the Rose opens with the story of both a lost manuscript and a lost traveling companion – a double tale of lost love. At a determinate political moment (Prague, August 16, 1968), the narrator is handed a nineteenth-century book written in French, which claims "to reproduce faithfully a fourteenth-century manuscript that, in its turn had been found in the monastery of Melk by the great eighteenth-century man of learning."[1] This seemingly uneventful proceeding leads to a series of quickly related adventures: Soviet troops invade Prague and the narrator leaves the city, reaches the Austrian border, journeys to Vienna, meets his "beloved," and then sails up the Danube with both manuscript and traveling companion. So far so good – the narrative can still account for the whereabouts of both companion and manuscript. However, before the end of the next paragraph and before the pair reach Salzburg, "one tragic night in a little hotel on the shores of the Mondsee," the traveling companion disappears with the manuscript in what is described as "an abrupt and untidy" ending of the relationship (xiv).

I have taken this much space to retell the story of the missing manuscript and the missing companion because there are a number of subtle problems embedded within it that relate to the discussion of gender and genre (how to say "I love you") in the postmodern romance. The medieval setting of *The Name of the Rose* reinforces the title's allusion to the *Romance of the Rose*. This might be enough in itself to legitimate a consideration of the novel in generic terms as a romance. However, the detective story adds two more confusing clues. Postmodernity has been understood as concerned with frames, and the framing narratives that present the novel turn explicitly upon the tropes of romance. Within the space of less than two pages, Eco's novel presents two different romances: a romance that involves a missing person, and a romance that involves a missing manuscript.

First the missing person. Because this character has a narrative life span of approximately three paragraphs, there may seem little cause for concern. Once the companion disappears, the narrator, although admitting a great emptiness in his heart, drops the search for his beloved and instead continues to pursue his manuscript research. Yet what is perhaps most strange about this romance, this affair of the heart, is not its brevity (which is strange enough) but rather the way in which the gender of the participants is or is not disclosed. The English translation fails to provide a way to determine the gender of the narrator until several pages into the narrative, when the narrator refers to himself as "a man of letters" (xviii). This is less of a mystery in the Italian version, when a past participle gives the gender away as early as the second paragraph (*affascinato*). In the case of the narrator, we could say, then, that the male gender of the narrator simply gets lost in the translation.

The gender of the beloved traveling companion, however, proves a much more problematic case. In both the English translation and the Italian text, s/he is never referred to by any determined gender reference: s/he is "my beloved," alias "the person with whom I was travelling" alias "a dear friend," and in each case the gender of the character goes unremarked. Thus, if romance is traditionally coded as a genre of and for women, and if romance is traditionally heterosexist in many of its premises, Eco's narrative does little to fall in with tradition. There are no discernable women taking part in the short three-paragraph romance, nor is there a particular appeal to female readers. Instead, there is one man, one manuscript, and one piece of guesswork.

What I would like to argue is that Eco's novel uses this break with generic convention and relies upon the indeterminacy of gender first to *displace* romance's traditional, heterosexist love interest between a male narrator and a female beloved, and then to *replace* it with a romance between the narrator and his manuscript. What the narrator pursues is not his beloved; we never hear from him/her again. Instead he goes after the manuscript, and a particularly mysterious historical manuscript at that. Yet to go in search of the manuscript without also searching for the beloved means that the narrator will have to find another copy of the manuscript . . . which is almost what happens. Instead of finding either the "original" fourteenth-century manuscript or another copy of the nineteenth-century French translation, the narrator ends up with "an Italian version of an obscure, neo-Gothic French version of a seventeenth-century Latin edition" of purportedly the same fourteenth-century manuscript, which we now know was a "work written in Latin by a German monk" (xvi–xvii).

It would seem, then, that with the manuscript recovered the story would end here: after a long search to regain his beloved manuscript (and not his beloved traveling companion) the narrator consummates his romance – takes possession of the object of his desires. But to end here would be to end on page xvii of the preface, and that would not be the stuff of best-selling novels. The recovery of the manuscript is not enough; it must also be "published." But why? Even the narrator informs us that he "finds few reasons for publishing" his Italian version of what is by now an obscure, adulterated text. Yet if the reasons for publishing are few they are significant and outweigh any concern for obscurity or faithfulness to the "original" text: "Let us say it is an act of love. Or, if you like, a way of ridding myself of numerous, persistent obsessions" (xviii).

An act of love. But an act of love committed for whom? The reader? The lost traveling companion? The better explanation would be that the act of love is committed both for and with the manuscript itself. The narrator "publishes" the manuscript, retells its story, because he finally feels "free to tell, for sheer narrative pleasure, the story of Adso of Melk" (xviii). Sheer narrative pleasure, the desire to commit an act of love and release accumulated obsessions, motivate publication. The romance *of* the text is the romance *with* the text. What we find in romance, according to Eco, is what reading and writing (what narratives) are all about – if writing once was thought to be a way to change the world, now it is simply positioned as a form of romance, an act of love, which gives the writer and the reader pleasure and consolation. Or as the narrator puts it:

> In the years when I discovered the Abbé Vallet volume, there was a widespread conviction that one should write only out of a commitment to the present, in order to change the world. Now, after ten years or more, the man of letters (restored to his loftiest dignity) can happily write out of pure love of writing. And so I now feel free to tell, for sheer narrative pleasure, the story of Adso of Melk, and I am comforted and consoled in finding it immeasurably remote in time (now that the waking reason has dispelled all the monsters that its sleep had generated), gloriously lacking in any relevance for our day, atemporally alien to our hopes and our certainties.
>
> For it is a tale of books, not of everyday worries, and reading it can lead us to recite, with à Kempis, the great imitator: "In omnibus requiem quaesivi, et nusquam inveni nisi in angulo cum libro" [In all things I looked for rest, and nowhere did I discover it except in a corner with a book]. (xviii–xix)

The tropes of romance appear once again: that which is remote from everyday life, temporarily alien to our present lives in its remoteness, is that which consoles us.[2] And perhaps curiously for a novel published in the 1980s, this pleasure of the text is not to be discovered in the romances of popular culture but in a medieval manuscript whose pleasure is described in an untranslated Latin quotation from à Kempis. And yet this manuscript will self-consciously evoke the plot twists and amorous interests (even in a monastery) of popular romance, not to say the plot structure of the detective novel. In the words of the dust-jacket description of the Italian edition probably supplied by Eco:

> Brother William will find himself required to clear up a series of mysterious crimes (seven in seven days committed within the precincts of the Abbey) which cover the labyrinthine and inaccessible library in blood. William will solve the case, perhaps too late in terms of days, perhaps too soon in terms of centuries, and in order to do it, he will have to decipher clues of every kind. . . . Difficult to define (gothic novel, medieval chronicle, detective story, ideological *roman à clef*, allegory) this novel (whose story is interwoven with History – because the author, perhaps untruthfully, insists that not a single word is his own) can perhaps be read in three ways. The first category of readers will be interested in the plot and its twists and turns, and will accept the long bookish discussions and philosophical dialogues because in those very pages are woven and dispersed the revelatory signs, traces, and symptoms. The second category will be fascinated by the conflict of ideas and will seek connections (which the author refuses to authorize) with the present day. The third will realize that this text is a network of other texts, a detective story of citations, a book made of books [translation my own].

In the novel, William of Baskerville, in the best tradition of Sherlock Holmes, solves a series of violent crimes by means of clues that draw upon a wide range of esoteric medieval and early Renaissance knowledge. In this sense, we have a detective story mingled with a dissertation on cultural history. The "solution" owes more to a mixture of the magical realism of Borges with the allegory of medieval romance: a mysterious lost manuscript hidden at the heart of a labyrinthine and allegorically arranged library. Furthermore, the text shares the tropes of historical romance in the way it is insistently set against the background of a society torn by conflict, both religious and political, so that the actions of the characters are constantly linked to the wider political stage of "History" in the best traditions of Walter Scott. Nor is the framework of historical romance devoid of a conventional love interest to accompany the struggle of a society emerging (if it did but know it) from the Middle Ages to the Renaissance. On the evening of the third day, in a scene narrated as a series of citations from Cistercian commentaries on the most famous allegorical commingling of romance and religion – the Song of Songs – we learn that Adso obtains the sexual favors of a beautiful young woman, "her neck as white as an ivory tower" (291).

Authenticity and anachronism: text and history

It is not merely the case, however, that we relinquish a romance narrative for the remoteness of a medieval manuscript only to find those tropes and citations once again in the plot of the manuscript. In choosing to publish this manuscript, in committing himself to committing an act of love, the narrator has worried from the very beginning about making love in the right style, about having the proper kind of romance. And on this score, our narrator is plagued by several questions: What style should he employ? Should he follow the Italian models of the day? Should he retain the Latin passages or should he translate them?

For the narrator, the correct answers to these questions will be the ones that allow him to remain faithful to his manuscript, that allow him to be properly authentic and historical. Yet being true to his love (the manuscript) is not that easy; in fact, it proves quite difficult. First, there is the problem of deciding exactly to what he must be faithful: the text that he holds is decidedly corrupt; as the narrator explains, at the most basic level he knows that "in translating Adso's Latin into his own neo-Gothic French, Vallet took some liberties, and not only stylistic liberties" (xvii). So to translate the text exactly as it stands is to repeat the corruptions, is to be unfaithful to the original manuscript. But this is not the only problem. Second, the narrator wants to publish an Italian version of the manuscript when in fact "Adso thinks and writes like a monk who has remained impervious to the revolution of the vernacular" (xvii). Already, then, any attempt to translate the manuscript into a modern, vernacular language betrays the style of the original Latin manuscript, a problem our narrator's Italian translation will share with Vallet's neo-Gothic French translation. Yet there remains in Vallet's version numerous Latin passages that "Abbé Vallet himself did not feel it opportune to translate" (xviii). And here is where the narrator must consider most seriously what it means to be faithful to his beloved manuscript. To retain all of Vallet's Latin passages would be historically authentic. Hence, the Latin passages could remain as the sign that the translator has been faithful to his beloved manuscript (a similar instance would be the fact that William Weaver, Eco's translator, decided to retain all the Latin passages that appear in the Italian novel in the English edition of *The Name of the Rose*).³ But this also seems to be the wrong choice; in the narrator's opinion it would amount to "a misplaced sense of fidelity to my source." After all, the "original" source was entirely in Latin, and what he is presented with here are fragments that do not necessarily "help" his translation. Instead of retaining all of the Latin passages, the narrator makes the following decision:

> I have eliminated excesses, but I have retained a certain amount. And I fear that I have imitated those bad novelists [*cattivi romanzieri*] who, introducing a French character, make him exclaim, "Parbleau!" and "La femme, ah! la femme!" (xviii)

The narrator is in a double bind here. He must be faithful to the original in order to avoid anachronism, yet authenticity produces the appearances of anachronism. That is to say, if the narrator retained all of the Latin passages he would be guilty of excess, perhaps even that kind of textual excess which we would associate with the historical romance. However, if the narrator were to decide to translate all of the Latin passages into modern Italian, the translation itself would sound anachronistic, would not sound "authentic" enough, and instead resemble a second-rate novel. So the best that the narrator can do is retain some of the Latin (to sound authentic) but not all (to eliminate the excesses of historical romance). Yet this method of transcription and translation does not seem to be entirely satisfactory either, for the remaining quotations will still give the manuscript the air of a second-rate novel – they will lend the text the "atmosphere" of history and the foreign intrigue which once again characterizes historical romances. It seems, then, that no matter what the narrator tries to do with his manuscript it begins to read like a historical romance.

If Eco's novelistic style is defined *by* the problem of anachronism and authenticity, which are associated with historical romance, it is also defined by the problem of woman, another concern of romance. Woman, in a manner of speaking ("la femme"), will once again mark the difficulties of style, of making love in the correct style. The problem with incorporating some of the Latin quotations will be that they evoke the style of bad novels of the type associated with male characters who try to speak about women. And this is precisely the type of novel from which the introductory remarks, through their avoidance of the traditional gender tropes of romance, have tried to dissociate the "manuscript" – a point further emphasized by the fact that Eco's novel is set in a monastery, whereas the "bad" romance/novel is identified by the "foreign" words, "La femme, ah! la femme!" (xviii). We could rephrase this and say that the problem of finding the right style in which to commit the act of love (with the beloved manuscript) is finally the problem of finding a style that decidedly tries to avoid women and the literature of excess (romance) that might be associated with them.

The pleasure of the text, the act of love, is not by the narrator's account something with which women are supposed to have any traffic. Eco's particular brand of romance will do more to erase the position of woman than it will to reinforce her role in the manner of traditional romance. Or at least this would be the strong reading of Eco's emphasis on the indeterminacy of the gender of the beloved and the clear gendering of the controlling narrator as male. Such a reading would be borne out by the fact that the only decidedly female character in *The Name of the Rose*, in the "manuscript," is not endowed with the gift of language.[4] It would appear, then, that the only way to avoid the excesses of romance and achieve historical authenticity is to silence women. Within the frame of a coy self-awareness about textuality, within a preface entitled "Naturally, a manuscript," problems of excess will be negotiated at woman's expense. Within the novel itself, the postmodern historical romance will go forward with woman silenced and burnt. In a postscript to the novel, as we shall see, a silent woman will allow a man to understand what postmodernity is.

All of the points which I have just raised, however, do not form a list of charges of sexism against Eco; rather what I am trying to do here is to suggest that Eco's ironic postmodernization of issues of genre and history is vitiated by being mortgaged to a classical portrayal of gender. This problematic intersection of gender and genre provides a threat to history, which Eco's text may try to avoid but which continues to haunt the narrative. The nature of this threat is not simply one of inaccuracy, which would presuppose that there was a way to write history properly, a way to be properly faithful to the original event, a proper style in which to commit an act of love. The tangled web of sources places us at a very great remove from any question of simple fidelity to an authoritative original. We are in a postmodern field, where history is always already something to be written. Rather, the threat that woman and the genre of romance pose has to do with the very meaning of history: they might threaten our understanding of history by suggesting that history might mean something more than itself. This may seem like a strong statement to make, for after all, isn't our concern for history based on the fact that it does mean something? In answer to my self-imposed question, I will first say simply, yes. But the difference in this case is that the force of the intersection of gender and genre is to make us reconsider *what* history means.

On the most basic level, the problem that woman and romance turn up is that the meaning or significance of history might have to do with more than just getting the dates straight – determining just which version of the manuscript one has (a nineteenth-century French translation of a fourteenth-century Latin manuscript, or a neo-Gothic French version of a seventeenth-century Latin edition of a fourteenth-century Latin text), or determining whether the manuscript is "genuine" (is it actually what it says it is?), or using the right style when editing the manuscript (translating a neo-Gothic French manuscript sprinkled with Latin quotations into vernacular "modern" Italian).

Yet these are precisely the types of concern that the narrator wishes us to believe are the prerogative of history. For it is this position that allows Eco's narrator to believe that one can write for the sheer pleasure of writing, read for the sheer pleasure of reading. According to his account, there does not need to be any concern for the historical force of events or the notion that writing might itself be an act with historical consequences. The past, and thus writing or reading about the past, puts us at a distance where past events are "gloriously lacking in any relevance for our day" (xix). The past is so remote in its temporality that it is "atemporally alien to our hopes and our certainties" (xix).

In reading and possibly believing in these words of the narrator, we must also recall that they are uttered by the same narrator who just happened to be in Prague in 1968. Eco could be articulating a post-68 sensibility, a lack of faith in the historical force of words. Yet it is also possible to understand what the narrator is saying here as a counter to what the text of the novel is actually doing. I would go so far as to argue that the novel is *not* asking us to forget the force of historical events but rather to rethink the ways in which this force is activated. That is to say, the "introduction" claims to substitute a manuscript for a beloved, the pleasure of antiquarian scholarship for the anachronistic excesses of the romance; yet, at the same time, the novel plunges into an explicit play with anachronism and romance – a use of ironic temporality that we will come to understand as the defining feature of Eco's postmodernity.

This turn to anachronism is not, however, mere gross historical error – the placement of modern railroads in a novel about the fourteenth century. Instead, for Eco and for the historical romance, anachronism is not so much a historical error as a way of rethinking history. On the simplest level, the use of anachronism confronts us with questions about how material is designated "historical." Although Eco's novel is rife with quotations from medieval sources, it is largely (of course) comprised of contemporary material written to sound as if it were medieval in origin.[5] Similarly, Scott concerns himself in *Old Mortality* with a title character who "was profuse in the communication of all the minute information which he had collected concerning [the Covenanters], their wars, and their wanderings."[6] Scott, like Eco, wants to make us believe that his characters carry the weight and words of history, because it is only on the basis of historical material that the romance story can unfold. Yet this "historical" material can only be recognized as historical because the characters of romance present it as such. The juxtaposition of periods as a defining feature of the anachronism is at work in the postmodern romance of Eco and Scott alike. The romance of Scott's *Waverley*, for example, depends upon its being poised at a point of transition between two worlds: the tribal and the modern. Committed to the modern by virtue of being a novel (tribes don't write novels, they sing songs), Scott's postmodern romance nonetheless evokes a nostalgia for the past with which modernity cannot finally come to terms. Eco's novel, like Scott's, is explicitly concerned with a point of passage between the medieval and the Renaissance, as evidenced by the concern with William's spectacles – a very "modern" invention for the Middle Ages. And at the same time it also constantly plays upon the twentieth-century reader's fascination with the past – a fascination, for instance, with the thought that spectacles, which are so familiar, could ever have seemed "modern." In this sense, both Eco and Scott must mark the historical as that which was written in the past, yet they must anachronistically write that very history as a trace in "modern" romance. As we shall see, the founding trope of historical romance is anachronism, the recognition of history's claim to write the past accurately in the present as inherently anachronistic. And to understand how this works with regard to postmodern romance, and to witness once again Eco's troubled relationship with gender, it is necessary to turn to his own anachronistic *Postscript to The Name of the Rose*.

Postmodern postscripts: an ironic temporality

The Name of the Rose is undoubtedly one of the most economically successful pieces of postmodern literature, and the *Postscript to The Name of the Rose* is Eco's own attempt to explain that success.[7] The fact that the explanation of success belongs in a postscript shows the extent to which *The Name of the Rose* can be considered postmodern. This is no modernist project, the success of which might be predicted on the basis of the degree of conceptual elaboration of grounds which precede the art object – the case in which a manifesto would dictate the structure of the narrative that follows it. The legitimate grounds of postmodern art can only be found *after* the event, in a time that the art work neither intersects nor produces. That is to say, the postmodern art work does not inhabit the time of its own success. Neither is it complacently inaugural (after the manner of the Eiffel Tower) nor does it produce the temporality in which it will have its effect (after the manner characterized by Marx's *Capital*).[8] Postmodernism effects a radically new relationship to time, which differs significantly from any modernist project. The distinguishing features of modernism's relationship to time – the condition of being either the inauguration or the determination of a historical project – are absent here. Instead, the bemused *belatedness* with which Eco confronts success, as success which is not so much unexpected as it is radically unthinkable (a best-selling novel about medieval theology with only one sex scene) is the mark of how little *The Name of the Rose* is a modern novel.

All of this is to say that the postmodernism of *The Name of the Rose* consists neither in the simple fact of being published in the 1980s nor in the use of certain formal techniques of an avant-garde – what might loosely be called pastiche.[9] The postmodernity of *The Name of the Rose* lies in its problematic temporality which the postscript most fully articulates. The postscript is written after the novel and yet contains material, both "historical" information about the Middle Ages and about Eco's process of writing, which precede the novel. That is to say, the postscript's narration is both the cause of and caused by (the effect of) the narrative that is *The Name of the Rose*.

In calling attention to this formal (anachronistic) property, I do not want to suggest that all novels with postscripts are postmodern. Novelists have long explained themselves in postscripts to their work; just as postmodernism is not simply that which follows after modernism, it is also not just postscript. What is crucial about the troubled temporality of *The Name of the Rose* is the extent to which, as a historical novel, it can only attempt to explain its *relationship to history* by means of a postscript, by means of an ironic temporality. This is as much as saying that a postaesthetics, an aesthetics of postmodernism, would consist of finding a way in which to articulate the troubled (and ironical) relationship that the art object imposes upon the historical. More simply put, the site of the postaesthetics must be an ironic postscript that casts doubt not certainty over the historical–aesthetic project.

And it is from this position of doubt, as opposed to certainty, that we can begin to make a distinction (even if it is not an entirely certain distinction) between ironic attitude and an ironic temporality. Returning to Eco's postscript once again, what we find is that for Eco the irony of the past is that there is a problem in recognizing it as historical:

> There is one matter that has amused me greatly: every now and then a critic or a reader writes to say that some character of mine declares things that are too modern, and in every one of these instances, and only in these instances, I was actually quoting fourteenth-century texts.
>
> (*PS*, 76)

The past somehow seems not other but altogether too familiar.

P.S. An Aside on Irony from the Rev. Dr Dryasdust F.A.S.

In making this association between postmodernism and irony, our author does not mean to call up the ghost of New Criticism as her ally. She is clearly not attempting to argue that Umberto Eco is really Cleanth Brooks in disguise; "The Well Wrought Rose" would not strike one as a very appropriate title for this chapter. If Brooks's focus on irony is as a device or attitude that unified the dissenting voices with a text, as a *perspective* from which one could view all the sides of the poem at once and synthesize partial and even conflicting attitudes and interpretations, postmodernism is an awareness of historical irony that cannot be mastered as a point of view towards history. Put simply, postmodernism is the recognition of the specifically *temporal* irony within narrative.

The significance of this distinction between New Critical ironic attitude and postmodern ironic temporality is a crucial one and

37

In many respects, the irony that what seems so familiar is really that which is most historical is what postaesthetics inherits from the modernist project. Modernism's treatment of the past may be understood by recalling the famous advertisement of the Philip Morris Company's plug for MOMA, which juxtaposes primitivism in modern art with primitive art. The caption at the top of the page reads: "Which is primitive? Which is modern?" and the point, of course, is that you would be hard-pressed to tell the difference.[10] Primitivism is being made familiar; that kind of shock is quite modern. What is modern, what is primitive, is what is universal and hence *true*. Decontextualized and dehistoricized, the primitive and the modern become one and the same, both equally present. Eco's example with regard to *The Name of Rose* shows the extent to which the modernist project succeeded in making the past present, in making it familiar and "true" in a way curiously aligned with an ironic attitude as explained by Brooks. In contradistinction to the modernist project, postmodernism seeks to recognize the past as past, as historical other; yet at the same time, postmodernism can only supply such recognition through retrospective (or post-scripted) irony – through an ironic temporality. It is no longer a worth examining in some detail. On the most rudimentary level, ironic attitude involves a distinction and disjunction between the literal and the figural – saying one thing but really meaning another, sarcasm and understatement being particularly controlled forms of irony. The general form of irony as an attitude would be the conscious employment of a figure of speech literally, or vice versa. This would distinguish "what a nice day," said of a thunderstorm, as an ironic comment rather than a lie. Instead of an attempt to deceive, there is a conscious misapplication of language.

A more complicated version of an ironic attitude can be found in the work of the New Critics. For Brooks, irony is "a device for definition of attitudes by qualification," and it functions to "throw light upon Coleridge's account of the imagination as the synthesizing faculty of the mind."[11] Put most simply, for Brooks, irony "accords with a wise recognition of the total situation."[12] The key words here, which help us to understand the modernity of New Criticism, are "wise recognition" and "total situation," because they make clear the humanist and organicist aspects of Brooks's claim. "Wise recognition" is a certain type of activation of the intellect (presumably performed by the intellectual who is in pursuit of the timeless, human truths of poetry) and consists of the recognition of the properties of a poem that extend beyond mere appearance, beyond the literal reading. Or to use Brooks's words to the same effect, wise recognition makes us understand that: "The 'form' of the poem is . . . much more universal truth which makes the modern and the primitive appear alike, rather it is ironical that we would confuse them. Unlike the modernist artist, the bemused postmodern author or critic is willing to point out that there *is* a difference, that the irony at play results not in synthesis but in difference.

But what is the difference? How does the ironic evocation of the past insist upon an uncanny otherness to the historical? Or: what is the effect of the postmodern condition of ironic temporality? The most crude effect is that within his postscript Eco is inviting us simply to see the difference between the past and the present through his usage of "historical" illustrations. Throughout he scatters photographs of medieval architectural elements and book illustrations. But rather than "identify" in the caption each photograph as historical artifact (such information is reserved for a list of illustrations at the beginning of the postscript) Eco provides as caption a quote from *The Name of the Rose*. For instance, on the page facing part of Eco's discussion of post modernism, we find a photo identified by the illustrations list as a mosaic depicting "Empress Theodora and her court," which dates back to the "middle of the sixth century," and can be found in "the Church of San Vitale, Ravenna." Yet when

than the precise set of rules and conventions mechanically [literally] apprehended. It is finally, the delicate balance and reconciliation of a host of partial interpretations and attitudes" (102).

Yet in speaking of "partial interpretations and attitudes," Brooks is not suggesting that an ironic attitude is a recognition of the incompleteness of the literary reading of a poem. Quite the opposite. It is important to understand that what Brooks is talking about is the *reconciliation* of the various aspects of the poem which are incomplete in and of themselves into the greater unity of the reader's ironic consciousness. Brooks is thus arguing that the wise recognition, which makes up the ironic attitude, does not simply recognize part of the picture, rather it sees the "total situation." This is another way of saying that an ironic attitude is a *perspective* from which one can view all the sides of the poem at once, from which one can synthesize partial and even conflicting attitudes and interpretations.[13]

There is, however, something very unsatisfying about Brooks's understanding of irony. Although he wants to believe that the universe is inherently contradictory and tensional, this recognition of difference does not last very long, since the function of "ironic awareness" is to put an end to difference or ironic uncertainty by making us entirely conscious of irony. In emphasizing the reconciliation of differences into an organic whole, in focusing on the "total situation," Brooks does not leave room for the possibility of irreconcilable differences which do not form a cozy whole. According to this photo appears in the context of the postscript, it is captioned with the following passage from *The Name of the Rose*:

At a merry signal from the abbot, the procession of virgins entered. It was a radiant line of richly dressed females, in whose midst I thought at first I could discern my mother; then I realized my error, because it was certainly the maiden terrible as an army with banners. Except that she wore a crown of white pearls on her head, a double strand, and two cascades of pearls fell on either side of her face. (Adso's dream in *The Name of the Rose*, p. 428)

(*PS*, 69)

Although we could argue that this is merely an instance of postmodernism as sales pitch, as self-promotion, such a position would not resolve the lingering question of the relationship between text and illustration. For the caption that Eco takes from *The Name of the Rose* does not simply explain the illustration nor does the illustration go very far in "explaining" the novel. Although the picture may have been a source upon which Eco drew for his novelistic description, the novel does not attempt to discuss directly the Empress Theodora but instead asks us to believe that Adso's dream of women is a re-enactment of the comedy, *Coena Cypriani*.

him, dissenting voices are always capable of being brought together, juxtaposed in the mind of the subtle reader. Yet as we shall see in the following chapter on Scott, such reconciliation is not necessarily possible. Scott's historical romance situates itself at the point where two radically heterogenous conceptual languages clash: where it is not a case of deciding on an ambivalence in language, where instead no common language exists. The assumption that the difference that irony makes can always be reconciled in a common language, a balanced attitude, marks the political limitations of the "New Criticism." It is this assumption, rather than any specific political bias, that has caused resistance to the New Criticism to arise from sites of political struggle where clashes of radically heterogenous languages occur, such as feminism and anti colonialism.

Along with the assumption of the underlying unity of all languages comes a privileging of the individual human subject in whose grasp of the ironic possibilities of that language all differences are reconciled. The problem lies here not so much in the specific cultural complexion of that subject (white male), as in the fact that this subject is presumed to be outside language. The subject stands before or behind language, using it, so that the irony that he (rarely she) finds in language is not extended to the subject himself. All the ironies of language are grasped in the mind of the subject. Recent developments in critical theory have taught us to consider the extent to which the subject's position is constructed

And the disjunction between picture and text does not stop here, for neither illustration nor caption seems to have anything to do with the accompanying text of the postscript. In short, the past, be it in the form of medieval mosaic or historical novel, doesn't simply illustrate the present, or vice versa. Authentication is not at issue. Rather, Eco's text forces us to think about the way in which the juxtaposition of word and image, of text and illustration, gives rise to a loss of meaning, to a moment of visual uncertainty.[14] In the postmodern condition of ironic temporality, the historical event as referent becomes problematic; any attempt at creating a meaning for the past is also the onset of a loss of meaning. Thus, the meaning that the modern detective William looks for with the aid of his spectacles cannot be discovered, just as the reader is not going to discover the truth about the Middle Ages within *The Name of the Rose* or about modernity within the *Postscript*.

This postmodern notion of ironic doubt rather than certainty about the past is perhaps nowhere more clearly illustrated than at the end of *The Name of the Rose*. After reading what has turned into over 600 pages of "manuscript," we are told by its "author," Adso of Melk: "And it is a hard thing for this old monk, on the threshold in language and therefore itself subject to the destabilizing play of linguistic irony. To put it crudely, once Benveniste has pointed out the extent to which our understanding of what it is to be an individual subject is affected by the linguistic function of the signifier "I," we cannot abstract that signifier from the potential for irony. Irony cannot simply be the property of a subject, his or her attitude, since irony may implicate the subject presumed to have the attitude: the joke may be on us, after all. Irony, that is, is not simply the attitude of a subject but the condition of subjectivity.

This is something we have recognized about the figure of the narrator in novels: the "I" that speaks is not exactly synonymous with the "I" that is spoken, the narrator is at once the origin of the novel and a character in it. As Derrida has noted, Poe's *The Facts in the Case of M. Valdemar* develops the *reductio ad absurdum* of this fact in the line "I say to you that I am dead."[14] The line points out the separation between "I" as referring to the enunciating subject (speaker) and to the subject of the enunciation (the "I" who is spoken). The difference between these two always opens the subject to the ironic play of linguistic ambiguity. As Derrida remarks, "I believe that the condition for a true act of language is my being able to say 'I am dead'. . . . 'I am dead' has a meaning if it is obviously false. 'I am dead' is an intelligible sentence. Therefore 'I am dead' is not only a possible proposition for one who is known to be living, but the very condition of the living person to speak is for him to be able to say,

41

of death, not to know whether the letter he has written contains some hidden meaning, or more than one, or many, or none at all" (610). Adso, reflecting upon his narration of past events, can't tell for sure what they mean or if they mean at all. And this predicament leads him, curiously enough, to occupy the same position as that of the only woman in the novel; in Adso's words, "All I can do now is to be silent" (610). Silence and uncertainty – the ironic relationship to the past.

Eco's novel could be said to end on a note of double uncertainty, for to cast doubt over the past is also to cast doubt over the future. The only certainty for Adso is the certainty of death, yet just what that death may mean is no longer clear. The event itself is certain, but the meaning of that event is not. While he once believed in the glory of divine revelation and elevation through death, Adso now sees the moment of death as a "sink[ing] into the divine shadow" which means silence, indifference, doubt. He even sees the future of his manuscript, lacking as it does in a divine purpose, as uncertain. Not inappropriately, then, the last words of the novel emphasize this point: "I leave this manuscript, I do not know for whom; I no longer know what it is about: stat rosa pristina nomine, nomina nuda tenemus" (611). Instead of finding the truth of or

significantly, 'I am dead.'"[15] To put this another way, the use of "I", which marks the immediate individuality of the subject is also the subject's giving up of individuality to become a pronoun, an explicitly empty linguistic mark, used before and to be used again. The "I" is in this sense an ironic reminder of the death of the subject as immanent possibility of the entry into language. To say "I" is always to admit one's transience. The "I" of the subject marks his or her division from itself: they can only situate the intimate immediacy of self-awareness as a fact of language.

The understanding of irony solely in terms of attitude is thus the failure to recognize the extent to which irony is the condition not merely of linguistic descriptions of the world, but also of the linguistic situation of the subject. It is a failure to recognize the ironic destabilization inherent in the position of the subject in language. More properly, we might say that irony is the condition of the subject in the temporality of language, in the face of language as the mark of death even in the affirmation of life. To phrase this less apocalyptically, the entry of the subject into itself through language is also an entry into a temporality that includes the subject's own disappearance or nonexistence (since language was used before, and will be used again). The effect of our awareness of the subject as situated by language is not to deny subjectivity (people do speak). Rather, it locates the subject as always in the grip of the ironic temporality that language carries with it: in which the assertion of the immediate, of about the past, we find the name of the rose – a name which we may or may not understand, just as we may or may not (depending upon our familiarity with Latin) understand the last sentence of the novel. Just what the rose might mean in the novel is what we can't decide. There are possible nominalist readings of the final sentence of the novel, but the sign (or name) of the rose is so rich in interpretive possibilities that it practically has no meaning at all. This is a point that Eco himself is not shy about making in his postscripted remarks:

presence, signifies only by virtue of the simultaneous evocation of mortality and absence.

Instead of following in the path of critics like Brooks and relying upon an understanding of irony as ironic attitude, I would like to suggest that for our author postmodernism is not an ironic attitude but the recognition of this specifically *temporal* irony in representation.[16] Postmodernism is an awareness of historical irony that cannot be mastered as a point of view toward history. Within the terms of postmodernism's ironic temporality, we are not surveying the ironical picture of world history from a single, synthesizing perspective as Brooks's literary analysis would recommend. Ironic temporality does not confirm what one knows or sees; rather it casts *doubt* upon the possibility of understanding at all.[17]

the rose is a symbolic figure so rich in meanings that by now it hardly has any meaning left: Dante's mystic rose, and go

(*Castle-Gate, York, 1817*)

lovely rose, the Wars of the Roses, rose thou art sick, too many rings around Rosie, a rose by any other name, a rose is a rose is a rose is a rose, the Rosicrucians. (*PS*, 3)

This is no instance of the certainty of New Critical irony; we can't resolve these different interpretations into any one synthetic reading which will render the truth of the text transparent. If there is anything that we can be certain about it is that what we do find is another text, concealing another text. Postmodernism, like the postscript, is not an attempt at making sense of the past, rather it is an attempt at revealing the troubled creation that is "a sense of history" – a sense of history that extends beyond the mere allusions provided by literary history. It is also not insignificant that such revelation takes place in a way that departs from the historical avant-garde. As Eco remarks in the *Postscript*:

The past conditions us, harries us, blackmails us. The historical avant-garde . . . tries to settle scores with the past . . . . The avant-garde destroys, defaces the past . . . But the moment comes when the avant-garde (the modern) can go no

43

further, because it has produced a metalanguage that speaks of its impossible texts (conceptual art). The postmodern reply to the modern consists of recognizing that the past, since it cannot really be destroyed, because its destruction leads to silence, must be revisited: but with irony, not innocently. (*PS*, 66–7)

Situating itself in counter-distinction to the modern as avant-garde, postmodernism must respond to the pressure of the past. Postmodernism cannot simply ignore the past; it must reproduce "historical" manuscripts. However, in suggesting this type of response to the past by postmodernism, I am not finally arguing that postmodernism produces either a metalanguage or a manifesto. Postmodernism is not futurism. Rather, in emphasizing the inescapable presence and future of the past, postmodernism stands in contradiction to projects such as those of the futurists. Put another way, postmodernism, as Eco sees it, cannot deny the historicity of the past, for that would be to fall into the destructive formalism – the technical production of silence – which exemplifies the avant-garde. Postmodernism makes history *function*; it does not reveal the meaning of history. The postmodern relationship between history and the art object is one in which both are dependant upon one another for their creation, but neither can straightforwardly explain the other. The text of the art object can't explain the illustrations of history, and the historical pictures can't gloss the text of art.

What's more, neither text nor object tells us when we are to be ironical. Unlike the manifestos of modernism, which emphasized understanding, and unlike Brooks, who believed in the importance and the possibility of spotting irony, postmodernism's ironic temporality calls into question the inevitability of such recognition and the necessity of understanding. As Eco puts it:

Thus, with the modern, anyone who does not understand the game can only reject it, but with the postmodern, it is possible not to understand the game and yet take it seriously. Which is, after all, the quality (the risk) of irony. There is always someone who takes ironic discourse seriously. (*PS*, 68)

Unlike Pound who believes that the modernist project can be kept going with the imperative, "Be modern," or the futurists who kept telling us to "Be electric," Eco is pointing out that you can't just say,

"Be ironical." There is always someone who will take the discourse seriously.[19] This is another way of saying that there is no pure certainty within the postmodern condition of ironic temporality. The subject is not reaffirmed as either universal or as that which is presumed to know.

The return of romance: the retreat of postmodernism

Up to this point, I have argued for the ways in which Eco articulates the postmodern condition as ironic temporality. However, Eco finally fails to deliver on a postmodernism that is rigorously attentive to the displacement of attitude by temporality. (This is no doubt some solace to those of us envious of his superstardom.) Eco's postmodernism does finally come back to a matter of ironic attitude closer to Romanticism and New Criticism than postmodernism, a failure which is inextricably linked to the position of woman in his text. We might say that the *Postscript* ends up by reinscribing the silent female as mark of the ironic attitude in much the same way as the closing sequences of the atrocious film version of *The Name of the Rose*, when the silent woman, instead of burning for her crime, appears at the side of the road as Adso and William leave the monastery. The film may not be so unfaithful to Eco as we might think, in its evocation of the romance trope of the ironic silence of woman.

In the *Postscript*, Eco defines postmodern irony in such a way as to bring us back to Brooks and the Romantics:

> I think of the postmodern attitude as that of a man who loves a very cultivated woman and knows he cannot say to her, "I love you madly," because he knows that she knows (and that she knows that he knows) that these words have already been written by Barbara Cartland. Still, there is a solution. He can say, "As Barbara Cartland would put it, I love you madly." At this point having avoided false innocence, having said clearly that it is no longer possible to speak innocently, he will nevertheless have said what he wanted to say to the woman: that he loves her, but he loves her in an age of lost innocence. If the woman goes along with this, she will have received a declaration of love all the same. Neither of the two speakers will feel innocent, both will have accepted the challenge of the past, of the already said, which cannot be

eliminated; both will consciously and with pleasure play the game of irony . . . . But both will have succeeded, once again, in speaking of love. (*PS*, 67)

The wisdom of postmodernism – postmodernism's ability to revisit the past – is once again made possible through a loss of innocence and a fall into irony: Eco's after-the-fall tale of postmodernism is a fittingly ironic replay of the oldest romance of all – the tale of Adam and Eve.

What is important, however, is that Eco reduces irony to a matter of attitude because of his inability to articulate the relationship between women and romance, between gender and genre, as they become the concerns of *both* "high" and "low" culture. It is not for nothing that Eco's postmodern romance narrates the story of a man in love with a "*very cultivated*" woman. We might wonder whether Eco's parable refers to everyman, but it is quite certain that it does not refer to just any woman. Post George Eliot and Virginia Woolf, if women have a problem taking part in culture it is of no concern to Eco; within his version of postmodernism women can, in fact, become such formidable representatives of culture that men have trouble speaking to them . . . or at least speaking to them of romance. And it is important that it is romance about which men have trouble speaking. Romance, as a narrative genre, seems to pose a problem within postmodernism. Interestingly enough, romance is not simply the genre of Eco's postmodern parable but (ironically) it is also the genre of Barbara Cartland. Significantly, it is this later type of romance that gives Eco, or Eco's male character, the most trouble. However much Eco tries to negate the fact (as he does in the opening remarks in *The Name of the Rose*), romance is still the genre *of* and *for* women in the field of mass culture. Eco comes to terms with this female genre only by making it the site of an ironic attitude: it is not the stuff Eco's very cultured woman *values*, rather it is precisely what she *knows* about and *devalues*. Thus, woman must be detached from her genre by the division of high from low culture, and Eco turns to Jamesian prose in order to do justice to his predicament. Eco reduces the postmodern condition to the fact that silly romances by silly women only get in the way of real romances by men, as Eliot might put it. Presumably, *The Name of the Rose* is to be preferred to Barbara Cartland's romances. In setting this priority, Eco diverts the problem *of* woman into a problem *for* women. Eco's postmodernism proclaims that real romance is a matter of culture, a matter of transforming mere acquisition of knowledge into cultural meaning, a position which starts ironically to echo George Eliot's pronouncements on "fellow feeling."

It would seem, then, that the thematization of romance is at the very heart of Eco's postmodernism, and that the only way we can succeed – recall that in Eco's parable both parties are supposed to have succeeded – "in speaking of love," in speaking across the cultural and historical barriers imposed by women and their popular romances, is to engage in the self-conscious and pleasurable (according to Eco) play of ironic citation of romance. Yet to make this argument is to go along with Eco's assessment of the postmodern predicament, and believe (falsely) that both the man and the woman succeeded in speaking. This, I would suggest, would be to fall into an ironic attitude, into the myth of the universal perspective.[20] Instead of following Eco quite so blindly into the land of metanarrative, we need to slow down a bit and reassess the relationship among women, history, and romance as they are situated *in* and *by* postmodernism.

To begin with, the question of postmodernism and women. Eco's *Postscript* articulates the postmodern romance, and likewise the romance of postmodernism, as a tale told by a man for men. Women, whether represented by the female character in *The Name of the Rose*, the women in the photo of the mosaic, or the very cultivated woman in the *Postscript*, are not allowed a voice or at least a voice any of the men can understand. Eco's situating of women as the silent other who silences men leads to the conclusion that women cannot actively participate in the discourse of postmodernism. Postmodernism becomes one more seductive technique, a way for men to talk to, or at, women. Put another way, postmodernism's attitude, and not its ironic temporality, is "that of a man," a man's voice heard in high-culture romance, in the postscript to Eco's successful novel. For Eco, women participate in postmodernist discourse only through their silence; their voice is to be found only within the "vulgar" pages of Barbara Cartland's popular romances. If we are to believe Eco, then women can either produce romance as popular culture (Cartland's novels, for instance), or they can become the narrated, very cultivated object of postmodern romance, which thematizes romance and representation as a problem for men.[21]

In taking Eco to task as I have just done, I am not isolating one example of postmodernism's "bad" attitude, which has as its significant characteristic an ignorance of the *force* of gender. Craig Owens, seemingly sympathetic to the plight of the silent woman, has this to say:

> The absence of discussion of sexual difference in writings about postmodernism, as well as the fact that few women have engaged in the modernism/postmodernism debate, suggest that postmodernism may be another masculine invention engineered to exclude women.[22]

What Owens does not seem to recognize is that it is not biological "sexual difference" which the postmodern debate ignores; Eco's texts are full of that. Rather, in each of these instances it is the force of gender *tout court* which is being ignored. "Postmodern" fashion is still draped on women's bodies as in *New York Times* advertisements. It is in this sense that, although Eco's postmodernism like Owens' does not exclude women *per se*, it is an instance of men putting women in their place. If much primitivism managed the "shock" of the primitive, then Eco's and Owens' postmodernism manages the "shock" of women. In a way, both Cartland's romance and Eco's postmodernism actually serve *modernism* by representing history as accessible escape rather than as that which is an irrecuperable other. Cartland offers women history as an escape from their own lives; Eco offers readers history as an escape from women. If much of modernism refused to acknowledge the transgression of primitive art, Eco's postmodernism and Cartland's romance equally ignore the transgressiveness of the figure of woman within history.

A post-postscript:
from an ironic attitude back to an ironic temporality

To end with the previous section would be to give Eco the last word (the postscript) on postmodernism and concede that postmodernism is only a fashionable attitude – is only modernism accessorized for a new season of wear. Instead of fashioning an image of postmodernism which makes it look like only another trendy term in this season's theory wardrobe, I would like to suggest a postaesthetics which would take the position that postmodernism and romance may offer something more disturbing than Eco is willing to consider – a less easy resolution of gender as history or history as gender. That is to say, the move I would like to make is from an ironic attitude back to an ironic temporality.

To do this would be to rethink the way that history can be represented or is a representation. Postmodern romance can then become a citation of the past that allows the past to inhabit a position that cannot be controlled within a realist narrative of modern history or produced, as it is for Eco, at the expense of the silencing (or burning) of women. Postmodern romance is potentially an uncanny way to evoke a past that is both displacing and displaced. This is a point that will become clearer when I turn to Scott in the next chapter, but for now it is important to recognize that when I refer to the particular way in which postmodern romance evokes the past, I am not simply trying to find another way to describe the transgressions performed in the name of the avant-garde. As Hal Foster explains, the avant-garde is a modernist project which "connotes revolutionary transgression of social and cultural lines."[23] Postmodernism, on the other hand, is characterized by resistance that "suggests immanent struggle within or behind" social and cultural lines. Where the avant-garde transgresses, postmodernism resists.[24] Although I have stated postmodernism's case as one which transgresses historical periodicity, this would more accurately be described as a *resistance* to historical periodicity in that the work which postmodernism performs is more than an exceeding of a boundary, a breaking of a law; it has to do with an opposing force that interrogates what's at stake - politically and aesthetically – in having historical boundaries and aesthetic laws in the first place.[25] Not transgression for the sake of transgression (the avant-garde) but interrogation in the form of a resistance which would consider the historical circumstances, the context in which we are necessarily located, at the same time as it acknowledges the impossibility of totally defining those circumstances.[26]

Thus, we could understand the failure of the avant-garde to be its tendency to place romance as the genre that allows the modernist categories of historical reality and unreality to function unchallenged. This would make for a romance that would be no different from that of Cartland's; it would prove merely escapist – the hole it would open in the synchronic field of the real (escape from the modern world) would be merely sutured in the diachronic field of historical possibility as a potential reality. In opposition to the avant-garde's understanding of romance, postmodern romance would be transformative and progressively resistant when it enters the diachronic field of history as a *constitutive unreality*, realizing itself in the synchronic field of culture. Romance does not offer alternative realities, rather it underscores the fictionality of the "real" and the unreality of culture. That is to say, culture becomes unreal like the romance myths that are an integral part of the narrative in Conrad's *Nostromo*. Although I will explore this concept in detail in chapter 3, suffice it to say for now that in Conrad's novel the cultural voice of the colonized is heard within the tropes of romance, while their oppressors speak realist history. Postmodern romance as synchronic genre, as ironic temporality, cannot simply be dismissed as unreal fantasy; rather it upsets the very "reality" of culture. Postmodern romance does not find history to be innately realist, and instead transforms history by refusing to escape the unreality of the event (the structural unreality that is the silencing of minorities) by exchanging it for the potential of an otherness too alien to be "reality."

History stops making sense. The aesthetics and the politics of postmodern romance are bound to the transgressive relationship it forges between a theory of history and a theory of culture. If, as Adorno suggests, Beckett's modernism obliterated the meaning that was culture, postmodernism – as it has become a question for the thematization of romance – attempts to revisit culture by refusing to dismiss the challenge of the past, by refusing to represent it either objectively (realistically) or subjectively (as a matter of attitude). Even if we take it seriously. The ironic temporality characteristic of the postmodern condition means, to recall my discussion of Lyotard in the Introduction, that we can never take hold of the "now" or "the present from which we can claim to have a right view over the successive periods of our history."[27] Postmodernism is not a "now" but a haunting, excessive return of past events.

Eco fails to understand this relationship to the past, and instead is haunted by the question of gender. But if Eco's failure defuses the radical potential of his version of postmodernity, this final recourse to political conservatism on Eco's part moves us to consider in the next chapter how postmodern romance can indeed function as a form of resistance which dislocates politics from the hegemony of the real, from the progress of capitalist "real" history. The progress of capitalism that Scott preaches, the assurance of historical progress, is accompanied by a progress of romance that can be understood only in terms of postmodernism's emphasis on the uncertainty of historical knowledge.

2

DELAYED IN THE POST: WALTER SCOTT AND THE PROGRESS OF ROMANCE

¹A footnote to history

Walter Scott is not the first author that comes to mind when one is drawing up a pantheon of postmoderns. Nor have the years since Scott's death been kind to his literary reputation. Despite the enormous admiration that writers such as Jane Austen and George Eliot professed for his writing in his lifetime, subsequent criticism has tended to treat Scott's popularity and success as the mark of something less than high seriousness. His slavish patriotism has prevented his inclusion by left-wing critics in their defense of the popular imagination. Thus Scott appears neither in F. R. Leavis's *The Great Tradition* nor in Raymond Williams's *Culture and Society*.¹ Only in Europe has he received a rather more favourable reception, such as in Georg Lukács's enthusiastic account of "Scott's exceptional and revolutionary epic gifts."²

And yet his development of the historical romance crucially opens the question of history to an interrogation that can be named as postmodern. His enormous output of novels is apparently dedicated to proving the inevitability of modernity, of Whig progress, whilst preserving the premodern as the locus of touristic nostalgia. On the other hand, the element of romance muddies the image of historical destiny and bourgeois commodification of the past. Scott's texts explode in a welter of textuality: marginalia, footnotes, parodic scholarship. And that textual excess revolves around the unstable relationship between something called history and something called romance, in a way that inclines me to refer to "historical romance," in Scott's hands, as "postmodern romance."

To pursue this distinction, it is useful to consider first that the majority of Scott's marginal annotations are organized as epistles and serve to remind us that a letter does not always reach its destination – or at least not always as quickly as it might. It is because of one such untimely delay in the post that the author of *Ivanhoe* adds a footnote to the printed text of his dedicatory epistle. Concerned that his "original" letter – posted to the learned antiquarian, The Rev. Dr Dryasdust F.A.S. – took twelve months to travel from Cumberland to York, the author writes a footnote addressing the problems involved in transporting historical correspondence:

> I mention this circumstance, that a gentleman attached to the cause of learning, who now holds the principal control of the post-office, may consider whether, by some mitigation of the present enormous rates, some favour might not be shown to the correspondents of the principal Literary and Antiquarian Societies. I understand, indeed, that this experiment was once tried, but that the mail-coach having broken down under the weight of packages addressed to members of the Society of Antiquarians, it was relinquished as a hazardous experiment. Surely, however, it would be possible to build these vehicles in a form more substantial, stronger in the perch, and broader in the wheels, so as to support the weight of Antiquarian learning; when, if they should be found to travel more slowly, they would be not the less agreeable to quiet travellers like myself.[3]

The burden of historical correspondence threatens both postal carriages and pocketbooks: packages either cost too much to be sent by rapid post or become too voluminous and weighty to be moved by common carriages. Yet for all the attention he gives to the fact that correspondence is too slow, for all his helpful advice about how it is the post office could best bear the weight of antiquarian learning, the author of *Ivanhoe* fails to mention *why* he, as an author of romance, is so concerned about the speedy delivery of historical correspondence. What's the hurry? What difference does it make if historical correspondence gets delayed? Isn't history the least "timely" of disciplines, the discipline concerned with that which has already taken place in the past? No matter how much the correspondence of historians is expedited, past events are not going to change. Or are they?

In a sense, history is always delayed correspondence: time

will always elapse between the happening (sending) and the narration (delivery) of the event. Historical correspondence cannot be delivered instantaneously; it is only by virtue of the very delay that historians seek to overcome that history continues to be possible. Historians are always trying to catch up on their correspondence.

The modernity of the postal service is afflicted by delay, slowed down by the burden of history. But we will go a little further. Modernity, modernist historicism, fails to correspond with or to itself because of the way a certain effect of the "post" introduces a temporal slippage to modernity. Modernity spreads with the "post" (the postmodern does not simply come after the modern, as we have noted). Yet the "post" inhabits the modern as an anxiety about the burden of history and how to come to terms with its weight. In Scott's letter, then, it is because of the delay of the "post" that history never quite corresponds with, or to, itself. And when history isn't itself, romance intervenes. Here we touch upon the crisis that Scott introduces to modernity by way of the historical romance. In Scott's novels, the clash between the assurance of historical progress and the burden of the past is given over to romance just as in his letter it is consigned to the postal service. In each case, what arises is a sense of the postmodern, as I have described it in my introduction: of history as predicament. Our sense of the past is displaced, incomplete, uncertain, marked by an excess of temporality.

The importance of Scott lies with his generic exploration of the historical romance: of a novelistic form that seems to contradict itself from the start by virtue of a double insistence. On the one hand, the narrative of the novel offers the structure of diegetic progress through time, be it as *Bildungsroman* (*Waverley*) or from initial crisis to resolution and closure (*Redgauntlet*).[4] On the other hand, the force of historical romance continually evokes the necessary burden of the past, haunting and limiting the progress that both Whig ideology and the form of the novel itself uphold. Nor is this paradox one with which we might accost Scott as being hopelessly mired in ideological blindness: it is something that his novels thematize insistently as the clash between historical realism and historical romance.

I have remarked that when history isn't itself, romance intervenes. Scott matters precisely because the encounter between history and romance in his writings takes place among a multitude of explicitly textual frames – dedicatory epistles, introductions, postscripts, prefaces, footnotes, appendices such as the letter with which this chapter opened. The obvious similarity to the mechanisms of Eco's text is not coincidental. The rethinking of the relationship between romance and realism, between modernity and the burden of history, by way of the displacement of textuality itself is not merely a nostalgic critique of reluctantly admired progress. Rather, modernity is confronted by an effect of the "post," a certain circuitry of the letter, upon which it depends and yet which it must suppress in order to take place. It is in this sense, by virtue of this evocation of the unforgettable that is forgotten in modernist historicism, that Scott's romance is postmodern. As such, Scott's novels provide a way to rethink the relationship between narrative and the legitimation of historical knowledge, to think otherwise than in terms of a simple opposition of real(ist) history to romance.

"All changes round us"

All changes round us, past, present, and to come; that which was history yesterday becomes fable to-day, and the truth of to-day is hatched into a lie by to-morrow.
(Introductory Epistle, *The Monastery*[5])

The question that remains is: what is the relation between history and romance? Toward the end of *Waverley*, the narrator remarks that "it is not our purpose to intrude upon the province of history."[6] Readers, characters, narrative: keep out of history. This is a romance; history can only come in as a reminder, as the narrator continues: "we shall therefore only remind our readers, that about the beginning of November the Young Chevalier . . . ." History is allowed into the pages of romance only as that which the reader of romance has forgotten.

The province that will be inhabited in the *Waverley* novels is that of romance, which Scott describes in the Introduction to *The Monastery*:

yet the province of the romance writer being artificial, there is more required from him than a mere compliance with the simplicity of reality, – just as we demand from the scientific gardener, that he shall arrange, in curious knots and artificial parterres, the flowers which "nature boon" distributes freely on hill and dale. (*M*, 23–4)

History may be the stuff of recollection, but romance is the art of arrangement; the realm of romance exceeds the simplicity of "reality," just as the scientific gardener exceeds nature.[7] Romance, like gardening, takes nature into the "province" of artifice. At the risk of sounding like some provincial simpleton, let me say that I am not sure quite where we are with this word. Does "province" refer to a region or district, a realm of artifice? If so, then romance may not have the same grounds as those of history; it must keep to the small plots around the house and eschew the grand historical sweep of hill and dale. Put another way, romance must not look like history any more than a tea party should resemble a military exercise, a woman a man. However interesting this argument may or may not be, I want to suggest that at any rate it does not exhaust the possible meanings of Scott's phrase. Scott could also be implying that romance is an artificial province, precisely a copy of history, history as simulacrum. Romance, it would seem, both is and is not like history.

We can take this interpretative problem yet a step further by asking which came first, the historical chicken or the romantic egg? Turning back to *Waverley*, both senses of historical romance (as the province of artifice and as the artificial province) seem to guide the structure of Scott's tale of Edward Waverley. On the one hand, romance and historical fact must be separated. Once Waverley's life ceases to be the stuff of romance, the novel must end, because, as a romance, it cannot start to look like history. As the narrator explains toward the end of the novel: "[Waverley] felt himself entitled to say firmly, though perhaps with a sigh, that the romance of his life was ended, and that its real history had now commenced" (*W*, 415). Youthful romance ends when the maturity of real history begins. A temporal barrier, the movement from youth to maturity, separates the province of romance from that of real history, and each side of that barrier has a different "look," contains a different arrangement of events. Thus to suggest that the distinction between romance and history is only a matter of age – youth needs to be reminded of history, maturity *is* history – would be to suggest that romance is something a reader outgrows, just as children do stuffed animals. Readers thus progress from romance to real history. If history has knowledge, it must, in essentialist terms, situate itself in opposition to fiction, to the fables of romance.[8] It must be possible, as *Waverley*'s narrator believes, *not* to intrude on the province of history, if that is what he proposes to do at the end of the novel, having outgrown the youthful reading of romances that led the young Waverley into his adventures.

But romance is not simply prehistoric, misty myth to be dispelled by the sunlight of historical fact. As Scott reminds us in *Waverley*, "indeed, the most romantic parts of this narrative are precisely those which have a foundation in fact" (*W*, 493). This apparently empirical link is supported by the fact that romance is acknowledged by Scott as structural to the nature of society. Society cannot just give up on romances, cannot just outgrow them: "The progress of Romance, in fact, keeps pace with that of society, which cannot long exist, even in the simplest state, without exhibiting, some specimens of this attractive style of composition."[9] As society progresses, so does romance. Even if the young Waverley apparently outgrows romance, society never reaches the point when it is too old for romance. Romance is not merely a form of fiction that pollutes the minds of Britain's youth, causing them to run off with the Jacobites. There is something distinct about the province of romance that makes it necessary for the state of society, in a manner analogous to the uncanny presence of the postmodern in modernity.[10]

What is distinct about romance is, however, difficult to understand. Scott engages in a complex, even contradictory, argument in order to claim that romance is both necessary to the history of society and yet clearly distinct from the factual authority of social history. The division between history and romance seems to have taken place in time. Scott claims that "romance and real history have the same common origin," and it is only over time (through history) that romance becomes distinct (*ER*, 267). Real history comes into being when the head of a tribe, the patriarch, "narrate[s] to his descendants the circumstances which detached him from the society of his brethren, and drove him to form a solitary settlement in the wilderness" (*ER*, 268). As Scott understands it, this narration is pure history; it contains "no other deviation from truth . . . than arises from the infidelity of memory, or the exaggerations of vanity" (*ER*, 268). However, real history has trouble holding its ground, for when the tale is retold by the patriarch's ancestors, it is slowly transformed into romance:

> The vanity of the tribe augments the simple annals from one cause – the love of the marvellous, so natural to the

human mind, contributes its means of sophistication from another – while, sometimes, from a third cause, the king and the priest find their interest in casting a holy and sacred gloom and mystery over the early period from which their power arose. And thus altered and sophisticated from so many different motives, the real adventures of the founder of the tribe bear as little proportion to the legend recited among his children, as the famous hut of Loretto bears to the highly ornamented church with which superstition has surrounded and enchased it. Thus the definition which we have given of romance, as a fictitious narrative turning upon the marvellous or the supernatural, might, in a sense, be said to embrace

————————————*quicquid Graecia mendax*
　　Audet in historia.

or, in fine, the mythological and fabulous history of all early nations. (*ER*, 268)

Our temporal coordinates seem to have been reversed – this time history is preromantic. If the individual gives up youthful romance for a mature sense of history, the process goes in the opposite direction to the development of society. In one sense – to echo the narrator of *Waverley* – real romance is mature (old) history. As history ages, as its stories get retold, it is turned into romance through the work of vanity, a natural love of the marvelous, and the desire on the part of kings and priests to hide their source of power. Romance reinvents history, retells the event in such a way as to lose the "original" history. The older a society gets, the more its early history comes to seem like romance. Which is of course what Edward Waverley has to say of his own early history, as recounted in the novel, *Waverley*.

To grasp the distinction of romance from history is to guarantee one's authority as a historian; however, the distinction proceeds from taking one's early history as romance. In this sense it does not so much mark the separation of romance from reality as their necessary entanglement. We discover that the real historian is not the person who sees the past clearly. Rather, the true or mature historian is that person who finds the past, or their own early years, romantic. History belongs strangely to the present, whereas romance is a sense of the past that *belongs* to the past.

Thus, Scott tries and fails to maintain a distinction between romance and history in *Rob Roy*. Scott's simple claim is that the Introduction tells "the history of the tribe," provides readers with "authentic" facts about Scottish tribal history, while the novel itself is "an old man's stories of a past age," the romantic adventures of the young Englishman, Frank Osbaldistone.[11] However, Scott seems skeptical of the viability of this distinction and questions the status of the introductory material:

> The history of the tribe is briefly as follows: But we must premise that the tale depends in some degree on tradition; therefore, excepting when written documents are quoted, it must be considered as in some degree dubious. (*RR*, 386)

The further clarification he makes here does not seem all that complex: authentic history is contained in written documents; tradition is transmitted as oral culture and is always unauthenticated hearsay. The problem Scott faces, however, is that the history of the tribe cannot be written without relying on tradition. The tale of history is inevitably contaminated by tradition and "must be considered as in some degree dubious," just like the pages of romance. The past must somehow always be romantic. Yet Scott does not stop here. Although this passage could be claimed as only another instance of the privileging of speech over writing, the very type of logocentric modernism that Derrida derides, Scott concludes the Introduction by revoking the privilege he accords to writing:

> I am far from warranting their exact authenticity. Clannish partialities were very apt to guide the tongue and pen as well as the pistol and claymore, and the features of an anecdote are wonderfully softened or exaggerated, as the story is told by a MacGregor or a Campbell. (*RR*, 435)

Everything that is a "written document" is not also a fact of history, is not necessarily the stuff of "authentic" history. It could also be part of the tradition of romance, of the very overflow and excess of textuality that threatens rational modern circulation. Patriarchal partialities guide both the tongue and the pen in such a way that makes final discrimination impossible. If the past must always be romantic, the historian must always be re-examining just where in the past romance may lie.

Whether Scott discusses their factual authority or their historical sequence, the entanglement of history and romance posts the way down the road of excess. Textual excess, the overflow of marginalia that paradoxically undermines the attempt to get to the heart of the matter – the problem of "getting the facts" – is repeated in Scott criticism. This effect of textuality is apparent when we consider the fate of modern historians who attempt to rationalize Scott's romances in the light of "present-day" historical scholarship. Their persistent failure marks the "fact" that romance is not merely the opposite of historical fact but a structural flaw at work within and against the discourse of historical fact, as postmodernism works within and against modernity.

This becomes apparent as early as Ranke, when he attempts to study the facts of the Middle Ages and compare Scott's representation with "source material." Not surprisingly this type of historical correspondence is not deliverable at Scott's postmodern address; according to Ranke, Scott's "history" is unverifiable and should be returned to sender as merely romance. It is Ranke who, in Scott's place, will write the realistic history which Scott failed to produce.

If Ranke claims to have solved the problems of historical correspondence, Georg Lukács is not willing to believe it. Apparently unmoved by Ranke's judgment of Scott, Lukács reinvokes Scott's claims to historicism and argues that historical realism, not romance, was after all the hallmark of Scott's novels.[12] Yet in Lukács's repudiation of the romance in Scott's work, there are, as A. O. Cockshut points out, historical inaccuracies:

> Such carefully considered historical passages give a particular air of futility to the extraordinary mistake in the date of the action of this novel [*Rob Roy*] made by Georg Lukács, who puts it "several decades" after *Waverley*, which deals with 1745. If several is taken to mean about three, this represents an error of sixty years. If it is generously taken to mean only two, it represents an error of fifty years. M. Lukács then proceeds to erect a complicated argument in economic history upon this gross error.[13]

In all of these critical exchanges, there appears a desperate attempt to "get it right," to find the real facts of history, to make

59

sure that the dates correspond. Yet, in romance there is an inevitable misprision of history. Romance must always lead to a confusion of fact with fiction, a confusion of history with romance.[14] Upon what is the harsh light of historical accuracy to be turned, then, if the past must be understood as mere romance?

The troubled and unstable distinction between history and romance shows us something crucial about modernity and its relation to tradition, because it allows us to understand the connection between romance and postmodernism. To simplify the analogy: the predicament of modernity is to have understood oneself in rejecting "inauthentic" tradition and yet to feel one's dependence on the tradition one has rejected – as Nietzsche might put it, one must visit museums in order to remember what history it is that one must forget, so as to live. Similarly, romance places the historian in the position of having to remember to forget, and thus reveals the Whig positivist historian of progress for what he is: always and only the historian of the present, of the miracle of today, whose historical grasp claims authority by virtue of its disregard for the burden of the past, whose mail coach is so strong-axled that it no longer feels the past as a burden. To be a realist historian is to forget the past by claiming that it is inauthentic. The repressed or "forgotten" past returns, however, as romance, as the post(al service) of modernity that feels the burden of the past, a burden that is manifested as textual excess, great heaps of an infinitely multiplying antiquarian correspondence.[15]

This is why in *Waverley* Scott saves his lengthy discussion of romance and history for the last chapter and titles it "A Postscript That Should Have Been A Preface." We can only begin to understand the relationship between romance and history on the margins of the text, and that relationship is one which confuses the proper place of the post, since romantic "obfuscation" has come to *precede* the history that the historian sees clearly. Here we should remember the "youthful romance" of Edward Waverley in recognizing that romance comes both before and after history, just as postmodernism comes both before and after modernity. That is to say, romance, which comes after real history as a kind of secondary colorization process, also comes before history, is the prehistory of historical culture, just as postmodernity precedes modernity:

This should have been a prefatory chapter, but for two reasons: – First, that most novel readers, as my own conscience reminds me, are apt to be guilty of the sin of omission respecting that same matter of prefaces; – Secondly, that it is a general custom with that class of students, to begin with the last chapter of a work; so that, after all, these remarks, being introduced last in order, have still the best chance to be read in their proper place. (*W*, 491–2)

We read first that which happened "last," and the effect is to find as close a correspondence to the present as possible. The history of reading is reading for the ending, reading for the present. The understanding of the relationship between romance and history belongs before the novel and so must be placed after the novel. Understanding the importance of events and their representation through history and romance is at best a chancy business because the discussion is always, in some way, out of place. At this point, we need to recognize that this spiraling of textual effects, this parallax of margins within which history loses its focus and proper place, is by no means secondary to the actions or events of history. For the history, or the romance, with which Scott deals is one in which an entire culture, that of tribal Highlanders, has already been condemned to historical marginality by the fact of "historical" writing, precisely because it is an *unhistorical culture*, in the modernist sense.

Scott's postmodernity will be wagered upon his treatment of an explicitly unhistorical culture, one which can appear in the text of historical modernity only as a marginal annotation, a footnote. However, he is not turning to romance in order to write a fuller history, the history of both sides. Instead of presenting a history structured as double-entry bookkeeping, Scott's inflationary footnotes and marginalia displace the notion of historical accounting. Through the encounter of history and romance Scott rethinks the necessity of history's erasure of the Highland tribes. The purpose of his "imaginary" romance is to preserve some idea of ancient manners (tradition), and this preservation is necessary because of the destruction brought about by the progress *of* modernity, progress in the *name of* modernity:

There is no European nation which, within the course of half a century, or little more, has undergone so complete a change

61

as this kingdom of Scotland. The effects of the insurrection of 1745 – the destruction of the patriarchal power of the Highland chiefs – the abolition of the heritable jurisdictions of the Lowland nobility and barons – the total eradication of the Jacobite party, which, averse to intermingle with the English, or adopt their customs, long continued to pride themselves upon maintaining ancient Scottish manners and customs – commenced this innovation. The gradual influx of wealth, and extension of commerce, have since united to render the present people of Scotland a class of beings as different from their grandfathers as the existing English are from those of Queen Elizabeth's time. The political and economical effects of these changes have been traced by Lord Selkirk with great precision and accuracy. But the change, though steadily and rapidly progressive, has, nevertheless, been gradual . . . . It was my accidental lot, though not born a Highlander (which may be an apology for much bad Gaelic), to reside during my childhood and youth among persons of the above description; – and now, for the purpose of preserving some idea of the ancient manners of which I have witnessed the almost total extinction, I have embodied in imaginary scenes, and ascribed to fictitious characters, a part of the incidents which I then received from those who were actors in them. (*W*, 492–3)

Modernist history, like the progress of modernity's economic system, obliterates the history of "ancient manners" along with the Highland tribes who practiced them. The battle of Culloden – 1745 – stands for modernist history as the site of its own "progressive" battle. Yet this site of modernist progress, this inscription at the center of modernist history itself, is also the site of a marginal erasure, of "destruction," of "abolition," of "eradication," to which Scott returns in the pages of romance in order both to illustrate the destructive force of modernist progress and preserve the memory of a culture modernity that would like to forget.[16] Romance assumes the burden of the past, is the memorial for a tradition that historians like Lord Selkirk, despite their precision and accuracy, fail to document. Unlike Selkirk's text that understands the consequence of change only as the history of the present, as *Observations on the Present State of the Highlands*, romance remembers the past as that with which it cannot come to terms, as that which is always never fully present or recuperable.[17] Where does this leave us if the discourse of historical fact denies the past's burden even while pretending to carry it? How is romance any more than the other side of this coin, a kind of senile nostalgia for the primitive, or a youthful primitivism, opposed to historical maturity? The answer is that Scott's is not modernist nostalgia, but a nostalgia for the past with which modernist history cannot come to terms.

We can no longer assume that modernist history "gets it right"; what it might mean to represent the past authentically is not certain. In making this point, I want to argue that Scott does not offer a mere escape from modernity; if anything Scott's romances confirm that modernity cannot be escaped because much of the work of modernity cannot be undone: we cannot bring back to life the obliterated Highlanders except in the pages of romance. What Scott can offer, by means of this explicit turn to romance, is an alternative to modernist aesthetics and modernist history. If modernity tries to forget the past, the postmodernity of Scott's romance tries to make it unforgettable, remind us that the past cannot be consumed like disposable packaging, or forgotten like directions written in a foreign language. Put another way, Scott's project is to remind us that we need to remember, that we can neither dispose of the past nor dismiss it because we don't understand it.

"We talk of a credulous vulgar"

We talk of a credulous vulgar, without always recollecting that there is a vulgar incredulity, which, in historical matters, as well as in those of religion, finds it easier to doubt than to examine, and endeavors to assume the credit of an *esprit fort*, by denying whatever happens to be a little beyond the very limited comprehension of the skeptic.

(Introductory, *Chronicles of the Canongate*[18])

If Scott's postmodernity marks a certain acknowledgment of the past, such acknowledgment is, however, an imperfect memorial to a culture condemned to be forgotten by modernity. Postmodernism always, in a sense, fails to do justice to the past, fails to produce the perfect memorial, at the same time

63

as it is nonetheless obligated to memorialize. The question that postmodernism must always ask is: How is it possible to remember the past, to carry the burden of history, without becoming modernist?

Scott's romances could be said to attempt to answer this question in the way that they constantly articulate themselves around a clash of cultures: Saxon and Norman in *Ivanhoe*, Highland tribe and capitalist modernity in the Jacobite romances upon which I am focusing. In each case, Scott's novels diverge from history to romance in order to figure this clash of cultures: one side is positioned as always already "lost" to history and historicism. Postmodern romance, unlike mere modernist nostalgia, finds a way to affirm this lost culture, beyond history, rather than merely mourn its passing from a historical perspective. It is in this sense that the tribal Highlanders are an "unhistorical" culture. In using the term "unhistorical" here, I am alluding to the inability of modernist history to come to terms with Highland culture, rather than claiming that it is in any way inherently static or unchanging – to claim that would be to become modernist all over again.

For the reader who finds that I have spent too much time at the edges of Scott's novels, in the margins, I shall now turn to this "central" concern – the marginalization of tribal culture – and focus on the way in which Scott's romances remember or memorialize it. The example that I have in mind is a scene from the first volume of *Waverley*, where the young Edward Waverley first encounters the Scottish Highlanders. At the risk of slipping into too much plot summary, let me say that this occurs shortly after Waverley has taken leave of his regiment in order to visit an old Scottish friend of his uncle, Baron Bradwardine. While staying with the Baron, Waverley feels "his curiosity considerably excited by the idea of visiting the den of a Highland Cacus," and thus inspired he decides to extend his leave in order to visit the Highlands (*W*, 133). In the course of his trip, Waverley ends up at the house of the Highland Chieftain Fergus Mac-Ivor Vich Ian Vohr, who treats Waverley to a Highland feast. Waverley is overcome by the prodigious quantities of food and drink, the loud music of the bagpipes, and the "clang of the Celtic tongue," as he describes it, yet what intrigues him most is the performance of the family *bhairdh*:

He seemed to Edward, who attended to him with much interest, to recite many proper names, to lament the dead, to apostrophize the absent, to exhort, and entreat, and animate those who were present. Waverley thought he even discerned his own name, and was convinced his conjecture was right, from the eyes of the company being at that moment turned towards him simultaneously. The ardour of the poet appeared to communicate itself to the audience. (*W*, 165–6)

The activities of the bard are unfamiliar to Waverley. He can but barely begin to think what function they may serve, and thus communicates to his host his own desire "to know the meaning of that song which appeared to produce such effect upon the passions of the company" (*W*, 166). But Edward's request is one with which it is not easy to comply. Just what the bard's song *can* mean to the English Edward Waverley is the issue that Scott's romance addresses in its attempt to memorialize the Highland tribal culture.

The revelation of the meaning of the bard's song is postponed; Waverley does not receive an explanation immediately. Rather, his host Mac-Ivor gives the job of explaining the bard's song to his daughter Flora, whom he describes as an "eminent" translator of Highland poetry. However, she postpones the explanation as well, arguing first that her father should "know how little these verses can possibly interest an English stranger" and that she can translate them anyway (*W*, 172). From the outset, the concern with marginalized cultures appears as a problem of translation, a problem that must be postponed. What could the history of the Highland tribes possibly ever mean to an Englishman? How could their significance ever be translated into the language of another culture? The answer, which Flora begins to explain to Waverley, is that, although the general contents of the songs can be described, translation is not really possible. The meaning of these songs is something that Waverley will never fully understand:

The recitation . . . of poems, recording the feats of heroes, the complaints of lovers, and the wars of contending tribes, forms the chief amusements of a winter fireside in the Highlands. Some of these are said to be very ancient, and if they are ever translated into any of the languages of civilized Europe, cannot fail to produce a deep and general sensation. Others are more modern, the composition of those family bards whom the chieftains of more distinguished name and power retain as the poets and historians of their tribes. These, of course, possess various degrees of merit; but much of it must evaporate in translation, or be lost on those who do not sympathise with the feelings of the poet. (*W*, 173)

While the translated poems may produce a "deep and general sensation," this sensation is still not that of the specifically local "original." Such translations are inferior because much of their merit has evaporated in the process of translation or has been lost on those who can no longer sympathize with the poet. These songs of the past are local: produced by *a* culture for *a* culture. They rely on situation – on the spontaneous retelling and alteration of the songs themselves in order to incorporate the scene of their own telling. As Flora reminds Waverley, "a bard seldom fails to augment the effects of a premeditated song, by throwing in any stanzas which may be suggested by the circumstances attending the recitation" (*W*, 173–4). Each time the bard retells the verses he is, in effect, telling a new poem, changing the verses to fit the moment. Any translation of the verses must necessarily lose this spontaneity if it desires to be faithful to the "original." But as we learned from Eco, it is impossible to be faithful to the manuscript that you love, and in this case the translation must betray the situation of its own production. Like Athelstane of Coningsburgh in *Ivanhoe*, one would be hard put to distinguish between translation and death for such texts.[19]

Part of the point of this passage is that the bard's songs can only have full significance, can only really have meaning, for the Highlanders for whom the bard performs. This is more or less the case, but Scott is also willing to confront the problem that these verses no longer even have significance for *modern* Highlanders. As Mac-Ivor puts it:

There are three things that are useless to a modern Highlander, – a sword which he must not draw, – a bard to sing of deeds which he dare not imitate, – and a large goat-skin purse without a louis-d'or to put into it. (*W*, 172)

The "modern Highlanders" (a contradiction in terms) are cut off from their own past, alienated, by virtue of the fact that it is made to seem useless and not worth remembering. The arrival of the meaning of the bard's verses is, for the modern

Highlander, permanently delayed by the progress of modernity. New economic systems, new ideas of social order, and new ways of thinking about the past make tribal culture outdated within the terms of modernity.

We can take this a little farther and say that capitalism is predicated on the universality of exchange, and modernist history is the form of the commodification of cultural value for capitalism. As such, it must be a universal language in which cultures can meet like commodities in a marketplace. If the condition of modernist history is capitalism's translatability into all cultures – its universal imperialism, as we shall see later with Conrad – then Highland tribal culture, by virtue of its insistence on its own *un*translatability and its *local* use value, is not properly historical and therefore not valuable according to the economic calculations of modernity.

What is important about Scott's romances, however, is that they are not willing to forget about Highland tribal culture, not willing to concede the conflict of cultures to the forces of modernity. Although Scott's narrative confesses that a full translation, an exact reproduction, of the bard's verses is impossible, it nonetheless insists upon the necessity of an imperfect attempt and indicates that it is the scene of *romance* in which this will take place.[20] Flora can thus lead Waverley "like a knight of romance" down a small path that "seemed to open into the land of romance," and then sing her "rude English translation" in rhyming couplets (*W*, 174–5). There is no doubt that these songs are not what the bard would sing; Flora "had exchanged the measured and monotonous recitative of the bard for a lofty and uncommon Highland air, which had been a battle-song in former ages" (*W*, 178). Yet they do have meaning for the young Englishman who is their audience. They ask him to "remember the fame that is flown!" and "remember Glenlivat, Harlaw, and Dundee!" and his response is such that the printed verses themselves can "convey but little idea of the feelings with which, so sung and accompanied, they were heard by Waverley" (*W*, 178–80).

These verses insist upon the importance of remembering the past, of remembering the cultures that modernist history wishes to obliterate because of their difference. If modernist history understands difference only as a certain sameness, as that which within the terms of its own imperialistic gestures it is willing to recognize as difference, romance can mark the difference of the bard's verses without indicating exactly what the use of that difference would be.[21] The poetry of remembrance is sung in the scene of romance, but that memorial is imperfect. The past as past is untranslatable into another culture; the past is always a different culture, lost to the "now" of modernity. What Scott's postmodern romances can do is make the burden of the past felt as burden because it is lost, because it is irrecoverable in a way that we will never know. As Flora explains to Waverley, "O you cannot guess how much you have lost!" (W, 180). That we cannot even begin to understand what it is we have lost, how much of the past is unrecoverable, untranslatable, for a different culture in a different time, is the burden that postmodern romance makes felt: the unpresentable exists, we know that something has been lost, but nonetheless it cannot be presented as such, even as the sure knowledge of loss (the negative moment of modernity).

Romance finds its postmodernity as it lays claim to the problem of translation (not being able to think the thoughts of the past), and it thus challenges the certainty of modernist history.[22] Postmodern romance serves to bring within the frame of novelistic narrative those values which remain ungraspable for modernist history. In this way, postmodern romance always questions legitimacy without legitimating itself. Rather than an admission of bad faith (or vulgar incredulity), this is precisely the affirmative power of romance, the point at which the work of mourning for the past that romance performs marks its own inability to come to terms with what has been lost: the simultaneous, impossible, presence and absence of the dead. Postmodernism has consistently turned to effects of translation, of carrying over, of metaphor, in order to trace the double scene of inscription and *erasure* that haunts the modernist writing of history. And Scott's postmodernity lies in his location of the problem of translation, the problem of the past as unrepresentable burden, in the scene of romance and of female sexuality, in Flora's "narrow glen" (175).

"Here are figments enough"

"Here are figments enough," I said to myself, "to confuse the march of a whole history – anachronisms enough to overset all chronology! The old gentleman hath broken all bounds – *abiit – evasit – erupit.*"

(The Rev. Dr Dryasdust, Prefatory Letter, *Peveril of the Peak*[23])

If romance is the scene of the translation of past events, it is also the scene of historical confusion, of a mixture of temporalities – what modernist history would call anachronism. As translated by romance, the past no longer seems to fit together properly; there are things that are out of place, in the wrong historical order. Judging by the standards of modernist history – committed as it is

> It may be that I have introduced little which can positively be termed modern; but, on the other hand, it is extremely probable that I may have confused the manners of two or three centuries, and introduced, during the reign of Richard the First, circumstances appropriate to a period either considerably earlier or a good deal later than that era.
>
> (Dedicatory Epistle, *I*, 530)

to a certain understanding of chronology – historical correspondence has certainly been lost in the post in the case of romance.[24] Yet, as I have argued earlier with regard to Eco, the kind of correspondence modernist history wishes to write, its claim to write the past accurately in the present, is itself anachronistic. The postmodernity of historical romance offers an alternative, not merely by being self-consciously ironic or anachronistic, but by insisting that *any* sense of the past, including that of modernist history, is in some way anachronistic. That is to say, if modernist history believes that historical correspondence is only lost in the post as a result of accident or inattention, postmodern romance would argue that anachronisms are always found in the post. To have a sense of the past, to take ironic temporality seriously, would involve acknowledging the necessity of translation and *a fortiori* the introduction of anachronism. Postmodern romance insists that we cannot know what it would mean to have an accurate sense of the past, because we are always losing and finding the unexpected in the post.

> It is true that I neither can nor do pretend to the observation of complete accuracy, even in matters of outward costume, much less in the more important points of language and manners.
>
> (Dedicatory Epistle, *I*, 526)

In making this claim with regard to Scott's romances, I am not really offering up anything "new." That his romances are anachronistic, that they include what modernist history would call "inaccuracies," is something about which Scott frequently reminds his readers. By the time he writes the Introduction to *Anne of Geierstein*, Scott is even making comparisons with regard to the degree of accuracy among his various novels. This is revealing

> I have to confess on this occasion more violations of accuracy in historical details, than can perhaps be alleged against others of my novels.
>
> (Introduction, *Anne of Geierstein*[25])

enough in itself, but to understand the significance of this confession I want to turn to another passage in which anachronism is made to play a role. In the middle of *Rob Roy* the narrative pauses so that the fictitious editor can add a footnote which points out an anachronism. In this case, we are asked to believe the fictitious editor

> This I believe to be an anachronism, as Saint Enoch's Church was not built at the date of the story.
>
> (Footnote, *RR*, 184)

who believes that he recognizes an anachronism. For the reader, as for the "editor," anachronism is a matter of belief; it depends upon testimony – "I believe that this was not so." Yet in insisting upon a belief *in* anachronisms, Scott's texts do not also suggest that anachronisms are something that should be purged from the text. Belief in anachronism does not lead to a historical inquisition of romance. Rather, in the textual marginalia Scott seems to be suggesting that writing (and reading) romance is made possible by the inevitability of anachronisms, which the reader may not recognize. This was the situation that Eco admitted encountering with regard to *The Name of the Rose*. Can we recognize the past as past? Do we notice the interjection of that which is inappropriately modern? In each instance the answer is: "not necessarily." The introduction of anachronisms (even when they are introduced in an introduction) is not something of which author, editor, or reader are in full control. Anachronisms creep

> besides the suppression of names, and of incidents approaching too much to reality, the work may in a great measure be said to be new written. Several anachronisms have probably crept in during the course of these changes.
>
> (Advertisement to the first edition, *RR*, 1)

into historical correspondence. There is no regulatory agency that can guarantee the regulation of anachronisms, because there is no such thing as purely authentic correspondence, no standard of modernist purity by which to judge.

If anachronism is inevitable, as postmodern romance would suggest that it is, what does it do to our understanding of the past? One way to answer this question would be to argue that our understanding of the past is not "improved" by merely acquiring an ability to recognize anachronisms (understanding that a train is out of place in a novel about the fourteenth century). Instead of simply offering to provide a warning label about its narrative contents – something to the effect of "beware of anachronisms" – postmodern romance questions the place of history through the attention it gives to anachronism. Historical anachronism is not simply error, it is the mode of experience of history, as tourists (and all of Scott's heroes are tourists) are well aware:

> Author. – I understand you. You mean to say these learned persons will have but little toleration for a romance or a fictitious narrative, founded upon history?

> Dryasdust. – Why, sir, I do rather apprehend, that their respect for the foundation will be such, that they may be apt to quarrel with the inconsistent nature of the superstructure; just as every classical traveller pours forth expressions of sorrow and indignation, when, in travelling through Greece, he chances to see a Turkish kiosk rising on the ruins of an ancient temple.

> Author. – But since we cannot rebuild the temple, a kiosk may be a pretty thing, may it not? Not quite correct in architecture, strictly and classically criticised; but presenting something uncommon to the eye, and something fantastic to the imagination, on which the spectator gazes with the pleasure of the same description which arises from the perusal of an Eastern tale.
>
> (Prefatory Letter, *PP*, 60–1)

The classical traveler is a modernist who saddens at the very thought of an anachronistic Turkish kiosk placed next to an ancient Greek temple. For the modernist, the only meaning for the past is as an orderly progression of events, and the only obligation the present has to the past is to keep the monuments of the past in the right chronological order. Just as modernist history wants to forget the Highlanders because they do not play a part in the progress of modernity, it must also protect the purity of the historical scene in which the play of progress takes place.

The modernist begs for historical order; romance refuses to oblige. The "Author of *Waverley*" argues that we need to understand the juxtaposition of different cultures and different temporalities not as historical inaccuracies, as anachronisms which blot the pure order of history, but as "something uncommon to the eye." In so many words, we need to learn how to become different kinds of traveler in the land of history. Not modernist travelers who cry at the sight of the kiosk next to the temple, but postmodern tourists who take interest in the uncommon juxtaposition of cultures and temporalities.

In making this claim I am not trying to sound as if I am a fan of Disney-style historical recreations. In using the phrase "postmodern tourist" I mean to suggest that a postmodern notion of history would be that which recognizes that we never actually inhabit the past or communicate with it directly through historical correspondence. We don't actually know what it's like to "live in history"; we are always just visiting. In that respect, the postmodern tourist is not all that different from Edward Waverley, Frank Osbaldistone, Darsie Latimer, or Alan Fairfield wandering around the Highlands and always in need of a trusty guide. History is over and forgotten as the necessary premise of modernist antiquarianism, but for the postmodern tourist it's always waiting to be discovered as the possibility of yet another uncommon sight in the landscape of romance. Whereas the antiquarian (Scott's figure for the modernist historian) is too busy trying to write historical correspondence to see anything "new" (the antiquarian is the classical traveler wincing at the new kiosk), the postmodern tourist, like Edward Waverley, has "time to give himself up to the full romance of his situation" (*W*, 138). In the time of romance, the tourist encounters the unknown as the locus of desire, rather than collecting souvenirs of the already known. In this sense, the antiquarian, in his desire to affirm the known, is closer to the hordes of souvenir-hunters, who value the signs of history only insofar as they are already exhaustively coded as historical (are already historical kitsch), than is our postmodern tourist.

This is not to absolve Edward Waverley and his avatars entirely from the charge of a certain patronizing commodification of the cultures they visit. What is important is that we should not simply dismiss the visiting Englishman touched by the sight of the Highlanders. For the force of Scott's romance lies in the fact that at certain moments in the scene of romance, as in Flora's narrow glen, the framework of the commercial traveler, the capitalist and modernist ideology of progress which the novels overwhelmingly support, is shaken. And at such points, history comes to seem more of a problem than a chronicle, while romance forces upon modernism a sense of the anxiety that constitutes modernity itself in its relation to the past. Romance here shares the postmodern in being the "constant," "nascent state" of the modern encountering its outer limit as something internal to its project.[26] For Scott, this problem is thematized in the conflict between romance and the "serious" history of the antiquarian: a conflict paralleled in the struggle between the novels themselves and the inflationary spiral of marginalia, in which the trivia of the romantic tourist or the parodic footnotes consistently turn out to be uncannily historically serious, not least in comparison to the researches of the Rev. Dr Dryasdust or the predictability of Scott's plots.

> Still the severer antiquary may think that, by thus inter-
> mingling fiction with truth, I am polluting the well of history
> with modern inventions, and impressing upon the rising
> generation false ideas of the age which I describe. I cannot
> but in some sense admit the force of this reasoning, which
> I yet hope to traverse by the following considerations.
>
> (Dedicatory Epistle, *I*, 526)

As I have illustrated earlier, there is really no need for Scott to defend himself against the imaginary antiquary's charge of "intermingling fiction with truth" (anachronism with accuracy), because the well of history is already polluted with modern inventions (the antiquary is, after all, a fiction). Romance as tradition (the residue of earlier modern inventions) is always at the bottom of the well of essentialist definitions of history. For Scott the issue is not what is essential to history but what is excessive about history. The difference between modernist history and postmodern romance is that the latter calls attention to the very things that the former would like to forget, and it does so in a very unmodernist way: through the proliferation of marginalia. It is as if postmodern romance cannot decide upon what is essential to its own genre – for Scott, there can never be too many marginalia. The postmodern condition of history and textuality is one of excess: history overflows the boundaries of narrative. That is to say the relationship between history and romance is negotiated in a proliferation of marginalia that continually interrupt the central text – dedicatory epistles, appendices, footnotes, and advertisements. And these negotiations are not easy to read, because the question asked by the postmodern condition of ironic temporality returns in another form: Do we take the marginalia seriously?

On the one hand, the marginalia have pretensions to be serious historical documents that address, in one way or another, the problem of anachronism. But on the other hand, the excessive return to a discussion of accuracy and anachronism begins to become one big joke – a joke made ever better by Scott's own Dr Dryasdust. In the prefatory letter to *Peveril of the Peak*, Dryasdust does not accuse the Author of *Waverley* of misrepresenting history (we all "know" that what the Author of *Waverley* writes is not history per se), rather he criticizes him for not taking history seriously enough. The "danger" his novels pose is that they cause readers to neglect real history. History, according to Dr Dryasdust, is not fun;

> Dryasdust. – But besides, and especially, it is said that you are in danger of causing history to be neglected – readers being contented with such frothy and superficial knowledge as they acquire from your works, to the effect of inducing them to neglect the severer and more accurate sources of information.
>
> (Prefatory Letter, *PP*, 62)

real history needs to hurt, as some of our more moralistic commentators, including Marxists, would say. Accuracy and "real" knowledge are severe taskmasters, unlike Scott's romances. The excessive marginalia, Dryasdust might claim, only add to the illusion that the reader is in any way acquiring a serious understanding of history.

Yet poor Dr Dryasdust is, after all, just another piece of marginalia, just another character to whom dedicatory epistles are addressed, just another fictional historical correspondent. And we don't know whether we should take him seriously either. The Author of *Waverley* doesn't think we should. The way he sees it, his novels act like a divining rod, indicating "where veins of precious metal are concealed below the earth, which afterwards enrich the adventurers by whom they are laboriously and carefully wrought" (*PP*, 63). The novels don't discourage an investigation of history, rather they indicate where such research should profitably begin. "The love of knowledge wants but a beginning," Scott argues. The reader will want to learn more, to find out "what the facts really were, and how far the novelist has justly represented them" (*PP*, 64). Romance initiates the reader's search for truth; it does not merely replace truth with lies. As I showed earlier with *Waverley*, romance does not neglect the past, rather it considers a past other than that which modernist history represents.

But do we take this seriously? Is the most serious discussion of history that which is produced by an author personified in a fictional prefatory letter?[27] If we do take the Author of *Waverley*'s words seriously, can we assume that a reader ever gets at the truth of history, ever finds out whether the novelist, the romancer, has done justice to the past? This is a serious question. Who speaks on behalf of the past in order to testify "this is not so"? The voice that testifies to anachronisms in postmodern romance is the voice of the present, and therefore not a reliable witness. Scott's postmodern romance makes us understand that we never can do justice to the past because the dead can never speak on their own behalf. Fictional characters can't sue their authors for misrepresentation; Dido cannot sue Virgil for damages in a court of law, as the Author of *Waverley* wryly points out to Dryasdust. History always misrepresents the past – introduces anachronisms, leaves out events,

> Dryasdust. – . . . But I doubt if all you have said will reconcile the public to the anachronisms of your present volumes. Here you have a Countess of Derby fetched out of her cold grave, and saddled with a set of adventures dated twenty years after her death, besides being given up as a Catholic, when she was in fact a zealous Huguenot. Author. – She may sue me for damages, as in the case Dido *versus* Virgil.
>
> (Prefatory Letter, *PP*, 65)

puts them in the wrong order. That is to say, anachronism is not merely incidental to history; it structures history.

". . . to mix once more in politics" (*AG*, 348)

Given such a "state" of affairs, the difference of romance from modernism (the postmodernity of romance) lies in the double evocation of both a burdensome past and the impossibility of our ever bearing that burden. This is not an occasion for despair, however; it is a challenge to thinking: How are we to deal with a past that cannot be represented historically? It is in this sense that I want to claim that the politics of romance do not merely lie in escapist nostalgia, that romance isn't merely the fantasy that keeps women eating chocolates and in the kitchen. Romance may also act as the site of a struggle with the politics of the representable, as locus for the articulation of cultural groups that are not simply minorities within a homogenous field, a small percentage of that population, but are radically excluded from the representable population, *a priori*. This, I shall argue elsewhere, is at least in part the encounter worked out in George Eliot's feminist romance and Conrad's account of imperialism.

Sticking with Scott for now, I want to end this chapter by talking about how romance evokes the absolutely irrepresentable. And this is not merely mysticism – the Highlanders are unhistorical. The politics of romance and postmodernism are not matters of accuracy or degree of sympathy *in* representation. Rather, the issue lies in the extent to which the rule of representation is displaced and comes to be felt (but not represented or shown) as itself political oppression.[28] And I want to stress here the issue of *extent*, for if Scott's novels do belie their conservatism at the points when they turn to romance in the face of the impossibility of writing a history of the Highlanders, nonetheless romance is not always at odds with representation.

For the purpose of clarity, we can distinguish here between a postmodern romance of the historical sublime or the unrepresentable and a more conservative romance of nostalgia. As we have seen, the distinction centers on whether the past appears as a threat to present representation, or as merely the present representation of what has been lost (the negative moment of representation, but a representation nonetheless). Let us compare the romantic sublime opening from Flora's narrow glen with the kind of nostalgic containment evident at the end of *Waverley*.

Importantly, what is at stake is the nature and effect of the frame, or margin. At the end of *Waverley* the exfoliation of marginalia no longer threatens the authority of history, rather a frame has been supplied that allows that past to be represented for the present without threat or displacement. The meaning of the past is reduced to portraiture – a painting of Waverley and Fergus in Highland dress:

> It was a large and spirited painting, representing Fergus Mac-Ivor and Waverley in their Highland dress; the scene a wild, rocky, and mountainous pass, down which the clan were descending in the background. It was taken from a spirited sketch, drawn while they were in Edinburgh by a young man of high genius, and had been painted on a full-length scale by an eminent London artist. Raeburn himself (whose Highland Chiefs do all but walk out of the canvas) could not have done more justice to the subject; and the ardent, fiery, and impetuous character of the unfortunate Chief of Glennaquoich was finely contrasted with the contemplative, fanciful, and enthusiastic expression of his happier friend. Beside this painting hung the arms which Waverley had borne in the unfortunate civil war. The whole piece was beheld with admiration, and deeper feelings. (*W*, 489)

The presence of words like "spirited," "ardent, fiery, and impetuous," "enthusiastic" and "fanciful" seem to connect the "genius" of the author and the "deeper feelings" of the viewer with the sublime of romance. However, everything remains in place, on the wall as in history, as a past whose burden is no longer oppressive, even if it seems "unfortunate." The meaning of the past as portraiture is "full-length," or life-size; yet this very realism marks the containment of the past in an accountable scale. That the painting is touristic kitsch is a fair guess for anyone acquainted with the tradition of Victorian representations of the Highlands. However, this owes less to any painterly demerit than to the handling of questions of *scale* and *frame*: to a containment within representation. History is turned into a souvenir. And in this instance Edward Waverley is no different from the more contemporary modern tourists who pose next to famous "historical" figures and have their photographs taken. Put another way, Waverley's portrait with Mac-Ivor gives viewers the feeling that he has lived in history. Yet this is, paradoxically, the very failure of the painting to do justice to a past whose threat, burden, and cry is that it cannot be represented. And indeed such

77

portraits are as useless as the arms that hang next to them; both prolong the illusions of modernist history, the illusion that to come to terms with the past is to do justice to it, that we can lay the ghosts of our exterminated ancestors definitively to rest.

If *Waverley* ends with a conservative bias, if it pretends to show us what the past means through representation, Scott concludes *Rob Roy* on a very different note: "Old Andrew Fairservice used to say, that 'There were many things ower bad for blessing, and ower gude for banning, like ROB ROY'" (*RR*, 383). Instead of realist portraiture, Scott gives us a proper name in capital letters and an excess of instructions for how to read it. Note that ROB ROY is here a "thing", so that the capitalized name appears doubled: both a reference to the hero and a sly metacommentary upon the moral import of the eponymously titled novel itself.[29] It is impossible to do justice to Rob Roy – he is both "ower bad" *and* "ower gude." Rob Roy, like the novel itself, exceeds the frame of realist representation and of modernist history. This is the instance in which postmodern romance can function as a form of resistance that dislocates politics from the hegemony of the real as realist. Rob Roy resists not merely the English army but also the equation of moral rectitude, rational representation, and historical realism. That is to say, Rob Roy is a resistance fighter but what counts is less actual military action than his capacity to expose an aporia in the real of historical representation: the bandit appears as contraband within the boarders of historical representation, throwing it into a double bind.

Dealing with the past is problematic. A preference for Rob Roy over the Edward Waverley/Fergus Mac-Ivor double seems somewhat easier. The danger of a certain oversimplification in my argument would be to assume that escaping modernist historicism and turning to romance in order to evoke and do justice to an irrepresentable past, the past of the oppressed, were in any way easy. If romance leads us to rethink the politics of realism, it does *not* do so in order to tell us what those politics "really" are. Rather, the representational framework of political judgment is opened to the play of desires which, emanating as they do from the excluded (women, lost tribes), are *a priori* irrepresentable.

How that play of unspeakable desire is to be handled is in no sense pre-established. Just as postmodernism is parasitic upon the modernism it subverts, so romance is always in an unstable relationship with the historical realism it displaces. In order to correct the binarism that has crept into my judgments on the conclusions of these two Scott novels, I want to turn to Conrad, whose importance for the romance and its politics lies not only in his encounter with empire but also in the way in which he develops a sense of the simultaneous necessity and impossibility of modernism as a way of thinking history.

3

ROMANTIC LETTERS AND POSTMODERN ENVELOPES: JOSEPH CONRAD AND THE IMPERIALISM OF HISTORICAL REPRESENTATION

Letter 1:
Monumental correspondence

Scott's romances did not deliver on all the problems of historical correspondence, even if they did point out the difficulties raised for history by postal delay or postmodern deferral. Joseph Conrad reopens this matter by reminding us that we don't always know how to treat such correspondence once it has arrived. In Part I of *Nostromo*, we are introduced to an American investor from San Francisco, Mr Holroyd, who gets some rather enigmatic mail:

> The Costaguana mail (it was never large – one fairly heavy envelope) was taken unopened straight into the great man's room, and no instructions dealing with it had ever been issued thence.[1]

The modern antiquarian, Dr Dryasdust, knew how to handle his correspondence once it arrived, but the uses of Holroyd's weighty envelope remain uncertain. And this goes for Conrad as much as for Mr Holroyd, since the weighty envelope is never opened, never returned to, in the novel.

If the imperialism that the novel documents is a discourse of historical readability – the insistence that destiny is *manifest* – then this is a piece of postmodern correspondence: whether postcard or cargo manifest itself, it remains unreadable. Indeed, the problem postmodernism raises for modernist history is that it refuses to issue instructions for dealing with historical correspondence. *Nostromo* situates this problem in the light of the geographical expansion of empire. For the modernist, Costaguana is the far-flung outreach of an imperial dream, whose life and events can only be inscribed at the center of western history by means of fragmentary messages. And this placement gives rise to a problem: how does one deal with a colony which both does and does not have a history of its own? Conrad's text recognizes the paradoxes of modernist historical imperialism inherent in this question: *Nostromo* confronts the breakdown of modernity's metanarratives in the face of the other that they seek to exploit. That is to say the postmodernity of Conrad's novel lies in the way it works without rules for dealing with this historical burden.

The appearance of Holroyd's envelope, the news from Costaguana, in the novel remains as enigmatic as its appearance in San Francisco; we never hear of it again. Which leads one to speculate . . . the history of the periphery appears at the metropolitan center in an envelope which is always already forgotten, yet which appears only at the cost of an act of forgetting – the stuff of romance.

Conrad's engagement with romance comes as a way to address the problem of missing instructions for handling historical correspondence – dealing with a country whose official history (*Fifty Years of Misrule*) is also explicitly unavailable, since the fictional author ("J.C.") holds the only known copy. Holroyd's postal problem becomes emblematic of the difficulty of writing a history that is not modernist, that is not bound by fixed rules. I want to suggest that Conrad's narrative does not simply forget about the problem of Holroyd's mail altogether, rather *Nostromo* patiently performs an investigation into the postal system of modernist correspondence. And the chief tool for that investigation is postmodern romance.

In arguing that Conrad stumbles onto a postmodern account of historical representation, I want to read *Nostromo* as a novel that repeatedly asks the question: What is modernist history? This is not a new question, either for Conrad or for this book. Scott's novels addressed this same question, but they did so in a rather formulaic way. As I've shown in the previous chapter, for Scott modernist history tells and retells the story of capitalism's progress, forgetting the cultures it wishes to obliterate. In proposing this brief summary, I'm not suggesting, however, that Scott's observations are either insignificant or "wrong". Instead, I am stressing that Scott takes us only so far, and what is important about Conrad's work, especially *Nostromo*, is the extent to which it confronts modernist history and traces the simultaneous necessity and impossibility of modernism as a way of thinking history – in the light, or the growing darkness, of imperialism.[2]

Conrad's engagement in these matters involves his situation as a writer of romances whose affinity with Scott is closer than we might imagine.[3] That romance is at issue for Conrad may be easily recognized in the titles of some of his novels: recall *The Rescue – A Romance of the Shallows* and his co-authored novel with Ford Madox Ford, *Romance*. Perhaps more to the point is the matter of setting or landscape. What Scotland was for Walter Scott, South America and the South Seas became for Conrad: the lands of romance, the "exotic" landscape of adventure. In Conrad's novels, romance turns boyhood adventure story, where swords swished and swashes buckled.

These affinities with popular romance/adventure tales have led some readers to take Conrad's work, like Scott's, less than seriously.[4] Others dismiss it as simply another co-option of romance for imperialistic ends, not unlike Ryder Haggard's *King Solomon's Mines*. Yet Conrad's use of romance, in its postmodern incarnation, situates it as not merely the sewer of colonial fantasy but also the site of a critical staging of history's *relation* to empire. Thus, for Conrad, romance serves a double purpose. Thematized within *Nostromo*'s narrative, it does indeed become the genre of choice for the tale of imperialistic adventure and desire; characters within the novel, as I shall later explain at length, write modernist history as romance and in the process reveal their own colonialist objectives. The romance of historical correspondence has imperialistic consequences, as Holroyd and Charles Gould (the director of Costaguana's San Tomé mine) make us well aware. Yet if modernist history, as a matter of historical correspondence, depends upon romance for its delivery, romance proves an unreliable courier. The uncertain generic construction of romance – its lack of rules for postage and handling – upsets both the imperialistic narrative of history as progress (Captain Mitchell's monumental cycle of technological development and governmental change) *and* the colonial narrative of history as adventure (Charles Gould's romantic adventure of mining operations in Costaguana). Romance ignores the "reality" of history and reveals that history is always a colonizing gesture, always a mode of discourse that silences some group – the colonialist events retold in *Nostromo* are, in the most obvious sense, the voice of the western colonizers. In order to understand this double articulation of romance, as both the theme of colonialist enterprise and the disruption of the claims of imperial history, we need to look more closely at the way in which Conrad's *Nostromo* examines modernist history and the politics of imperial expansion.

Letter 2:
Romance purchases the stamp of history

To look more closely at *Nostromo*, however, is immediately to encounter a problem, for the novel is notoriously difficult to read. It seems that examining modernist history proves a confusing task. Unlike action-packed adventure stories, where we follow the hero or heroine from one exotic location to the next, Conrad's novel challenges the reader even to follow the action, much less understand the sequence of events. *Nostromo* jumbles the chronological order of events so much that the novel can read like one long challenge to the way in which we are accustomed to think of the historical novel. Conrad's departure from the temporal conventions of realism are numerous. To take examples from the beginning of the novel, the narrative obscures the temporal relationship among the first three chapters. The action in chapter 5 takes place eighteen months before that of chapter 3, and all the while the text still does not inform us as to when the action in chapter 3 did occur. If that is not enough, the novel repeatedly gives away its own ending: part 1, on more than one occasion, refers to technological and governmental "progress" that will befall the Costaguana of the novel's closing pages; the prefatory Author's Note discloses the eponymous character's death and the action itself forms the narrative sequence of the final chapters of the novel. To make matters more confusing, elusive references, like those to Dr Monygham's imprisonment, occur before any explanation or description of the actual event enters into the narrative. In a similar vein, the novel makes references to characters' names before we have any idea who the character might turn out to be. And on and on.

Yet *Nostromo* is not a novel in which Humpty-Dumpty cannot be put back together again; as countless critics have demonstrated, it is perfectly possible to piece together the sequence of events once you finish reading the book.[5] But somehow doing a critical cut-and-past(e) job on the narrative sequence seems to miss the point. The effect of Conrad's crumpling of the astral time-sheet, so as to juxtapose events from different chronological moments, is to call attention to the way in which events get remembered and given meaning by modernity. Modernist history's stress on a sequence that reveals progress – progress created by linking cause and effect through time – guides the structure of *Nostromo* through its noticeable absence. In *Nostromo* Conrad does not examine modernist history strictly on its own terms; examining history involves more than making sure that events are presented in the sequence proper to modernist history or its cohort, realism. There is, as *Nostromo* makes evident, more than one way to fit together the events of the narrative.

But where are we to discover the new rules for arrangement? This is the question that Conrad's narrative postpones answering. And following that lead, I shall also postpone my answer. In this state of deferral, I want to call attention to the way in which a sense of the postmodern, as an ironic juxtaposition of temporalities, arises in *Nostromo*. I've referred to this temporal condition of postmodernity before with both Eco and Scott. But the condition is somewhat different here. Whereas the clash of temporalities within the work of Eco and Scott involves centuries, for Conrad the collision occurs within modernity itself and concerns a matter of conflicting months, days, hours, even less. Modernist history does not correspond to itself, is divided from itself and not just from Eco's Middle Ages or Scott's tribal culture.

That Conrad calls attention to this failure of correspondence (or more precisely the failure to read correspondence) through his use of postmodern romance is by this time self-evident. But the significance of this intersection of romance and history is not as easy to understand, for it returns us to the question of rules, brings us back to the moment of deferral. On one hand, romance orders events in the name of modernist history; that is to say, it provides aesthetic rules for the manipulation (delivery) of historical correspondence. Yet, on the other hand, romance seems not to provide any rules at all; the novel's overall structure – its commitment to postmodern romance – keeps getting in the way of imperialistic tales of adventure by dissolving or failing to provide noncontradictory rules. So whereas romance seems to provide an unproblematic narrative ordering of events in the name of modernist history, it also relies on the use of ironic temporality, a temporality without rules, that challenges the validity of modernist history and scrutinizes its relationship to imperialist politics.

In order to trace this dual movement, by which the generic tropes of romance refigure our understanding of the historical assurances that they seem to install, we must look more closely at the historical mosaic of the novel. *Nostromo* pieces together conflicting tales of romance that rely on modernist philosophies of history for their construction and validation, in a way that poses to each an unanswerable question: What is history? The validation of historical correspondence takes place only by means of a cancellation stamp: the postmark.

Letter 3:
Delivering history

Romance delivers modernist history by several different routes. And it is possible to make some sense of them by examining the way in which Conrad's text activates incommensurate accounts of modernist history that correspond to Hegel's systematic revelation of Spirit in *The Philosophy of History* and Nietzsche's description of modernist history in *The Use and Abuse of History*.

Postmark: Berlin, 1837

One way of putting the events together in *Nostromo* forms a tale of romance and adventure that illustrates the imperialism of Hegelian world history. Conrad's history of the imaginary Costaguana picks up world history at the stage Hegel would describe as the manifestation of the dialectical nature of history in the progress of Enlightenment or *Aufklärung*.[6] As Conrad tells it, the Costaguana port of Sulaco was for years sheltered from technological progress by virtue of its geographical location. The natural barrier that repelled "modern enterprise by the precipices of its mountain range, by its shallow harbour opening into the everlasting calms of a gulf full of clouds" (*N*, 64) now finds itself overcome by modernity's steam-powered ships and railway expertise. And with this technological invasion, Sulaco is no longer historically important as the former center for Spanish missionary zeal, the seat for "the highest ecclesiastical court" (*N*, 62); it has instead entered into the golden age of modern progress. As the chairman of the railway explains:

> We can't give you your ecclesiastical court back again; but you shall have more steamers, a railway, a telegraph-cable – a future in the great world which is worth infinitely more than any amount of ecclesiastical past. You shall be brought in touch with something greater than two viceroyalities. (N, 63)

Imperialist history situates importance in the future; that is to say, it forgets about the importance of the past in order to make way for "something greater" – modern technology. In accordance with Hegelian notions of the progress of world history, Enlightenment technology supplants religion, and religion's only role, as we see with Padre Roman and Bishop Corbelàns, is to support material interests. The future, as modernist history tells it, lies in the realization of material interests, not in bringing back Catholic enthusiasm.

In the age of modernity, the institution symbolic of capitalist progress supplants the institutional authority of the Church: "the San Tomé mine was to become an institution, a rallying-point for everything in the province that needed order and stability to live" (N, 119–20). This passage is especially revealing because it illustrates the way in which modernist history (as Hegelian world history) views the past as that which must be overcome. In this case, progress actually forgets the past as past tense and narrates it as an event that can only be understand as the promise of future progress, as the future perfect. World history inscribes progress as infinite, as that which belongs to the domain of the future perfect. The tale of imperialistic adventure must continually move forward, just as capitalism must forever expand in order to exist. Thus, the mine, as an institution supplanting the Church, supplants its own powers by giving birth to a new state.[7] Dialectical history cannot help but progress.[8] Holroyd even could be said to see the future as the third and final stage of Hegelian world history, foreseeing as he does the reintroduction of religion – the shift Hegel would describe as the reconciliation of church and state, the supplanting of history and Objective Spirit.[9]

Postmark: Basel, 1874

Hegel's system of world history, the progressive manifestation of the Spirit of Being, is not, however, the only philosophy of modernist history which can neatly present the case for imperialism. Conrad puts to this use what Nietzsche would define as monumental history. Nietzsche looks at this type of history as a transcription of the past that is useful to "modern man" because it makes it known "that the great thing existed and was therefore possible, and so may be possible again."[10] For Nietzsche, "the simplest and commonest example" is found in "the inartistic or half-artistic natures whom a monumental history provides with sword and buckler."[11] And the same could be said of Conrad's use of monumental history in *Nostromo*. Not only can the history of Sulaco and Costaguana be constructed as a romance/adventure narrative attempting to justify the claims of empire, but the characters in *Nostromo* also form a collection of histories of "great" men, all of whom see their own lives as tales of adventure, as romances that justify and are justified by imperialism. Swords and buckles of sorts are flying everywhere in the imaginations of Conrad's characters.

First of all, Charles Gould, the Senor Administrator of the San Tomé mine and El Rey de Sulaco, "perceived that he was an adventurer in Costaguana, the descendant of adventurers" (*N*, 311). He spent his boyhood dreaming about the silvermine forced on his father in a government repayment scheme, and then went on to turn his father's concession into a profitable capitalistic enterprise, separating the actual business of the mine from "the Old Man of the Sea, vampires, and ghouls, which had lent to his father's correspondence the flavour of a gruesome Arabian Night's tale" (*N*, 80). Such epistles of monumental history may not seem particularly significant in themselves, but a boy's dream of treasure and romance quickly materializes into a legitimation of imperialism disguised as evocations of morality, memory, and myth. These are letters sent C.O.D.: capital accumulation on delivery. At first, like any extension of empire, the mine is supposed to bring "law, good faith, order, security":

> Only let the material interests once get a firm footing, and they are bound to impose the conditions on which alone they can continue to exist. That's how your money-making is justified here in the face of lawlessness and disorder. It is justified because the security which it demands must be shared with an oppressed people. A better justice will come afterwards. That's your ray of hope. (*N*, 100)

In the name of romance and adventure-turned-material-interests,

87

Gould perpetuates the notion that the justification for capitalism is the justice of capital.

Conrad does not, however, lead us to believe that one man is capable of carrying out the romance of capital single-handed. Holroyd, the receiver of enigmatic correspondence, shares Gould's "insatiable imagination of conquest" (*N*, 94). Like Gould, the sense of adventure afforded by running a silvermine in South America fascinates Holroyd. Yet this great man, whose "massive profile" significantly resembles "the profile of a Caesar's head on an old Roman coin," has an imagination of conquest that surpasses even Gould's. For Holroyd believes that he was not only running a "great enterprise" in the shape of the San Tomé mine; "he was running a man!" (*N*, 98). Holroyd's ambitions of conquest fall nothing short of introducing "a pure form of Christianity into this continent" (*N*, 275), seeing through Hegel's third stage of world history, as I've argued earlier. Religion and romance once again justify the ways of imperialism.

Perhaps the most insistent example of monumental history, of sword and buckler working in the name of imperialism, is the eponymous character. Nostromo starts out by assuming the role of the working-class Italian hero who can solve any problem for the forces of imperialism in Costaguana. He is, in modern terms, the knight that can fail in no quest. But Nostromo's mythic position – his very status as the hero of monumental history in all its romance – is what functions to legitimate the far-reaching effects of imperialism. Nostromo is the working-class-knight-turned-capitalist himself, in the tradition of Dickens's Gradgrind.[12]

If each of these characters represents individual instances of the writing of monumental history as romance, Conrad also provides a character who acts as the historian who puts together the various tales of great men in order that he may write his own authoritative monumental history. Captain Mitchell is the eyewitness who saw it all, who was "in the thick of things from first to last" (*N*, 280). He always looks out for history in the making and generally finds it everywhere.[13] There is really no end to Mitchell's historicizing, because, like the fins on a Cadillac, the romance of monumental history has a built-in obsolescence which is the very mark of the newest and most progressive. That is to say, you can never stop narrating history, because there is always more progress to come. Needless to say, Mitchell proves rather insistent and long-winded, but his monumental style is worth recalling:

> Monygham arranged it all. He went to the railway yards, and got admission to the engineer-in-chief, who, for the sake of the Goulds as much as for anything else, consented to let an engine make a dash down the line, one hundred and eighty miles, with Nostromo aboard. It was the only way to get him off. In the Construction Camp at the rail-head, he obtained a horse, arms, some clothing, and started alone on that marvellous ride – four hundred miles in six days, through a disturbed country, ending by the feat of passing through the Monterist lines outside Cayta. The history of that ride, sir, would make a most exciting book. (*N*, 401–2)

Mitchell grinds the sordid tale of imperialism and bloody revolutions into a script that would seem suitable for today's television miniseries market. Effects are depicted at the expense of the causes, as Nietzsche would put it.

In spending as much time as I have detailing the ways in which Conrad represents monumental and world history as imperialistic romance, I do not want to suggest that Conrad's novel is merely a series of complicitous imperialist versions of modernist history. History, for modern men (if not modern women), can consist of more than this, and Conrad's novel extensively confronts the possibility.

In order to see how it does this, I want to turn back to some of the obvious problems with Hegelian world history and Nietzchean monumental history. In many respects, as I have illustrated with *Nostromo*, Hegel's argument for the progress effected by the expansion of Enlightenment capitalism is simply an elaborate justification of imperialism. The idea that historical progress might be the conquest by the Spirit of Being of the otherness of a world is parallel to the description of imperialism as the expansion of those races most in tune with the forces of progress into the dark corners of the globe. That is to say, Hegelian thought is imperialist in so far as it is an attempt to overcome the world's otherness, the otherness of historical happening in which the Spirit must reveal itself.

On one level, imperialism can be seen to operate as the obliteration of difference (whether of gender, race, or historical events) by means of technology. Conrad describes this technologization in Sulaco as "the material apparatus of perfected civilization which obliterates the individuality of old towns under the stereotyped conveniences of modern life" (N, 109). Technology only recognizes its own reflection, which it calls "convenience." In turn, anything that we might call individuality is reduced to an inconvenience that can be done away with by technological mechanization. The scattered references throughout the novel to the installation of technological advancement – telegraph lines, cable cars, and the like – serve not only as a celebration of progress; but in the way that Conrad refers to them it is as if there is something ominous about this invasion of technological expertise. Rather than a celebration of modernity, Conrad's text suggests that modernity's arrival is a cause for concern, sort of an imperialist version of *Invasion of the Body Snatchers*.

Nietzsche's warning about the mechanism of monumental or cumulative history mentions just this point. If we are to learn anything from the examples of the past, Nietzsche explains, then "many of the differences must be neglected, the individuality of the past forced into a general formula and all the sharp angles broken off for the sake of correspondence."[14] In *Nostromo*, monumental and world history delivers events only as tales of progress – the future-perfect quest narrative of and for capital. The sharp angles that get broken off are the voices that would speak out against the progress of capitalism, would give the narrative a jagged edge.[15] Monumental history silences possible discontent (which eventually would overthrow the imperialist system) by channeling such energy into a "dance round the half-understood monument of a great past."[16] Here history, not religion, is the opium of the people. Even Pedrito Montero leads a revolution, not because he wants to mount any kind of effective resistance to the hegemony of imperialism, but because he wants to be like the powerful Duc de Morny, about whom he has read in French works of monumental history.[17] From France to Costaguana, monumental history perpetuates itself by relying on its own system of false analogy – a postal service delivering false correspondence.[18]

Postmark: Sulaco, 1875–6

Conrad's novel provides an opportunity for us to see why we should not trust our correspondence to the hands of monumental or world history. There is, he suggests, even the possibility that one day these letters may fail to reach their destination. In a declaration that has a somewhat contemporary ring in its apparent articulation alongside revolutionary socialism, *Nostromo*'s Cardinal-Archbishop warns the colonizers: "Let them beware, then, lest the people, prevented from their aspirations, should rise and claim their share of the wealth and their share of the power" (*N*, 422). The future may hold something other than the progress of capitalism.

In the Cardinal-Archbishop's brief speech, Conrad's novel articulates the possibility that there are ways to write modernist history other than as monumental or world history; it may be possible to handle historical correspondence so as to narrate the fall of capitalism and the rise of socialism. Yet Conrad's novel does not seem to offer a philosophy of history that would explain how we are to write this kind of history, for one of the problems Conrad lays out in *Nostromo* is that there is something unsatisfactory about all history and likewise all philosophies of history.

Consider the other possibilities. Nietzsche mentions antiquarian history, the patient cataloging of the past in the tradition of Dr Dryasdust. Captain Mitchell, the great monumental historian, also has a bit of the antiquarian spirit in him. But Conrad, like Nietzsche, does not take antiquarian history as a serious option or challenge to imperialistic history. It is as if Conrad recognizes the same problem that Nietzsche identifies when he argues that "there is always the danger here that everything ancient will be regarded as equally venerable."[19] Or, as Conrad says of Mitchell, "almost every event out of the usual daily course 'marked an epoch' for him or else was 'history'" (*N*, 121). Antiquarian history equally fetishized all past events; the past is valued simply for its status as "past," in a way reminiscent of the consumer rage for antique furniture. Modern man in the sway of antiquarian history is no more than a walking encyclopedia, as Nietzsche would say.[20]

If Conrad dismisses antiquarian history, he does take into consideration an equivalent of Nietzsche's modern critical history. According to Nietzsche, critical history "breaks up the past" by interrogating it remorselessly, and finally condemning it.[21] And this is what Don Avellanos's *History of Fifty Years of Misrule* attempts to do. As the title suggests, Avellanos interrogated the past fifty years of Costaguana's history and condemned it as misrule. Avellanos hoped that the people who read his history would learn from it and make Costaguana into "an honourable place in the comity of civilized nations" (*N*, 143). However, the only noticeable effect that his work has on Costaguana is as a contribution to its litter

91

problem. The revolution interrupts the printing, and Decoud finds the pages "floating upon the very waters of the harbour," "littering the Plaza, floating in the gutters, fired out as wads for trabucos loaded with handfuls of type, blown in the wind, trampled in the mud" (N, 213). Critical history is so much litter.

Finally, lest we think that Conrad has also thrown romance to the winds for its complicity with imperialist history, there is another way of writing history that relies once more upon romance narratives. This history has the status of myth and is composed by "the common folk of the neighbourhood, peons of the *estancias, vaqueros* of the seaboard plains, tame Indians coming miles to market" (N, 39–40). Their stories tell of the way in which "many adventures of olden time had perished in the search" of Costaguana's deadly "forbidden treasure" and attest to the presence of ghosts that continue to protect the treasure (N, 39–40).

The persistence of the legend of the forbidden treasure, whether or not the ghosts which are said to protect it have any material status, is a way for the exploited natives of Costaguana to discourage imperialist entrepreneurs from further exploiting them. And it is also a way to retain a memory of the exploitative nature of imperialist adventures. Although Conrad gives myth a certain historical status within his novel, he also makes it clear that this unofficial story does not stand in the way of the progress of modernity – telegraph lines and engineering are not afraid of ghosts. The ghosts and superstitions of myth do not scare modern capitalists and serve only as yet another indicator of imperialism's disregard for native culture and tradition.[22] Modernist history dismisses myth, and the "native" voices in Costaguana fall silent in the face of imported legitimation – modernist history. This is what Nietzsche worries about when he says that history is foreign invasion. Even the category of "native" in the narrative of Costaguana begins to lose all meaning, for being a "native" of Costaguana now means being an imperialist son or daughter born in the country. In this way, modern history is always a colonizing gesture. It is impossible to write history otherwise, because modern history is always a tale told by western voices and seen by western eyes, authorizing versions of "otherness."[23]

Letter 4:
Return to sender

Faced with the dilemma of modern history, one way in which postmodernity could respond would be to forget history altogether. Simply leave its troublesome correspondence alone, much like Conrad did with Holroyd's mail. Postmodern romance would then stand in place of modern history, delivering remembrances of things past without having to negotiate the weight of colonialism. Certainly, this is the direction in which Scott's texts lead, and it is also part of what Nietzsche has in mind. Nietzsche argues that for action to be possible history must be forgotten; "life in any true sense is absolutely impossible without forgetfulness."[24] This "art of forgetting," or the "unhistorical" as Nietzsche calls it, is the necessary corrective to modernity's excess of history – the night in which all cows are historians.[25]

That action is made possible through forgetfulness could also be Conrad's point in the almost endless series of revolutions that form part of the social and political fabric of Costaguana. For what else is revolution besides action made possible by forgetting historical prescription? Yet as de Certeau points out, revolution's relationship to history is not one of simple forgetting:

> Revolution itself, that "modern" idea, represents the scriptural project at the level of an entire society seeking to *constitute itself* as a blank page with respect to the past, to write itself by itself (that is to produce itself as its own system) and to produce *a new history* (*refaire l'histoire*) on the model of what it fabricates.[26]

In this view, revolutions are a modern attempt to erase modern history in order to make it even more modern. Historical produce must be fresh; new and better routes for delivery must be found. Yet the work of revolution does not do away with history altogether. If revolution is a gesture of self-erasure within modern history itself, then forgetting history in the name of revolution produces action which simply reinscribes a new history that needs to be remembered – all action once again is performed in the name of history, in the name of "making" history. Thus, Captain Mitchell would be the perfect revolutionary historian, because he is always one to recognize "history in the making," to unself-consciously understand the modern historicity of revolution. This alone should warn us that postmodern suspicion of "progress" is not simply reactionary, even if we had failed to notice the oppressive effects of the historical metanarratives of "revolution" in the Soviet Union and the United States. Historical memory is suppressed rather than vindicated in revolutionary enlightenment.

Such is the lesson of even Nietzsche's claim that the past can be overcome through the mediation of monumental history. The historical actions that monumental history records incite us to their imitation and hence their forgetting as they are surpassed in order to allow us to act. Yet the mode of this imitation is never straightforward, what we imitate is not simply real action, but romance:

> As long as the soul of history is found in the great impulse that it gives to a powerful spirit, as long as the past is principally used as a model for imitation, it is always in danger of being a little altered and touched up and brought nearer to fiction. Sometimes there is no possible distinction between a "monumental" past and a mythical romance, as the same motives for action can be gathered from the one world as the other.[27]

How can we forget about history if we can't distinguish it from romance? If action is predicated on the forgetting of history, what happens when we confuse history with romance? To answer these questions it is important to recognize that Nietzsche is not worried about history as such but about history as a mode of representation: we tend to imitate a fictional account, a romance, rather than replicate "real" historical action.

Nietzsche articulates an important problem that occurs when we first acquire a sense of the historical:

> Then [the child] learns to understand the words "once upon a time," the "open sesame" that lets in battle, suffering, and weariness on mankind and reminds them what their existence really is – an imperfect tense that never becomes a present.[28]

Language makes possible the child's awareness of the burden of the past, yet the language that performs this work is the rhetoric of romance – "once upon a time" and "open sesame." So history, which is the burden that we must forget in order to enter the romance of unhistorical action, to come into our destiny, is always already part of romance, just as romance is always already part of history. Romance exists impossibly on both sides, past burden and

94

future freedom: condemning the present to the imperfect tense. In a radical sense, the historical event, like existence, is unhistorical in that it must be understood through the rhetoric of romance. But then the unhistorical as romance is also strangely historical, because it gives voice to the events of the past. To put this another way, history is always "the yesterday of romance," a phrase borrowed from Conrad's *Romance*.[29] In effect, Nietzsche notices the same problem that Scott sees – the origin of history is confused with that of romance. And the unhistorical – the art of forgetting the historical – proves difficult to perform.

It will come as no surprise that I want to rename Nietzsche's "imperfect tense" the "future anterior" of postmodernism. To return after so many pages to Lyotard: "*Post modern* would have to be understood according to the paradox of the future (*post*) anterior (*modo*)."[30] This is the temporality announced in the belatedly apocalyptic opening of Derrida's *Dissemination*: "This (therefore) will not have been a book."[31] The future anterior insists upon the fact that what passes for our "present" is not a fullness or a presence, since it is always marked as the potential past of our own future: postmarked, as it will have been. Insofar as the "now" is thinkable, it is as the possibility of its passing, its becoming a moment among others in a future history: that time in the future where even our own future will be the past. For the modernist, artistic production is organized according to rules delineated before the fact: the present fills the future and guarantees its truth as present. Postmodernity, by contrast, involves a recognition of the artistic event as unforeseeable, unpredictable. As Lyotard puts it, "The artist and the writer, then, are working without rules in order to formulate the rules of what *will have been done*."[32] To say this is not willful self-blinding: it is a refusal to abstract the present from history as the single point from which a perspective on history can be adopted, an insistence upon the way in which any act of writing is written across by a temporality that it cannot itself inhabit, suspended in quotation marks as it were.[33] In place of the living present comes the recognition of presence as a lost object, grasped only in its passing. The present is always a reconstruction from an imaginary absence, just as *Nostromo* can only be understood as history by virtue of a critical rereading. In this sense, its contemporary epigraph comes from another South American allusion, the title song of Terry Gilliam's film *Brazil*, which reminds us that: "Tomorrow was another day." History cannot be written, as such; but this does not make us nihilists.

Rather we should recognize that history will have been written, whether we like it or not. Engaging in arguments about what history will have been, we take responsibility for our actions, yet we do not ground them in a truth of what history *is*.

At this point we become aware of how the postmodern linking of history and romance as intractable twins violates the assurances of historical critics such as Georg Lukács, for whom the historical novel presents an "artistically faithful image of a concrete historical epoch" and marks the "outside" historical material as it enters the "inside" of the literary text.[34] I would like to argue that Conrad does not subscribe to Lukács's postal service for delivering historical correspondence. Instead, we can discern *Nostromo*'s postmodernity in the way it evokes the historical novel not to confirm the distinction between history and romance but rather to call that distinction into question once again.

This is perhaps nowhere more apparent than in Conrad's Author's Note, a familiar enough type of disclaimer in which he reveals the "sources" for *Nostromo*. Conrad insists that "his principal authority for the history of Costaguana" is his "venerated friend, the late Don José Avellanos" whose work, *History of Fifty Years of Misrule*, proved indispensable. Of course, Avellanos is a character of Conrad's own invention, and Conrad, not surprisingly, is "the only person in the world possessed of [the] contents" of the text in question (*N*, 31). The extratextual "historical" sources are actually the product of romance – part of the narrative of *Nostromo*. Rather than mark the distinction between history and romance, Conrad seems further to confuse the two. And yet the text makes references to "historical" materials of a more verifiable or marked sort – Garibaldi, Spanish conquerors, South American countries, acts of imperialism, the "accuracy" of which Norman Sherry has documented at length.[35] What, then, is Conrad getting at here? As if anticipating this question, he offers an explanation in the Author's Note:

> the few historical allusions are never dragged in for the sake of parading my unique erudition, but that each of them is closely related to actuality; either throwing a light on the nature of current events or affecting directly the fortunes of the people of whom I speak. (*N*, 31–2)

According to Conrad, historical allusions in *Nostromo* are not mere displays of the author's knowledge; instead, they affect the action in some crucial way. And yet the historical allusions of which Conrad speaks refer to a fictional text – *Fifty Years of Misrule*. The historical novel, as Conrad understands it in *Nostromo*, tries to hide its own fictionality rather than mark the "history" it contains. That is as much as to say that the extratextual authority of the historical novel is itself a fiction.[36] For texts like *Nostromo* – for postmodern romance – *history is the illusion of allusion*: the illusion that something exists outside the text to which romance may make an allusion. Thus, romance is not simply the aesthetic vehicle that transports historical messages into the literary text, the aesthetic envelope that contains historical correspondence. Romance and history are inseparable, much like a fold-up aerogram – which turns out to be an economical way to post historical correspondence after all, even if its destination becomes uncertain.

This complication (or fold) is not, however, merely theoretical; literature is not simply caught between the genres of romance and history. Rather than phrase the problems of modernist history solely in terms of an inability to read the address on the aerogram (is it to be delivered to romance or history?), I want to argue that history itself is caught between the theoretical claims of the philosophy of history and a literary activity of writing. Along these lines, Hayden White has shown us the reliance of history on literary tropes.[37] Yet we can go even farther than White's claim, because textual difficulties are not just history's weakness but the effect of participation within what, following Derrida, we may call a generalized economy of textuality.[38]

The problems with historical writing, that is, are not simply epistemic issues. Instead of simply worrying about whether history is as realist as modernism claims, and proving, by means of some rather well-known maneuvers, that history depends on perspective, I want to argue for an understanding of the temporality of writing, or its historicity, as undermining the writing of history. While modernist philosophy of history operates by forgetting the textuality of history, postmodernity insists upon the textuality of history. That is to say, postmodernity claims history *as* a text – as a kind of letter or correspondence. Suspicion of claims to locate a real history of action that would be innocent of effects of textuality is merely the most obvious corollary of this. Perhaps more interestingly, and in a way that disbars any simple claims that history is *only* fiction, the philosophy of history itself relies upon the very interdependence of the historic and the literary that it seems to deny.

Hegel, philosopher of history, thus tries to forget the literary despite all his claims for the aesthetic. Hegel's dialectical progression of history rests upon the attempt to do away with an envelope, an envelope that I shall take literally as a certain materiality upon which letters depend, and which I shall therefore name the literary:

> Spirit – consuming the envelope of its existence – does not merely pass into another envelope, nor rise rejuvenescent from the ashes of its previous form; it comes forth exalted, glorified, a purer spirit.[39]

As Hegel would have it, history (as Objective Spirit) is the coming into being (*parousia*) of the Absolute; it is the presencing double movement of the *unfold*ing and *infold*ing of Spirit. The sheet of history is doubly folded, so that it both is and is not an envelope. History, as the development of Spirit in time, *becomes its own envelope*, and history is always in the process of being consumed by Spirit. Rather than self-sealing, this envelope not only opens but destroys itself. In Hegel's postal system, there is no need for the literary envelope to perform the activity of delivering history: history delivers itself, or reveals its meaning, by being consumed by Spirit. In this sense, the very extent to which history is liberated from the literary vehicle of its representation is only the mark of the way in which history becomes literature and, as such, destroys itself. The very activity of delivery is Spirit itself. And such an explanation depends upon being able to differentiate clearly between history and the literary, the very terms that are conflated in this conflagration of envelopes.

The work of modernist philosophy of history, from Hegel through to Jameson, is a process that *forgets* the textuality of history, that forgets the inextricable relationship between history and literature.[40] It first claims that only some texts or some parts of texts are history, and then it forgets the textuality of history, arguing that history is not a text at all but an idea (which either has not yet been arrived at through texts or is inaccessible and therefore only "knowable" through texts).

In dealing with the double relation of history to romance and to literature respectively, the same pattern governs our argument. At the level of form, the historical genre is inextricable from the romance genre against whose secondariness it defines itself. As content, historical meaning is inextricable from the literary envelope against whose secondariness it defines itself; that which should be outside, nonserious, dispensable, recurs at the grave heart of truth itself. Postmodernism is the recognition of this problem, of the extent to which modernist history can only be history, in its own terms, by virtue of a steadfast refusal to consider the textuality of history, actually to confront the textuality of the question that remains unanswerable for modernism – what is history?[41] This is the question that postmodernism insists must be re-posed as – what will history have been? In phrasing the question of history in this way, postmodernism is not insisting that nothing is real and that everything is a text; rather postmodernism insists that our understanding of the real in terms of explicit contradistinction to the textual is a problem.[42]

Because of a refusal to admit the textuality of history, modernist history remembers events in much the same way as the meaningless memorials in Sulaco. At the beginning of the novel's sequence of events, the memorial of the royalty whose "very shadow had departed from the land" no longer commemorates anything at all for the common people:

> for the big equestrian statue of Charles IV at the entrance of the alameda, towering white against the trees, was only known to the folk from the country and to the beggars of the town that slept on the steps around the pedestal, as the Horse of Stone. (N, 72)

By the end of the novel, even the memorial itself has been forgotten:

> "The equestrian statue that used to stand on the pedestal over there has been removed. It was an anachronism," Captain Mitchell commented, obscurely. "There is some talk of replacing it by a marble shaft commemorative of Separation, with angels of peace at the four corners, and bronze Justice holding an even balance, all gilt, on the top. Cavaliere Parrochetti was asked to make a design, which you can see framed under glass in the Municipal Sala. Names are to be engraved all round the base. Well! They could do no better than begin with the name of Nostromo." (N, 401)

The novel does not so much accumulate events as erase them in becoming historical: its progress is the ever-greater forgetting of the past. For Captain Mitchell's solicitude to protect the name of

Nostromo from oblivion is wagered upon his readiness to consign the signs of another past to obscurity as "anachronism," irrelevant to the abstract rationality of geometrical forms and "universal" concepts such as peace and justice. We remember anachronism from Scott and Eco; in its usage Conrad keeps his distance from modernism, reminding us by a homophonic interpolation that Justice remains brazenly guilty, even when her bronze is "all gilt." Indeed, historical justice for modernism is merely an even balance of guilt. The opulence of commemoration obscures the force of the event – gilt is laid over guilt. Modernism, charting the value of events as a "place" in history, leaves no room for the names that will not be remembered, the stories that will neither be told nor commemorated. Within the terms of modernist history, the souvenir of the organic community is mass-produced; the South American tribe is wiped out by the ethnologist who praises it; the Sulaco revolution returns as memorial coffee beans called "*Tres de Mayo*" (*N*, 399); and Avellanos's authentic history of Costaguana takes its place in history only as wastepaper.

This forgetting and erasure is not an accidental lapse, it is the structural corollary of the imperialism of modernism's claim to write a history that can be, in principle, universal, whose "meaning" is unaffected by the site of its inscription. As with the names carved on the monument to "Separation" this is a history written nowhere and everywhere, inscribed on the grid of rationality itself. Indeed the independence named "separation" is not a freedom to be local so much as an independence from any local context, a flight into the universal, a self-imperialization rather than a national liberation. We may rethink "separation" as both independence and the alienation from the concrete out of which the concept, the abstract universal, arises. Sulaco is like a South Vietnam, freed from itself to be more in tune with the technological rationality of western modernity.

For Conrad, to remember the force of the event, to write a history that can be other than self-imperialization, will be to remember a disaster, the disaster of imperialism as it is implicated textually. That is to say, history will have to be written, not from a different viewpoint or with a different technique, but otherwise than as itself. To write history otherwise than itself is to break with the modernist mode that seeks to determine historical truth as the suppression of textuality and a pointing to something outside textuality. Rather, Conrad the postmodernist always confronts history with the textual (or political) economy of its inscription. And this final failure to decide what history *is*, this insistent asking of what history will have become, demands that we remember, as in a postscript, that the message of history can only be delivered in an envelope of romance which, as the literary or the unhistorical, it is the burden of the philosophy of history to forget. Thus, the narrative confusion of *Nostromo* proceeds from the fact that no single narrative position in the novel embodies such a "perspective." Conrad, in this sense, doesn't even present himself as a postmodern storyteller. That is to say, the dispersal of modernist narration is not recuperated by any character; the dispersal's only figure is a bulky envelope that never issues instructions for its reading. The deferral of decidability, upon which postmodern romance insists, makes possible the delivery of history as writing, while suspending any decision as to the genre of that writing. In this sense, postmodern romance is the history of the unhistorical, of what real or realist history can't account for. The human necessity of forgetting (recognizing the past as other to oneself) is constitutive of postmodern romance but cannot be incorporated within it. In the terms of postmodern romance, we are like Nostromo, who "would never understand what he had done" (*N*, 463).

Conrad poses an important question to modernist philosophy of history when he asks in *The Rescue*, "Who could tell what *was* real in this world?"[43] If modernist history forgets the "unreality" of events – always "knows" what *was* real, postmodern romance forgets their "reality" – insists that the real of the past is not self-evident. This involves refusing the "reality" of chronological meaning in the interests of evoking signs of differences buried by history (the primitive or unhistorical indigenes) that can only be decided after the fact. Even the most disillusioned literary formalism finds itself inadvertently turning back to Nietzsche: the question is not merely what was real, but "Who compels you to judge?"[44] To write the history of the forgotten is not an epistemological but a textual problem. Rupturing the self-sealing envelope of imperialist progress is impossible either from the inside or the outside. That is to say, to send astray the message that imperialism addresses to itself (postmarked "destiny"), we must ask an interminable, unanswerable question, a question that must be answered yet cannot be, an ethical question: "What will history have been?" The fragmentary question that romance poses.

4

HEROINES AND HERO WORSHIP: WALTER SCOTT'S UNCERTAIN WOMEN AND GEORGE ELIOT'S UNCERTAIN ROMANCE

Toward a conclusion

I began with a question of gender, asking Eco why the invocation of the romance genre allowed the suppression of woman within the narrative of postmodernism's ironic sophistication. And then, turning to Scott and Conrad, I seem to have repeated that very same gesture myself – telling a story about romance's involvement with the masculine genres of historical realism and imperialism. Has romance merely become the woman of the world of genres, the dutiful, if occasionally flighty, helpmate of serious historical inquiry? My delay in directly confronting the issue of gender has been precisely in order to displace any such ready association of romance with woman, the simple understanding of romance as *the* female genre.

The association is easily made because romance is so closely linked to gender. In the world of contemporary marketing, romance is woman's genre, whatever sexual politics individual romances may espouse. I want to argue, however, that romance should not be understood as built upon the foundation of an assumed gendering. This argument may seem counter-intuitive in the face of the marketing practices of supermarket book sections, which mark romances as a woman's genre in less time than it would take to check the "F" box on a form that asks: "SEX?" Yet just as the identificatory marker of biological sex – please check "F" or "M" – simplifies the ways in which bodies are marked by gender, an

102

understanding of romance as woman's genre simplifies the ways in which romance addresses the question of gender. Rather, gender is at issue in romance not simply because romance is a gendered genre but because romance functions as a locus where the question of gendering is negotiated.[1] I choose to turn *back* to gender so that gender doesn't appear to be stable, something to which romance "happens." Romance doesn't simply reflect or deflect women's experience; instead, the historical romances of Walter Scott, and the more diffuse "romance practices" of George Eliot (from which biography is inseparable as text), seek to engage the question of what female gender might be. Thus, for example, gender is only an *issue* for Scott's women, for his female characters. There is nothing to be said about the male sex, qua gender, but female gender is always a question.

In this sense, romance is not simply the other half of realism, realism's weaker vessel; romance asks the fictional question of female gender even as it poses the question of its own generic identity. The extent to which romance involves not simply a reflection but a rethinking of gender for Scott and Eliot, the extent to which gender becomes confused and multiple (for Scott), is illuminated by the way in which more overtly postmodern writers like Acker and Derrida turn to romance tropes in order to effect a radical dispersal of gender identities. The return to gender (and return to Freud, Marx, or Saussure is an exemplary postmodern trope) will permit us to understand the way in which romance does not simply carry the burden of the oppression of the female gender. In a more complex sense, romance engages the relegation of woman to the status of the gender that is not self-evident.

The community of feminism and postmodernism is not a step on the way to demystifying or revealing the truth of woman's gender so much as an engagement with the way in which gender has always been a women's issue, a recognition that the question "What do women want?" is a patriarchal one. Which is a way of replying to Dr Monygham's remark in *Nostromo* that "Women are so very unaccountable in every position and at all times of life" (*N*, 276). If an orthodox feminism has sought to demand that women be accounted for (Gilbert and Gubar), and a more apparently radical trend has sought to transvalue and reaffirm woman as the unaccountable (Cixous), the lesson of romance is that feminism might do well to be suspicious of either method of accountancy. Why should women be confronted with their gender as a question? Why, that is, is gender itself a "women's issue"? In the next two chapters, I shall argue that feminism requires a more radical dispersal of gender and sexuality.

"Varium et mutabile"

"Varium et mutabile semper femina."
(*Aeneid* iv: 569, *Redgauntlet*, 372)
"Your sex are not thinkers, you know – *varium et mutabile semper* – that kind of thing."
(*Middlemarch*, 35)

But let us begin with the promised return to Scott, in order to see how woman is burdened with the question of gender and nonetheless remains unaccountable for Scott as well. All of Scott's women seem to live a curious double life. On the one hand, they act intrepidly to save the hero from the consequences of his own stupidity.[2] On the other hand, this action is performed only to permit the renunciation of action for what can best be described as a life of inordinate dullness as either the hero's wife or a member of a convent.

To illustrate the significance of this claim, I want to return to *Waverley*, this time focusing on the role female characters play in the novel. As we saw in chapter 2, Edward Waverley's recognition of the importance of the Highland tribal past is necessarily mediated by a woman: Flora Mac-Ivor as translator. The historical and cultural rifts between men, the heterogeneity of tribal and modern, mean that men can't understand each other without a woman performing the role of mediator. Edward would never have taken up arms with the Highlanders had it not been for Flora's explanation of the value of preserving tribal culture. In effect, Flora furnishes Edward with the necessary cultural education which enables him to act on behalf of the Highlanders.

Yet Flora does not function as the sole catalyst for Edward's actions. That Edward does not remain a Highland supporter and instead returns to the Hanoverian fold is the work of yet another woman – Rose Bradwardine. But just how significant a role Rose plays is something of which Edward remains unconscious at the time and only learns later in the novel, after the fact. Since Scott's reader is almost as confused as Edward by the intricacies of his fate, I think it is worth recalling the sequence of events. Having fought

under Mac-Ivor against the Hanoverian troops – a commitment that
has even at one point led to imprisonment – Edward finds himself
accidentally separated from Mac-Ivor's company just before the
fatal charge of the English Cavalry that annihilates the "plaids"
beside whom he has been fighting. Edward then undergoes a series
of perilous adventures, as he journeys back to London and later
to Tully-Veolan. Upon this return to bourgeois society, Edward
learns that Rose is "the author of [his] deliverance" (*W*, 444–5).
Through her secret missives and behind-the-scenes action, both
Edward and the reader learn that it was Rose who earlier negotiated
with Donald Bean Lean to rescue Edward from the Cairnvreckan
dungeon, where he awaited execution under the prescriptions of
martial law. As Edward finally realizes:

> To Rose Bradwardine, then, he owed the life which he now
> thought he could willingly have laid down to serve her. A little
> reflection convinced him, however, that to live for her sake
> was more convenient and agreeable, and that, being possessed
> of independence, she might share it with him either in foreign
> countries or in his own. (*W*, 450)

Flora rescues Edward from blinkered Britishness and acts as the
catalyst for his taking up arms with the Highlanders, while Rose
rescues him from the British court martial so as to permit his eventual return to British society without outstanding convictions.

If the work Rose and Flora perform on Edward's behalf were
to stop here, that alone would be significant, but Rose's influence
on Edward's action extends even further. For it is his amorous
involvement with Rose that releases Edward, finally, from a more
desperate involvement with the Jacobite cause. The Chevalier
Charles Edward Stuart himself sanctions ("umpires": *W*, 402) the
engagement of Edward to Rose, which is also Edward's continuing
engagement with British society (it is, after all, in Hanoverian
society that they are married). In this sense, Rose mediates Edward's
divided loyalties, which is to say, his masculine relations with both
his Jacobite "brother adventurers" and the Hanoverian father-
figure of Colonel Talbot (who likewise sanctions the marriage at
the end of the book).

We can begin to make sense of what is going on here if we
recognize that first of all "woman" has a double action. Flora
and Rose both engage in perilous adventures, in disguise, to bring
about events in the face of the irresolute or paralyzed behavior of

male characters (the Chevalier and Edward respectively). And they also serve a mediating function between radically divided groups of men: Flora as translator, Rose as universally approved spouse. It is important to understand that this latter mediating function is not simply that of woman as the passive object of exchange between men against which we feminists have so justly railed. For the point is not that men in Scott's novels are using women to solidify other relationships (male bonding) but that there *is no conceivable relationship* between a Highlander and a Britisher, between a Jacobite and a Hanoverian, except as women "make it happen."

What I am arguing here is not that Scott is in any simple sense a feminist or even that Rose Bradwardine is a protofeminist guerrilla. What could seem more blatantly patriarchal than packing off heroines to a convent or consigning them to domestic obscurity as wife and mother? Yet even if these are blatantly patriarchal narrative practices, rather more is at stake than meets the eye in Rose's matrimonial arrangements or Flora's literary mediations. That is to say, it is not enough merely to acknowledge Scott's sexism. Significantly, the obscurity of Flora's convent or of Rose's eventual married life as Mrs Edward Waverley clashes with, rather than continues, the political function of their roles as translator and fiancée, just as much as retirement is obviously a falling off from their cloak and dagger escapades. The discontinuity between this classic "romance" conclusion (which Scott shares with Harlequin or Mills and Boon) and either women's action or women's mediating passivity in the novels seems worthy of our attention.

Granted, from a feminist perspective it is disturbing, if not entirely surprising, that in the face of women's action and mediation Scott must return to classically confining roles for women as the outcome of romance. But the question is why Scott's texts, concerned as they are with the postmodern temporality of "historical" events, have trouble accounting for women. One way to begin to answer this question is to draw a comparison between Scott and Eco. To backtrack for a moment, recall that Eco believes that romance has been the genre of and for women (the point that his male character understands ironically when he tries to speak to the "very cultivated woman"). In order to re(en)gender romance as postmodern, Eco attempts to exclude women altogether. As I argued in chapter 1, in Eco's patriarchal marketplace we purchase knowledge of the postmodern at the expense of a modernist inscription of gender. If Eco finally tries to exclude women from both history and romance, Scott does concede that women play a crucial role, whether as mediators or translators. Yet however important woman's role is for Scott, hers is ultimately a limited and clearly defined part: no improvisation or expansion allowed in this script. As with Eco's *The Name of the Rose*, a representation of the past should only be possible by finally expelling woman from it, or so the conclusion of Scott's and Eco's novels would like us to think.

I've spoken already of the way in which Flora and Rose are banished to obscurity at the end of *Waverley*, but the closing moments of *Rob Roy* provide an even stronger example of the way in which Scott expels female characters from his narrative conclusions. Scott ends *Rob Roy* without actually accounting for Diana Vernon's life with Frank Osbaldistone. The narrative space accorded to these events is small, yet the events are startling:

> How I sped in my wooing, Will Tresham, I need not tell you. You know, too, how long and happily I lived with Diana. You know how I lamented her. But you do not – cannot know, how much she deserved her husband's sorrow. (*RR*, 382)

Within the space of two sentences (Frank's words to his friend Will), we learn that Diana did not, after all, end her days in the convent as she had planned; instead, she marries Frank, lives happily ever after, and then mysteriously dies. This is a lot of narrative ground to cover as quickly as Scott does, and the result provides a striking contrast to the relatively leisurely narrative pace of the rest of the novel. Such compressed narration allows Scott to conclude the novel by evoking the impossible historical and ethical case of doing justice to Rob Roy. In order to end with Rob Roy, Scott has to kill off Die Vernon, who has by this time taken over as the focus of the novel's attention and Frank's curiosity. It is as if Scott can bring the past back into the ambit of representation, come to terms with the strange legacy of tribal culture for which Rob Roy stands, only if he expels woman from that representation. And conventional tropes of romance (courtship, engagement, and eventual marriage of the heroine and hero) are precisely the narrative elements that allow Scott to dismiss women from his conclusion.[3]

The incongruous necessity that Die Vernon live up to her name, that she die so that the novel can live up to *its* name and be about Rob Roy, returns us to the significance of the discontinuity of women's roles in these novels: it is as if Scott believes that romance will define woman for him and that, in turn, romance's formal generic requirements will dictate the position that her figure will occupy. That is to say, since romance is traditionally the genre of and for women, Scott seems to rely on the requirements of the genre to dictate what position woman is capable of taking in the narrative. Scott banks upon the literary form of romance to take care of the question of gender. Once more, woman's figure is an aesthetic concern for men. The assumption that a solution to the problem of gender could be elaborated on the basis of a formal aesthetic manifesto, that woman is most herself as represented in "woman's art," structures the modernist understanding of the relationship between gender and genre. However, I want to argue that romance opens onto the postmodern as "woman" does not correspond to her own "figure," either to herself or to the tropes of the genre appropriate to her. Postmodernity returns to haunt Scott's work when romance finds woman as in excess of herself, too romantic for romance.

Before exploring the complexities of this statement, I want first to turn to a few simple examples of the way in which Scott's female characters are in excess of the figure of woman to which they are supposed to correspond. To put it bluntly, they are always too much. Either they exhibit excessive behavior like Rose Bradwardine, who is "too frank, too confiding, too kind" and thus without "the sort of beauty or merit which captivates a romantic imagination in early youth" (*W*, 121); or even more frequently they are simply creatures whose qualities are so exalted, so excessive, that they cannot be described by the terms of human nature. Thus Flora is "exalted above the ordinary daughters of Eve" (*W*, 187) to the point that she becomes Waverley's otherworldly attendant, his "fair apparition" of the sublime (*W*, 175); Die Vernon is Frank's "beautiful apparition" (*RR*, 43); Darsie Latimer describes Lilias Redgauntlet as a nymph with lovely eyes (*Redgauntlet*, 123); and in *Ivanhoe* Rebecca faces charges of sorcery for possessing qualities deemed unnatural for any human woman (*I*, 402–4).

Yet however simple these examples may be, the implications of Scott's excessive female figures exceed, if you will, the mere mention of their excessiveness. To explain the significance of their excess, I want to return to a point I made in chapter 2. There I argued that the paradigmatic statement of the postmodern valance of romance was the description of Rob Roy as "ower bad for blessing, and ower gude for banning" (*RR*, 383). If patriarchy tropes action as a male prerogative and passivity as female duty, my strong claim is that we can rephrase this statement for all of Scott's heroines so as to find them "ower romantic for action and ower romantic for passivity."[4] To put this another way, the involvement of woman as figure *in* romance and as the figure *of* romance, both feminine ideal and the figure who invokes romance in order to translate or mediate between men who are "really" radically divided, unfixes the patriarchal definition of female gender as idol or whore. In order to become the passive woman of romance, the feminine object that Scott believes that the romance genre defines for him, woman must *act* as the bearer of romance tropes. Whether disguised adventurer or mediator opening a space beyond conventional patriarchal representations of the real, woman *as* romance engages a play of female desire that is uncontainable within the generic definition of woman *in* romance. Thus, in order to become women, they have to act in a way that is other than the truly or really "feminine" woman that romance offers.

Gender thus becomes unfixed in Scott's romance, in the very genre that purports to ascribe the most heavily encoded or stereo-typed gender roles to men and women. Not only do women cross gender boundaries to act like men, they are never simply at home in their femininity. This is perhaps most obviously borne out by the frequency with which Scott's heroines are either described as in some way masculine or, even more obviously, appear in men's clothing. In *Waverley*, for instance, Flora may have "possessed the utmost feminine delicacy" (*W*, 168), but she also

> bore a most striking resemblance to her brother Fergus; so much so, that they might have played Viola and Sebastian with the same exquisite effect produced by the appearance of Mrs Henry Siddons and her brother, Mr William Murray, in these characters. (*W*, 167)

Flora looks like Fergus, but somehow Fergus doesn't look like Flora – despite his kilt, he remains the utmost exemplar of masculine toughness. This one-way traffic in resemblances, even as it confines woman to the status of copy of the male, allows the heroine of romance to cross-dress convincingly with a regularity that makes it a structural principle.

Scott's insistence on female masculinity becomes an even more noticeable part of Die Vernon's character in *Rob Roy*. The first time Scott introduces her, she is wearing clothing that resembled "those of a man, which fashion has since called a riding-habit" (*RR*, 40). And it is indeed her habit to ride roughshod over gender conventions. Later on, her directness of address is compared to "the style one gentleman uses to another" (*RR*, 119), and even Die herself wishes to transform her own gender role when she tells Frank Osbaldistone: "Endeavour to forget my unlucky sex; call me Tom Vernon, if you have a mind, but speak to me as you would to a friend and companion; you have no idea how much I shall like you" (*RR*, 51). As we saw with Flora, once again the heroine (or "Tom-girl") "puts on" masculinity. And if we are to believe what Die Vernon goes on to say, then the reason for this is that women cannot act as women, they can only act if their femininity is forgotten:

> In the first place, I am a girl, and not a young fellow, and would be shut up in a mad-house, if I did half the things that I have a mind to; and that if I had your happy prerogative of acting as you list, would make all the world mad with imitating and applauding me. (*RR*, 87)

Gender hampers the heroines of romance, yet it is their recognition of gender stereotypes and their ability to cross the boundaries they establish that make the narrative action of the entire novel possible. Scott's masculinized women, his "fair Amazons" as he calls both Die Vernon and Helen Campbell, like the disguised Rose and the militant Flora, cloak their gender so as to bring about narrative closure. Yet just as Fergus does not resemble Flora, cross-dressing in order to bring about plot resolution is not a symmetrical process. Whereas female figures are mobilized, male figures are immobilized. Darsie Latimer is paralyzed by being disguised as a woman, explicitly unable to move because of the fact that he is "muffled [in] the extreme folds of the riding-skirt with which he was accoutred" (*R*, 343). This is perhaps not so startling in that it seems to conform to the pattern by which the male is active and the female passive. However, gender roles fall into a double jeopardy in the light of cross-dressing. The paralysis that strikes Scott's heroes is not simply a matter of donning women's clothes, as in the cases of Edward Waverley and Frank Osbaldistone. Each is consistently overwhelmed, stupefied, and confused so as to be unable to act. Darsie's transvestism is only the strong figure of the persistent condition of paralysis that besets Scott's heroes; that it is so figured may allow us to call it "hysterical." Cross-dressing seems to operate entirely within gender stereotypes, yet it has the effect of disseminating those stereotypes in two senses. First, heroines adopt "unnatural" male costume as if born to them, with an ease that we can only call "natural." Second, male figures are consistently prey to hysterical paralysis: the best case being that most heroic and romantic of romantic heroes, the Chevalier Charles Edward himself. It's as though the gender stereotypes exist to mark both the inability of the characters to abide within them and the structural necessity of their transgression, as cross-dressing women aid "feminized" men.

Perhaps the problem here lies with the assumption about the polarity of gender stereotypes that has governed our reading, with the extent to which we have embraced Scott's patriarchy. We might remember Lacan's caveat about female homosexuality: "we still have to take up the naturalness with which such women appeal to their quality of being men, as opposed to the delirious style of the transsexual male."[5] As I have noted, cross-dressing by women produces a new sense of ease, while the crossover of men, though no less structurally implicit in the romance narrative, produces the symptoms of hysterical paralysis. It's as though it were more natural for women to become men. This dissymmetry might seem to make the patriarchal suggestion that gender is naturally male. But it also undermines the patriarchal definition of the female gender; the female becomes something far more complex, multiple, and disguised. Disguise seems no longer a merely secondary attribute of the female; women's gender remains a problem for the patriarchy.

As romance works, apparently to establish a fixed ratio or clear relation between genders, a postmodern effect occurs as the poles of gender dissolve and gender positions become fluid and multiple. If we presume that Scott's intentions remain within the patriarchal paradox of woman as virgin and whore, what actually happens in the novels is that women do not simply put on disguise in order to act like men at certain points: rather, the female gender becomes not so much a gender (in any strict oppositional sense) as a disguise. Postmodern romance becomes the site in which gender disguise reveals gender as disguise. Thus, woman does not simply put on disguise in order to act. She is never simply passive, because her gender, *as such*, is a disguise. That is to say, woman can act because she is cloaked (her gender is hidden).[6] In this sense, when

111

the heroine of romance "acts" as "passive" translator or mediator she is every bit as disguised as the woman in male clothing.

This relationship between woman, gender, and disguise is articulated most dramatically in the case of another disguised woman, Lilias Redgauntlet, who is metonymically represented as her cloak – as Green Mantle. In the folds of the cloak or veil which is the consistent form of Scott's female disguises – for Rose, Green Mantle, Diana Vernon – we can read a figure of woman which resists simple accommodation to romance stereotypes. In one sense, the description of Lilias's appearance to Alan Fairford clearly genders the cloaked and mysterious miracle-worker of the romance plot as a female figure:

> Her dress was, I should suppose, both handsome and fashionable; but it was much concealed by a walking-cloak of green silk, fancifully embroidered; in which, though heavy for the season, her person was enveloped, and which, moreover, was furnished with a hood.
>
> The devil take that hood, Darsie! for I was just able to distinguish that, pulled as it was over the face, it concealed from me, as I was convinced, one of the prettiest countenances I have seen, and which, from a sense of embarrassment, seemed to be crimsoned with a deep blush. I could see her complexion was beautiful – her chin finely turned – her lips coral – her teeth rivals to ivory. But further the deponent sayeth not; for a clasp of gold, ornamented with a sapphire, closed the envious mantle under the incognita's throat, and the cursed hood concealed entirely the upper part of the face. (*R*, 80).

All Alan sees is a mouth, a lipped orifice sheathed by the larger folds of the hood, and fastened with a small button or clasp at one end. One doesn't have to resort to a diagram to find here in the masked face of woman a fantasmic figure of female genitalia: labia majora, labia minora, clitoris. The connection between cloaking and the female is reinforced by Alan's jocular remarks to Darsie concerning his susceptibility to female charms, teasingly provoked by Darsie's first vision of Green Mantle:

> Thou wert once caught, if I remember rightly, with a single glance of a single matchless eye, which, when the fair owner

withdrew her veil, proved to be a single in the literal sense
of the word. (*R*, 47–8)

Again, woman is masked. And the mask is woman, is what makes
woman the object of male desire. Yet woman is also disguised, for
under the mask lies the grotesque socket which is the object of both
male desire and revulsion – the Medusa's head indeed. Woman is
paradoxically placed as both the disguised object and as the disguise
for the object, a paradox which plays out the contrary drives of
desire and revulsion that form the condition of the patriarchal
perception of women.

Donning the androgynous cloak, woman is mobilized only by a
disguise which – even as it hides her gender – is the very figure of
the folds of her sex. Woman is not simply put in her place by the
generic moves of the romance plot; she is not merely disguised as
a man and then returned to womanhood and the ministry of the tea
table in her master's house. Instead, woman is always implicit in
disguise; her disguise is the outward wearing of her inward gender.
Scott's text suggests that woman is disguised as herself – a self
which threatens the male order as does the Medusa's head. The
folds of her disguise mark the potential horror of what it hides –
Green Mantle's *vagina dentata*. Thus woman cannot simply drop
her disguise to return to subordinate married life with the hero.
For what would the intimacy of the marriage be if not one more
revelation to Waverley, to Alan Fairford, to Frank Osbaldistone, of
the folds of the heroine's disguise?

All of this is to suggest that woman is uncertain because the very
anatomy of her gender is a disguise of gender. Thus simple gender
reversals do not bring about resolutions in romance in the way that
cross-dressing traditionally functions in comedy. The crisis in the
social construction of gender produces the uncertainty of female
gender not merely as the unaccountable resolution of the romance
narrative but as its problematic origin. The figure of woman
unleashed by postmodern romance (as opposed to the realism
of comedy's work-a-day fantasies) destabilizes any attempt by
romance to define itself, to recognize itself, in reference to gender.
Although I will explore this point in more detail when I discuss the
work of Kathy Acker and Jacques Derrida in the next chapter, in
this context let me just say that there is not an essential description
of gender that characterologically stabilizes itself once the question
of romance is brought to light. Postmodern romance offers a model

113

not simply of feminine escape from reality through disguise but of feminine *resistance* to male reality through a recognition of gender roles as disguises.

Eliot, Scott, and Lewes: romance on the fly

However much the deployment of postmodern romance in Scott's novels liquefies gender boundaries, those novels nonetheless consistently conclude with reinscriptions of a very traditional understanding of gender. The potentially radical political move that would use a notion of gender disguise to argue for the fluidity of gender boundaries becomes derailed. Scott's texts favor instead a notion of gender disguise as that which only serves to hide the "real" divisions of gender which the novels must reveal in their conclusions.[7] This final conventional turn on Scott's part is at the expense of any confrontation of the problematic intersection of female desire and high culture. As I have shown is the case with Flora Mac-Ivor in *Waverley*, Scott's understanding of women's relationship to culture is as translator, as mediator. Female characters in Scott's novels participate in culture as translators and mediators to effect "real" cultural relationships between men – in Flora's case, between her brother Fergus and the young Edward Waverley. Flora has no say in what that culture might be; rather her role is "postmodern" in that her job is to supervise the delivery of Highland tribal culture to its modern addressee Edward Waverley.[8] Flora is a postal supervisor who has little say in the contents of her deliveries.

In order to readdress the delivery of cultural correspondence in the name of female desire, I want to turn to George Eliot's "romance practices." One reason for this is perhaps self-evident, for as Deirdre David points out, "from the moment of George Eliot's appearance in print, the issue of sex and gender intrudes itself upon almost all critical discussion of Eliot's work."[9] In a sense, Eliot reproduces the figure of Scott's heroines: unable to appear in public as herself. Whereas Die Vernon went so far as to say to Frank Osbaldistone "Call me Tom," Mary Anne Evans insists that her readers call her "George." Authorial cross-dressing, like the masculine "disguise" of Die Vernon and the cloaking of Lilias Redgauntlet as Green Mantle, once again situates the female as the site where gender is a problem that has to be negotiated.

By suggesting this type of reading of Eliot's work, I am not, however, trying to make a case for George Eliot's undying commitment to feminism or for that matter to postmodernism. I think that Deirdre David is right when she calls Eliot a "timid feminist" at most, and, as I will go on to illustrate, much of Eliot's writing owes more to a modernist understanding of culture and history than it does to what I have been describing as postmodern. [10] Yet in stressing the way in which Eliot does make use of "postmodern romance," I want to suggest that her work has something to say about the relationship between female desire and culture, which is easy to overlook if we focus only upon the way in which Eliot's novels could be considered as quintessential examples of literary realism. Eliot's postmodernity does not lie primarily within the central narratives of her novels; these narratives would be better characterized by their relentless drive to be accorded the modernist plaudit of high seriousness. Rather, the mark of Eliot's postmodernity is to be found in the peculiar obtrusion of the biographical: the introduction of a marginal femininity that is at odds with a realist representation of an explicitly engendered organic culture.

It may at first seem strange to discuss Eliot's work in terms of romance and not realism. For Eliot's debt to romance – from F. R. Leavis's granting Eliot a place in the great tradition of realist novels, to Elaine Showalter's more recent christening of Eliot as "Queen Realism" – has usually either been ignored in criticism of her work or has been dismissed as a momentary lapse on the part of the author of *Adam Bede*, who defended the realism of Dutch genre painting. [11] Even Daniel Cottom's lengthy discussion of the relationship between romance and realism in Eliot's novels concludes with the familiar privileging of realism. [12]

In arguing for the persistence of romance, in a reading of Eliot that mingles Eliot's biography and criticism with textual analysis of her literary works, I won't so much be going "outside" the novels as indicating the extent to which the novels are unable to remain "inside" themselves. The expulsion of romance, that is, never quite takes place as it should in the novels. I want to argue that Eliot's treatment of romance both invokes a traditional understanding of culture against romance and produces an innovative understanding of romance which is resistant to the dominant understanding of culture. Eliot rejects romance as a silly female desire for uncultured knowledge, as she tells us in her often quoted essay, "Silly Novels By Lady Novelists." Eliot's disdain for the romance narratives of silly women causes her to attack the escapist romance that

115

understands history as a grab-bag of facts, akin to "the pictures clever children sometimes draw":

> you will see a modern villa on the right, two knights in helmets fighting in the foreground, and a tiger grinning in a jungle on the left, the several objects brought together because the artist thinks each pretty, and perhaps still more because he remembers seeing them in other pictures.[13]

Romance depends upon anachronism and disregards a serious understanding of culture, for in these silly novels by silly women culture is reduced to "mental mediocrity," clothed in "a masquerade of ancient names." To put this another way, "knowledge remains acquisition, instead of passing into culture."[14] Eliot's appeal here, as I will go on to illustrate in more detail later in this chapter, is to an Arnoldian notion of culture, of the best that has been thought and said – a best which, as has often been remarked, preserves and defends the middle class's right to rule.[15]

Yet even if Eliot's understanding of culture in this 1856 essay seems to anticipate that of Matthew Arnold, other moments in her work suggest that a different reading of romance and a differing relationship to culture is possible. Thus I will be arguing that Eliot appeals to romance for an account of female desire which is at odds with the standards posed by bourgeois Victorian culture – a radical impulse in the bosom of conservative realism. This is the possibility of a postmodern cultural vision founded upon an alternative understanding of romance: a romance of history blurs the distinction of private desires from public actions and disdains the single "truth" of realism. Eliot's work understands, at least in part, the romance of women's desires as "postmodern" rather than unrealistic or foolish. That is to say, if realism can only deal with woman by relegating her to romance, by classifying romance as the inferior site of the construction of feminine identity, sexuality, and culture, postmodern romance can offer a way of revaluing the complex and contradictory aspects of female discourse.

The first site at which I want to examine the worrying excess of female desire is in Eliot's relationship to Walter Scott, which is characterized by a gushing sentimentalism and feminine submissiveness uncongenial to those who would wish to praise Eliot as a rational realist and feminist. If Eliot's use of romance has been downplayed by her critics, her consistent admiration for Walter Scott has also failed to attract much critical attention. Eliot's interest in Scott is, however, well-documented throughout her letters and essays. For instance, in her 1855 essay, "*Westward Ho!* and Constance Herbert," Eliot argues that Scott "remains the unequalled model of historical romancists [sic], however they may criticize him."[16] Gordon Haight, one of the few commentators to recognize Eliot's debt to Scott, goes so far as to claim that it was Scott who "first introduced her to the writing of fiction."[17] Scott was not merely an inspiration to Eliot – he was also, it seems, a sort of hero for her in the spirit of Carlyle's *Heroes and Hero Worship*. As Lewes writes: "Scott is to her an almost sacred name."[18]

There can be little doubt that Eliot wrote in only the highest of terms about Scott. Yet what are we to make of this biographical material? Why would "Queen Realism" choose the king of historical romance for her consort? One way to understand this odd coupling would be to look at the way in which Scott's romances influenced Eliot's own work. The most obvious instance is certainly *Romola*, in which Eliot set out self-consciously to write a historical romance in the mode popularized by Scott. George Henry Lewes called *Romola* Eliot's "historical romance," the term also used by Eliot and her publisher John Blackwood in correspondence that mentions the novel.[19] Writing to John Blackwood in 1860, Eliot explains: "When we were in Florence I was rather fired with the idea of writing a historical romance – scene, Florence – period, the close of the fifteenth century, which was marked by Savonarola's career and martyrdom."[20] However "fired" Eliot may have been by the idea, the actual writing of the novel proved to be rather problematic for her. Looking at her attempts to come to terms with the writing of this novel, we find that Scott figures in her attempts to prepare for the project. In her journal Eliot records that she reread Scott's *The Pirate* (and Bulwer Lytton's *Rienzi*) in the summer of 1861, while trying to devise a plot for the novel that was to become *Romola*.[21]

Blackwood repeatedly encouraged Eliot, stressing her ability to write in the genre of historical romance. As Blackwood put it in a letter to her:

> Savonarola and his times is a splendid subject for you, and you have such a power of imparting reality to every thing you write that your Romance will not read like Fiction. I expect that you will return Historical Romance to its ancient popularity.[22]

Blackwood acknowledges Eliot's ability to impart a sense of

"reality" to historical romance, which will not detract from but rather heighten the novel's value. What we should note here is that the problem, about which Blackwood offers reassurance, concerns the opposition of realism to romance and Eliot's difficulty in crossing the border between them. As Lewes, Eliot's romantic partner, indicates in a letter to Blackwood, Eliot's ability to write the romance is hampered by her inability to conceive of history in anything other than realist terms – as the product of research and scholarship:

> At present she remains immovable in the conviction that she *can't* write the romance because she has not knowledge enough. Now as a matter of fact I know that she has immensely more knowledge of the particular period than any other writer who has touched it; but her distressing diffidence paralyses her.
>
> This between ourselves. When you see her, mind your care is to discountenance the idea of a Romance being the product of an Encyclopedia.[23]

The possibility of writing romance paralyzes Eliot. She believes that historical romance must proceed from an encyclopedic knowledge of the past – knowledge which always seems out of her reach. Eliot seems to have convinced herself here that you can never know enough about the past to write romance. According to Eliot, one must finish with realism before one can write romance, or, put another way, for Eliot romance must always come after history.

If Eliot's admiration of Scott led her into this encyclopedic predicament, nothing could be farther from Scott's postmodern romances than such an understanding of the relationship between history and romance. As I have argued in chapter 2, for Scott, romance is indeed connected to the possibility of historical culture (it is through romance that we have a chance of remembering the past). However, remembering the past is not made possible through the accumulation of a primary stratum of mere historical "facts." Rather than promoting a false sense of historical accuracy secured by the reading of encyclopedias, Scott's postmodern romances reveal the inevitability of anachronism as the mode of historical experience.

Eliot simply does not grasp the structural significance of anachronism for Scott. Since Eliot believed that anachronism was the very trademark of silly novels by women, it seems that she would go to some lengths in order to avoid anachronistic references in *Romola*. Her modernist commitment to the accuracy of historical information causes Eliot to fill her novel with "historical details," as if she believed that their accumulation would give a sense of what it would be like to "live in history."[24] Such a commitment also leads her to worry over the possible appearance of "real historical facts" as anachronisms within her own romance. Unlike Eco or Scott, who took the play and inevitability of anachronism for granted (even when that meant the impossibility of distinguishing anachronism from period details), Eliot tried to write a purely historical romance, in which possible anachronisms are rigorously accounted for.

Thus, for Eliot, historical romance demands a commitment to historical accuracy in the wake of the threat posed by tourism. As she explains in the case of *Romola*, romance must militate against anachronism:

> The general ignorance of old Florentine literature, and the false conceptions of Italy bred by idle travelling (with the sort of culture which combines Shakspeare [sic] and the musical glasses), have caused many parts of "Romola" to be entirely misunderstood – the scene of the quack doctor and the monkey, for example, which is a specimen, not of humour as I relish it, but of the practical joking which was the amusement of the gravest old Florentines, and without which no conception of them would be historical. The whole piquancy of the scene in question was intended to lie in the antithesis between the puerility which stood for wit and humour in the old Republic, and the majesty of its front in graver matters.
>
> I suppose that our beloved Walter Scott's imagination was under the influence of a like historical need when he represented the chase of the false herald in "Quentin Durward", as a joke which made Louis XI and Charles of Burgundy laugh even to tears, and turned their new political amity into a genuine fellowship of buffoonery.[25]

The ignorance bred by "idle travelling" leads to a false understanding of culture by means of the collection of souvenirs – the combination of Shakespeare and musical glasses. That is to say, ignorance of "real" culture causes a misunderstanding of the signs of culture so that, in this example, the joke is read as

119

contemporary humour invented by Eliot rather than a historical depiction of practical joking. Likewise, when Eliot describes the architecture in the Via de' Bardi, *Romola*'s narrator explains: "But quaint as these buildings are, some of them seem to the historical memory a too modern substitute for the famous houses of the Bardi family, destroyed by popular rage in the middle of the fourteenth century."[26] Eliot insists on calling our attention to the distinction between the old and the new, even when that distinction occurs within "history" itself. Historical events may have introduced what appears to the modern eye as an architectural anachronism, but a proper understanding permits an accurate perception of history.

As Eliot sees it, such faithfulness to historical authenticity parallels Scott's. Yet despite her lengthy reference to Scott's *Quentin Durward*, nothing could be farther from Scott's postmodern understanding of historical representation. If Scott's postmodern romances continually remind us that we must have a touristic relationship to past events and can never know what it's like to "live in history," Eliot insists on trying to make the past present, to reconstruct a history from which her own position as writer is excluded. We can thus understand the irony of Neil Hertz's explanation of Eliot's effort when he argues that "*Romola* is both a Victorian humanist's effort to reconstruct a moment in the past and a story of a similar effort, that of the Florentine humanists, to piece together the fragments of classical civilization."[27] The paradox is that in her attempt to occlude the contemporary in a pure historical reconstruction, Eliot blindly repeats the past as utterly contemporary, as she attempts to reconstruct historically a great moment of historical reconstruction. And most importantly, Eliot still thinks that anachronism plays no proper part in the writing of history, rather than realizing that the Florentines' efforts share with her own writing the heroic task of romance – flagrant anachronism. For all of her efforts to be faithful to her heroic Walter Scott, in *Romola* Eliot can only understand the historical romance by way of a very traditional notion of historical realism. She attempts to provide an encyclopedic and accurate depiction of the cultural tensions of Renaissance Florence, and the failure of the novel is not so much a failure of accuracy as one of romance. It's not that the history related in the novel is insufficiently exciting so much as that it appears only as a history written *from elsewhere*. Eliot's resistance to anachronism blinds her to the extent to which postmodern romance is always metahistorical, is about what history may come to have meant. Hence, Hertz's brilliant observation on the parallel acts of historical reconstruction is simply *not present* to the novel, as Eliot writes it. History as such is never in question in the novel, as it is for Scott, because the questions that romance raises about the force and meaning of history, questions of what kind of anachronism a reconstruction may be, are never posed by Eliot who defers them to the problematic of accurate reconstruction.

Eliot's most obvious attempt to imitate Walter Scott's romances leads her far afield from his postmodernity; I would go so far as to suggest that, perhaps ironically, *Romola* is the novel of Eliot's that is the most thoroughly grounded in a modernist notion of history, that most completely fails to face up to anachronism as a necessity. *Romola* is not an aberration on this count, for in *Daniel Deronda* Eliot also encounters a quasi-postmodern architecture with the same high seriousness. Speaking about the architectural integrity of his house, Sir Hugo explains that: "Additions ought to smack of the time when they are made and carry the stamp of their period. I wouldn't destroy any old bits, but that notion of reproducing the old is a mistake, I think."[28] Rather than reproducing the old (the task of *Romola*), here Eliot's character turns his attention to the juxtaposition of historical periods, a notion to which I have earlier called attention with regard to Eco's ironic temporality. Eliot's character does not, however, go so far as to anticipate Eco, for we also learn that "Sir Hugo's reasons for not attempting to remedy the mixture of the undisguised modern with the antique" was that "in his opinion [it] only made the place the more truly historical" (*DD*, 469). Rather than explore the implications of an ironic juxtaposition of historical periods, Sir Hugo's architectural appreciation depends upon an appeal to the "authentic" – a belief that an architectural style may be true (authentic) to the period from which it was designed. Thus the modern coexists with the medieval but not in such a way as to make confusion of the two possible; instead each makes the other only that much more historical, more clearly separated and proof against anachronistic intermingling. History, then, would not need to be reconstructed, since it would already have preserved itself in clear and distinct succession.

I've argued for the relative failure of Eliot's novel of historical romance on the grounds that the postmodern work of romance is rigorously excluded in favor of modernist historical realism, which moves me to the paradoxical position of finding Eliot less open to the play of female desire than Sir Walter Scott.

Eliot's attempts to develop a universal culture of fellow-feeling in her novels have often been cited as feminist resistances to the heartlessness of patriarchal capitalist society.[29] Yet an examination of the Feuerbachian counter-religion of the organic community as it is inflected in Romola's progress to the domestic sphere of nurture shows a distinct patriarchal strain to the community of women established at the end of the novel.

Romola proceeds from amanuensis to a Miltonic blind father to an unfortunate marriage to Tito, who also forms a quasi-bigamous if progenitively successful union with the archetypal "dumb blonde" (actually brunette) Tessa. Romola responds to marital dissatisfaction by a similarly archetypal displacement of her energies into good works and religious enthusiasm. After the death of both Tito and Savonarola and Romola's discovery of Tessa, the novel concludes with Romola's living with an increasingly obese and dormant Tessa and her two children. Romola tutors the son of Tessa and Tito, leaving their daughter to the care of Tessa herself in the latter's few, and ever more infantile, waking hours. Romola is praised as Madonna in her overcoming of religious prejudice and succoring of a Jewish child, in her awareness of a universal human culture of fellow-feeling, an organic community that is nonetheless explicitly masculine. In short, Romola has become a Madonna figure, the lumpish Tessa merely the biological conduit of her tutorial relation to her husband's son Lillo. She is thus a Madonna not merely by virtue of religious devotion but also in that she has an abstract relation to "her" son, born without birth pangs as well as conception, in this case. And if the practical details of the matter seem closer to the presumed experience of St Joseph than of the Virgin Mary, that serves to underline the extent to which this is a paternal, masculine relation, as abstract as the "legal fiction" of paternity. The intellectual supremacy of Romola over Tessa, who attends the scene contentedly looking on or happily falling asleep, is deeply masculinist, even without the educational privileging of Lillo over his sister Ninna.[30] If Eliot praises Romola as "the Holy Mother" (R, 646) prior to her settling with Tessa, this model of feminine virtue turns out to be the achievement of an entirely paternal and patriarchal relation to the activity of child-rearing.

Nor is this an incidental weakness on Eliot's part. The universal modernist community of human nature is built upon an abstraction: the abstract universal of human nature. And the privileging of the abstract over the concrete is precisely the privileging of the paternal over the maternal in the activity of naming children. Eliot does not fail to be a feminist because she slips up in making Romola too like a man, but because her modernism inscribes the abstract patriarchal relation as the highest achievement of human culture. As Deirdre David puts it, "Romola is certainly a humanist ideal, but hardly a feminist one."[31] If this were the only direction in which Eliot's indebtedness to Walter Scott led, then my argument would nicely confirm all the claims for Eliot's "true" relationship to realism. If Eliot grounds her fiction in an appeal to modernist history and historical realism after all, her interest in Scott would appear to be tangential or misguided at best. I would like to suggest, however, that it is possible to understand Eliot's relationship to Scott in another way: if her interest in historical romance seems to privilege historical realism over female desire, an excessive desire nonetheless recurs as a kind of "romantic interest" in the figure of Scott, a practice of reading Scott's romances, which combines with Eliot's own authorial cross-dressing to emplot a marginal biographical romance.

I want to take another look at the scene of Eliot's worship of Walter Scott, beginning with Eliot's remarks about the Centenary Festival in celebration of Scott's birthday. Although a conscious avoider of large celebrations and the crowds that go with them, Eliot at first agreed to be the Festival's honored guest and sit at the head of their dinner table. However, she later declined this invitation, offering a rather curious explanation:

> I worship Scott so devoutly that I leaped out foolishly with a consent to go to Edinburgh, feeling that I should have a good happy cry at seeing any honors done to his memory. But I am altogether thankful that the step was not irrevocable. The journey and the fuss would have been intolerable to me. Edinburgh will look fine with the crowds streaming along Princes Street, but I doubt whether anything else will be satisfactory.[32]

Her devout worship of Scott causes her initially to accept the invitation; yet she later withdraws from the scene of public worship not simply because of her health but because she fears that the celebration will not be satisfactory. So instead of traveling to Edinburgh, she celebrates Scott's birthday privately, at home, working on her next novel – *Middlemarch*.

Yet why would Eliot feel such a need for private worship or have such a fear of public disappointment? There is something unique about Scott for her which makes any public celebration inadequate. For Eliot, evoking Scott is a scene of private emotion rather than public display. Her devotion to Scott involves the intimacy of reading aloud; a deprecating remark about him is felt by Eliot as a personal grief and a "heart-wound":

> I like to tell you that my worship for Scott is peculiar. I began to read him when I was seven years old, and afterwards when I was grown up and living alone with my Father, I was able to make the evenings cheerful for him during the last five or six years of his life by reading aloud to him Scott's novels. No other writer would serve as a substitute for Scott, and my life at that time would have been much more difficult, without him. It is a personal grief, a heart-wound to me when I hear a depreciating or slighting word about Scott.[33]

In her preference for private worship over public display, Eliot curiously reproduces the figure of one of Scott's heroines, unable to appear in public as herself. For just as Green Mantle in *Redgauntlet* only reveals her face, only shows herself as Lilias when serving privately at her guardian's table, George Eliot only reveals herself to be Mary Ann Evans worshipping Walter Scott when writing letters or reading at home. The public may know about her devotion to Scott, but they are not allowed to witness it.

And yet however much Eliot's relationship to Scott is a personal one, one not on view to the public, she also incessantly cites Scott within public view. Attendance at public ceremony is too much; purely private communion not enough. References to Scott in her novels and essays act as a form of transmission between public knowledge and private emotion.

The relationship between Eliot and Scott, which is also Eliot's relation to romance, can only be fully understood in biographical terms precisely because Scott's historical romances were, for Eliot, inseparable from his biography:

> All biography is interesting and instructive. Sir W.S. himself is the best commentary on the effect of romances and novels. He sacrificed almost his integrity for the sake of acting out the character of the Scotch Laird, which he had so often depicted.[34]

It is Scott's "integrity," his total moral vision, which is threatened:

not so much by his writing of romances but because he has clearly been caught up in reading his own work. The effect of romance for Eliot's work has to be considered in terms of biography because Eliot's work was, in large part, an attempt to relegate romance to the marginal incidental weaknesses of biography, lest it threaten the "integrity" of her work. And of course the flagrant "immorality" of Eliot's own life as unmarried companion to Lewes was a constant threat to the high moral claims that her novels made. Her biography gave grounds for the charge that her critique of orthodox bourgeois morality was less in the name of a higher moral vision than an attempt to excuse her own immoral behavior.[35] If Scott's integrity was threatened by taking his own romances too seriously, Eliot's integrity could only be guaranteed by taking her own novels very seriously indeed, which is to say by reading her own novels as anything but romances.

Thus, when women read romance the moral nature of female desire is at stake in Eliot's novels – but also in her own life, as we can see from the inscription George Henry Lewes wrote on the flyleaf in a set of the *Waverley* novels (a sizeable present of forty-eight volumes) which he gave to George Eliot:

> To Marian Evans Lewes, The best of Novelists, and Wives, These works of her longest-venerated and best-loved Romanc-ist are given by her grateful Husband 1 January 1860.[36]

The biggest fiction of all forty-eight volumes is contained on the flyleaf, for George Eliot was never married to Lewes. By living openly with Lewes, by playing the *fictional* role of his wife, Eliot risked scandal in a way that merely being his covert mistress would not have. It seems appropriate, then, that Eliot's biographers remind us of the moment "when Mrs Congreve asked [Eliot] to what influence she attributed the first unsettlement of her orthodox views" on religion, and Eliot answered quickly, "Oh, Walter Scott's."[37] Eliot, who elsewhere dismisses romance as the product of and for silly women and then writes her own conservative historical romance with *Romola*, also finds in reading Scott's romances the force with which to resist orthodoxy. Romance, the genre of the formulaic and silly orthodoxy that Eliot ridiculed, is also the literary form that provides a space for her resistance to bourgeois moral orthodoxy.[38]

In this light, we should not be too quick to dismiss biographical romance as incidental, for the grounds of the cultural *transformation* of knowledge offered in Eliot's novels lies in a critique of orthodox bourgeois morality apparently inspired by Scott's romances, and played out biographically as a romance on the flyleaf of romance. The humanist orthodoxy of her novels leaves no space for romance, excludes it; yet Eliot gets her unorthodoxy, her challenge to bourgeois morality, from reading Scott's romances. In the novels, as I illustrated with *Romola*, the unorthodox actions of her heroines tend to be inscribed within a greater orthodoxy. However, Eliot is not simply monolithic – the scene of the subversive play of female desire for Eliot is not the *writing* of romance, but the *reading* of romance. When romance is read, female desire is in question in a manner that raises crucial feminist questions. Eliot's relation to feminism requires biographical consideration not simply because she is a biological woman but in order to understand how, for herself as for her heroines, the reading of romance (the genre which the novels appear to exclude) is the site where female desire sets to work. Women's reading in Eliot's novels is something of an elusive and surreptitious process, and the reading of reading requires more detailed attention to specific moments in those texts than has characterized my analysis up to this point.

Reading romance

Eliot's heroines are consistent readers of romance, whether literally like Maggie Tulliver or *more metaphorically*, in the way they figure their ambitions to themselves, like Gwendolen Harleth. This is by no means a uniform process, as the opposed figures of Dorothea Brooke and Rosamond Vincy in *Middlemarch* illustrate, each of whom channels her life according to the textual fantasies of various kinds of romance. Given their respective fates with Casaubon and Lydgate, we might be tempted to interpret this entirely negatively; in such a reading Eliot would argue that women read romances because their unreality is analogous to the fantasy life to which nineteenth-century British society condemns female desire. Indeed, the failure of Rosamond's marriage is doubtless an effect of her own failure to inquire into the economic basis upon which the romance genre effects narrative closure in matrimony. Romance might thus seem to be a form of ideological social control, keeping female desire in the realm of the unreal. That is to say, reading romance would be what keeps women silly, to use Eliot's phrase.

Yet there is more to reading romance than silliness, as Eliot's novels suggest. After all, Dorothea's union with Ladislaw despite the "dead hand" of Casaubon's will seems to come straight out of the genre fiction that was Rosamond's downfall. And what are we to make of the eminently sensible Mary Garth's addiction to reading Walter Scott? Female desire is not merely imprisoned within the fantasy world of romance: romance seems to be the terrain upon which female desire can work, outside the testamentary realism that enacts male desire as law. If the representation of female desire is incommensurable with the objective cultural field that is the purview of realism, then it is as readers of romance that Eliot's heroines explore a space beyond that of their author's own overt representational strategies. As readers of romance, Eliot's women produce a counterplot to patriarchal law – for good or ill, surreptitiously subversive or merely superstitious. Eliot may not have been a romance author, or even a feminist by today's standards, but as feminist readers of Eliot we need to repeat that practice of surreptitious, covert, romance reading – even within the text of Eliot's own "realist" novels.

We commonly think of *Middlemarch* as a triumph of literary realism in its survey of the rural bourgeoisie. However, romance functions as a sort of social glue in the novel, for it is Walter Scott's novels, rather than any political or social commitment, that the community holds in common. We might almost say that Scott's novels are what brings together the social fabric, given that such a large number of the characters read Scott. When asked whether women fall in love with men they already know, Mary Garth turns to Scott and Shakespeare for examples, citing *The Pirate* and *Waverley*. Importantly, she does not allude to them as novels, repeatedly referring to the cases of Minna and Flora Mac-Ivor as "my experience."[39] Female experience is not only gained through reading romance, it is inseparable from romance.

Nor is reading romance solely a female activity. Mr Trumbull reads the prose, Lydgate the poetry.[40] Mr Brook calls on Scott as the author who could have "worked up" a local event – a Methodist preacher caught poaching (*M*, 428). The Garths, often thought to be autobiographical, are a family united most when contemplating Scott's romances. After an epigraph extolling Scott's virtues, chapter 57 opens with a scene in which Jim Garth reads aloud from *Ivanhoe*, and the children are acting out the archery scene (*M*, 616–17). In *Middlemarch*, paragon of the realist novel, romance is not simply escapist fantasy but the ground of the everyday experience of community itself.[41]

Yet if romance is always a part of everyday life, it is not always the same romance. What we observe in *Middlemarch*, which is not apparent in Eliot's other novels, is the repeated employment of varying romance tropes by the different characters. Rosamond Vincy views her life as "a social romance" in which "a stranger was absolutely necessary" (*M*, 145). The stranger who takes on this role is, of course, Lydgate, and Rosamond at first finds him to be every bit the "crown-prince" she expected (*M*, 475). Lydgate likewise relies on romance. His romance is both "the other passion, sung by the Troubadours" (*M*, 173) and the romance of scientific discovery; he is ready to "transform life into romance at any moment" (*M*, 387). Similarly, Celia thinks her husband, Sir James, is a smiling prince with "a chivalrous nature" right out of a romance (*M*, 99, 319). Will Ladislaw draws on a different stratum of royal hierarchy: his romance casts Dorothea as queen, Casaubon as the fire-breathing dragon, and himself as the knight in shining armor who, of course, rescues the queen from the dragon (*M*, 511–12). Finally, if we are to believe Will's interpretation, Dorothea also "must have made some original romance for herself" in order to marry Casaubon in the first place (*M*, 241).

This rather confused pervasiveness of the reading of romance in *Middlemarch* is more directly focused on the figure of Maggie Tulliver in *The Mill on the Floss*. Unlike Scott's romances, however, Eliot's novel of rural life does not provide any of the conventional settings for romance. The narrator, for instance, remarks:

> It is a sordid life, *you say*, this of the Tullivers and Dodsons – irradiated by no sublime principles, no romantic visions, no active, self-renouncing faith – moved by none of those wild uncontrollable passions which create the dark shadows of misery and crime – without that primitive rough simplicity of wants, that hard submissive ill-paid toil, that child-like spelling-out of what nature has written, which gives its poetry to peasant life. Here, one has conventional worldly notions and habits without instruction and without polish – surely the most prosaic form of human life.[42]

Eliot forsakes Scott's sublime Scottish landscapes, in which passionate actions and poetic rewards find their place. And in so doing, Eliot dismisses the superficial trappings of historical romance.

There is, as she points out in this passage, nothing that seems extraordinary about the action she portrays in *The Mill on the Floss*; the uncommon features of romance seem expurgated. However, the emphasis here must be on *seem*. In the passage Eliot prefaces her remarks with the phrase "you say," and in so doing she anticipates the reader's response to the "prosaic" world of the Tullivers and Dodsons. But rather than take up the same position as her imagined reader, Eliot asks us to examine the overlooked, the unseen – what could be called the romance in everyday life. In keeping with this emphasis on the everyday, the extraordinary impulse or romance in the novel originates in a very ordinary place, in the character of Maggie:

> A girl of no startling appearance, and who will never be a Sappho or a Madame Roland or anything else that the world takes wide note of, may still hold forces within her as the living plant-seed does, which will make a way for themselves, often in a shattering, violent manner. (*MF*, 320)

Maggie may indeed appear ordinary, but there are extraordinary forces within her that have violent effects. And these violent forces are the potential for female desire which can neither be represented within the formulaic conventions of silly romance nor appropriated by the containing strategies of realistic fiction.

With the character of Maggie, Eliot explores the potential force of female desire. But in doing this, Eliot is not so much concerned with the fluidity of gender boundaries (Scott's focus) as she is disturbed by the way in which gender roles have become straitjackets for women. For Maggie, reading romance becomes a way to test the boundaries of gender roles and at the same time they serve to show her the force of those boundaries. Time and again in *The Mill on the Floss*, Eliot reminds us of Maggie's inappropriate behavior and appearance; Maggie continually fails to conform to the standards set for her by virtue of her gender. For example, Tom scolds Maggie, telling her that she's "always in extremes" (*MF*, 503); Mr Wakem finds her "rather dangerous and unmanageable" (*MF*, 545); Mr Riley observes her and tells her father that since she is a woman Maggie has "no business wi' being so clever" (*MF*, 66). Like Scott's heroines, there is something excessive about Maggie's character.[43] Yet Maggie's excessiveness is even more threatening, as her youthful resemblance to "a small Medusa" suggests (*MF*, 161).

A refuge for this inappropriate, unmanageable heroine is found in the pages of romance. To begin with, Eliot describes the social space into which Maggie can retreat for comfort by making a reference to Scott. Referring to the sanctuary, Alsatia, which Scott depicts in *The Fortunes of Nigel*, Eliot describes Maggie's actions:

> But Maggie always appeared in the most amiable light at her aunt Moss's: it was her Alsatia, where she was out of the reach of law – if she upset anything, dirtied her shoes, or tore her frock, these things were matters of course at her aunt Moss's. (*MF*, 139)

Aunt Moss's comforting lawlessness explicitly figures Eliot's allusion to romance as an escape from the novelistic laws of social realism.

More directly, however, Maggie turns to reading romance, specifically the works of Scott and Byron, as an escape from the restrictions imposed by daily life:

> if she could have had all Scott's novels and all Byron's poems! – then perhaps she might have found happiness enough to dull her sensibility to her actual daily life. And yet . . . they were hardly what she wanted. She could make dream-worlds of her own – but no dream-world would satisfy her now. She wanted some explanation of this hard, real life. . . . If she had been taught "real learning and wisdom, such as great men knew" she thought she should have held the secrets of life; if she had only books that she might learn for herself what wise men knew! (*MF*, 379)

Romance is posed here as mere escape, not as a solution to Maggie's "real" problems. That is to say, women read romances to dull their sensibility, while real learning and wisdom is contained within the books that great men read.[44] Rather than the dream world posited by romance, Maggie yearns for the "real" explanations of life, which she believes are given to men.

Opening her brother's schoolbooks, Maggie thus expects to find the answers for which she longs. Yet the search for real explanations leads back to romance, as Maggie turns away from Tom's books and thinks of Walter Scott once again:

> Then her brain would be busy with wild romances of a flight from home in search of something less sordid and dreary: –

she would go to some great man – Walter Scott, perhaps, and tell him how wretched and how clever she was, and he would surely do something for her. (*MF*, 380–1)

Maggie's romance is about romance itself: if Scott's romances can't help her, then Scott, the great author of romance, will. But this appeal to Scott offers only temporary solace, for romance – and even the figure of Walter Scott himself – cannot ward off the intrusion of everyday realism:

But in the middle of her vision her father would perhaps enter the room for the evening, and, surprised that she sat still, without noticing him, would say complainingly, "Come, am I to fetch my slippers myself?" (*MF*, 381)

Eliot blatantly introduces the law of the father as the obligation to return to the mundane, ordinary existence of "realism" which demands of Maggie that she fetch slippers instead of Walter Scott. Maggie can only stay outside the law, only stay within the pages of romance, for so long.

Eliot continues to suggest that romance remains unsatisfying, unfulfilling, for women when she has Maggie encounter Philip in the Red Deeps:

Maggie had looked at the back too and saw the title: it revived an old impression with overmastering force.

"The Pirate," she said, taking the book from Philip's hands. "O, I began that once – I read to where Minna is walking with Cleveland – and I could never get to read the rest. I went on with it in my own head, and I made several endings; but they were all unhappy. I could never make a happy ending out of that beginning. Poor Minna! I wonder what is the real end. For a long while I couldn't get my mind away from the Shetland Isles – I used to feel the wind blowing on me from the rough sea." (*MF*, 401)

Although the titles of Scott's novels retain an "overmastering force," Maggie cannot get away from the problem of making romance end happily for the dark heroines. Maggie has read far enough to realize what Scott himself must also have thought – that it would be impossible to make the romance end happily for the raven-haired Minna.

The felt unreality of romance endings seems to have much to do with the reason Maggie gives Philip for refusing the volume (even though she has trouble not reading the volume once it is placed in her hands). Explaining her refusal to Philip, Maggie says:

> It would make me in love with this world again, as I used to be; it would make me long to see and know many things – it would make me long for a full life. . . . But not for me – not for me. . . . Because I should want too much. (*MF*, 402)

Romance itself, with its alternative visions for women, creates desires that Maggie feels are excessive. A full life is not only unobtainable, it is literally unthinkable for Maggie. The full life that might become desirable for the dark woman would itself be full of too many desires, desires which must remain unspoken. Romance, therefore, carries the prospect of dissatisfaction for women as a structured principle implicit in its opening.

Through this continual return to realism that highlights the impossibility of romance, is Eliot suggesting that romance offers only temporary and inferior outlets for female desire? That Maggie next renounces romance for the teaching of Thomas à Kempis would suggest that the answer is yes. However, Eliot's novel does not give up on romance that easily. Philip convinces Maggie that she is "shutting [her]self up in a narrow self-delusive fanaticism which is only a way of escaping pain by starving into dullness all the highest powers of [her] nature" (*MF*, 427). In effect, Philip argues that religion (Kempis) proves more self-delusive than romance (Scott), and he encourages Maggie to read Scott once more.

And yet Maggie's return to Scott doesn't seem to get her anywhere. She finishes *The Pirate* and discovers that it ends just as she suspected – the dark Minna does not marry her lover, Cleveland, while her sister, the fair Brenda, marries the alternative protagonist, Mordaunt Mertoun. What's more, Maggie finds that this pattern repeats itself in *Ivanhoe* and *Waverley*. Maggie longs for a narrative that she has yet to find in romance and thus asks Philip: "If you could give me some story, now, where the dark woman triumphs, it would restore the balance – I want to avenge Rebecca and Flora Mac-Ivor, and Minna and all the rest of the dark unhappy ones" (*MF*, 433). Scott's dark heroines are, like Maggie, the unhappy ones. So Philip suggests to Maggie that she "avenge the dark women" herself (*MF*, 433). But Maggie retorts: "Philip, that is not pretty of you, to apply my nonsense to anything real" (*MF*, 433).

In each instance, Maggie grounds her argument on the separation of romance from reality; although romance might be acceptable for the temporary escape from unhappiness, it offers no "real" solutions: "blond" romance, which ends happily, is mere escape (the blond Lucy is not held up as the answer), "dark" romance, which would be realized as the transformation of reality, is impossible.

Maggie's understanding of the impossible realization of dark romance is underscored by the people of St Oggs, who judge Maggie's behavior by the standards of "blond" romance. Their response to her potential elopement with Stephen Guest is "what a wonderful marriage for a girl like Miss Tulliver – quite romantic!" (*MF*, 620). But Maggie refuses to take the "romantic" path offered to her and resolves to give up both Stephen and Philip. By not conforming to the topoi of "blond" romance (she is a Minna not a Brenda), Maggie is judged immoral and sentenced to social exile; even the good intentions of Dr Kenn cannot absolve her. Sanctioned transgression has its limits, and Maggie's problem is that she attempts to be more socially transgressive than the gender borders of "blond" romance make allowances for.

Yet I do not want to suggest, as would any upstanding member of the St Oggs community, that Maggie's more transgressive version of romance has no force whatsoever. The transformative power of Maggie's dark female imaginings lies in the extent to which they threaten the decidability of the boundary between reality and romance. Dark romance seems impossible, unachieved, because it would be the birth of a *real* female desire of which realism is unable to speak in representation – as much for George Eliot as for Maggie. The reading of romance threatens the distinction between reality and romance by offering a dark or unspeakable desire which cannot be dealt with by realism, and yet which is too authentic to be dismissed as merely escapist romance. To put this another way, dark romance is the unrepresentable in female desire. Thus, *The Mill on the Floss* fails to present any effective resolution for the problem of the relationship between romance and reality. The only alternative Eliot finds for Maggie's unhappiness is death, and Maggie's (as well as Eliot's) vision of the social realization of dark romance dies with her.[45] That is to say, in *The Mill on the Floss*, romance always becomes displaced in that it can only imagine the fulfillment of female desire in an impossible future – a future that can never exist for the dead Maggie. The fellow-feeling for which Eliot's text argues can only come about at the expense of Maggie's death.[46]

It is tempting to draw a parallel to *Middlemarch*, where the limitations of blonde Rosamond's silly romance vision contrast the wider scope of the dark-haired Dorothea's engagement with romance.[47] Hair color is, however, far too frivolous an issue to provide a consistent litmus test for female moral orientation in Eliot's novels. If the function of romance, its place in a total moral vision, is unclear, the effects of romance-reading are determined by gender in *Middlemarch*. Romance may fail for men, but that is an external threat – as in Lydgate's lack of funds. The failure of a female romance is a failure from the inside, as it were – women cannot shrug it off and return to a "reality" of publicly sanctioned desire (such as monetary or parliamentary ambition), since they have none. Rosamond's failure is inherent in the limitations of her reading of romance; Dorothea realizes her aspirations with Ladislaw only by virtue of the "sacrifice" (*M*, 896) of herself to anonymity. That is to say, she relinquishes any wider realization of romance, either as general social redemption or blazing public love affair.[48] The realization of female desire has to remain as surreptitious as the reading of romance in the realist novel.

In *Daniel Deronda*, this problem splits the novel in two – literally, if we are to accept the critical judgments of F. R. Leavis. However, Leavis contrasts the sinewy realism of Gwendolen Harleth to the mere romance of Daniel Deronda. Alerted as we are to the condition of "romance reader," we may produce a rather different account of the two possibilities – seeing Gwendolen Harleth as a private reader of romance constrained by public realism, in contrast to the publicly activated historical romance of Deronda's Zionism.

Like the characters in *Middlemarch*, Gwendolen Harleth's experiences are represented as being patterned on silly romances: the novel describes Gwendolen as a "princess in exile" waiting for prince charming (Grandcourt) to rescue her from the perils of obscurity or finally the perils of poverty (*DD*, 53). Gwendolen, as the representation of an insignificant woman appealing to silly novels, illustrates the serious problem of the denial of cultural understanding to women. Women are forced, by the way in which society limits their experiences, to be dull. As Gwendolen herself comes to recognize: "Her mother's dullness, which used to irritate her, she was at present inclined to explain as the ordinary result of women's experience" (*DD*, 483). The real dullness of women is a product of the way in which their desires are caught up in the conventions of silly romance. Like Maggie or Mary

Garth, Gwendolen derives her notion of experience from reading romance. As Eliot puts it: "Gwendolen's uncontrolled reading, though consisting chiefly in what are called pictures of life, had somehow not prepared her for this encounter with reality" (*DD*, 193). Reading romance proves an inescapable part of culture for women at the same time that it fails to serve as adequate preparation for the "reality" that they will encounter.

On the other hand, Deronda's romance is a reading of the historical past that issues upon the wider public stage. For Deronda, the tropes of romance provide the structure for a cultural understanding of his past, much in the fashion of Scott's Darcie Redgauntlet or Edward Waverley. The gendering of the hero as male seems to allow Eliot to run closer to Scott than in the overt historical romance of *Romola*. Yet just as Gwendolen Harleth is not a straightforward romance heroine, neither is Daniel Deronda's character obviously associated with romance. As Eliot first explains it:

> To say that Deronda was romantic would be to misrepresent him; but under his calm and somewhat self-repressed exterior there was a fervour which made him easily find poetry and romance among the events of everyday life. And perhaps poetry and romance are as plentiful as ever in the world except for those phlegmatic natures who I suspect would in any age have regarded them as a dull form of erroneous thinking. (*DD*, 245)

Deronda is not "romantic" in the way silly novels would understand the term, and his interest in romance cannot simply be dismissed as "erroneous thinking." Eliot returns to this issue later in the novel, describing Deronda's connection with romance more directly:

> And, if you like, he was romantic. That young energy and spirit of adventure which have helped to create the world-wide legends of youthful heroes going to seek the hidden tokens of their birth and its inheritance of tasks, gave him a certain quivering interest in the bare possibility that he was entering on a like track – all the more because the track was one of thought as well as action. (*DD*, 573–4)

Romance returns as a description of the action that motivates the inception of worldwide legends, the discovery of cultural origin and the perpetuation of traditions. And, as we learn, for Deronda this romance works itself out by way of his commitment to Judaism. Eliot unites romance with a unified moral vision, in Deronda's drive to unify the culture of the Jewish people:

> The idea that I am possessed with is that of restoring a political existence to my people, making them a nation again, giving them a national centre, such as the English have, though they too are scattered over the face of the globe. (*DD*, 875)

However, this community will arise only through separation and as the separation of a self-conscious minority.[49] Furthermore, it is an exclusively male romance. Deronda's marriage to Mirah rather than Gwendolen is more properly merely the external sign of his more profound marriage to her brother, Mordecai. As Mordecai remarks to Deronda, "It has begun already – the marriage of our souls" (*DD*, 820). Real marriage occurs between men. As Deronda's mother puts it, the male homosocial relation is the true meaning of matrimony within Jewish culture as it is represented in the novel:

> To have a pattern cut out – "this is the Jewish woman; this is what you must be; this is what you are wanted for; a woman's heart must be of such a size and no larger, else it must be pressed small, like Chinese feet; her happiness is to be made as cakes are, by a fixed receipt." That was what my father wanted. He wished I had been a son; he cared for me as a makeshift link. (*DD*, 694)

Eliot stresses the exclusionary structure of the public romance, the Zionist epic. This exclusion is not only racial; it is also explicitly masculinist.

The impossibility of public romance, or epic, for women is the lesson that Dorothea learns at the end of *Middlemarch*:

> A new Theresa will hardly have the opportunity of reforming a conventual life, any more than a new Antigone will spend her heroic piety in daring all for the sake of a brother's burial: the medium in which their ardent deeds took shape is for ever gone. (*M*, 896)

These two stories share an exclusionary desire with the Zionist movement – Theresa's converts, like Antigone's actions, place women in an *alternative* public space. According to Eliot, feminine epic is no longer possible; transformative narratives of female desire have given way to a public culture which is much less conducive to the strong representation of female desire. Eliot suggests, instead, that female desire now has to work in an "unhistorical" way:

But the effect of her being on those around her was incalculably diffusive: for the growing good of the world is partly dependent on unhistoric acts; and that things are not so ill with you and me as they might have been, is half owing to the number who lived faithfully a hidden life, and rest in unvisited tombs. (*M*, 896)

We are not told by Eliot *why* the days of Theresa and Antigone are over. The failure of public romance for women (the lack of a feminine epic) is linked to the totalizing, organic vision that underpins Eliot's moral reasoning. It is not so much that history has no space for women as that Eliot's realist project of modernist claims of moral universals cannot deal with a *separate* female desire, a romance of dark women.

In speaking of Dorothea's problem of genre, the failure of public romance, Eliot performs a *diametrical misreading* of her own examples:

Theresa's passionate, ideal nature demanded an epic life: what were many-volumed romances of chivalry and the social conquests of a brilliant girl to her? . . . Many Theresas have been born who found for themselves no epic life wherein there was a constant unfolding of far-resonant action . . . but after all, to common eyes their struggles seemed mere inconsistency and formlessness; for these later-born Theresas were helped by no coherent social faith and order which could perform the function of knowledge for the ardently willing soul. (*M*, 25)

According to Eliot, epic disappears along with the unified culture of coherent social faith and order in which female desire could find a public articulation. Yet Antigone's act was the *transgression* of that order, Theresa's a *retreat* or withdrawal from that *social* faith. A similar contradictory impulse of separation structures Eliot's account of the appearance of female desire, which can only be spoken in the terms of the romance of the fairy tale: "Here and there a cygnet is reared uneasily among the ducklings in the brown pond, and never finds the living stream in fellowship with its own oary-footed kind. Here and there is born a Saint Theresa" (*M*, 26). The universal community of moral humanism, the coherent social faith and order for which Eliot argues in her novels, is a modernist goal. Yet if Eliot argues for the organicism of community, the necessity of fellow-feeling, why do the Saint Theresas who are motivated by this vision need to depart from the stream of fellowship? There seems to be no space within this modernist vision of a coherent humanist social totality for the alterity or specificity of the feminine.

I could be even blunter and say that "fellow-feeling" demands precisely that we "feel" like "fellows," as men. If the vision of organic integration is presented as a female yearning for change and a more totalized society, the entry into public community is to be purchased only by the renunciation of the dark specificity and difference of female desire.[50] Given that female desire can find public expression only as a romance of separation, women are sacrificed for the social whole. They either become anonymous and unhistorical, living a merely private romance like Dorothea, or they encounter romance as the limitation and failure of their own desire, like Rosamond Vincy.

Eliot's realism of the organic totality cannot include (or make representable) woman's desire; the public romance, the epic of female desire, appears as an unthinkable separation, private romance appears as anonymity, failure, or drowning. That female desire is never achieved should alert us to the real stake in Eliot's invocation of the romance genre. A return to *Daniel Deronda* that allows us to note the parallels between Dorothea and Gwendolen may help us to understand Eliot's divided relation to romance. For Gwendolen shares Rosamond Vincy's romance (waiting for Grandcourt) yet is marked by the wider public aspirations of the social reformer Dorothea:

> She rejoiced to feel herself exceptional; but her horizon was that of the genteel romance where the heroine's soul poured out in her journal is full of vague power, originality, and general rebellion, while her life moves strictly in the sphere of fashion; and if she wanders into a swamp, the pathos lies partly, so to speak, in her having on her satin shoes. (*DD*, 83)

Daniel Deronda explicitly poses the issue of romance between public and private spheres. Like Dorothea Brooke, Gwendolen is caught between a limiting realization of orthodox "romance," with its patriarchal conventions, in the private sphere, and a wider public romance that appears unrealizable, even swamping.

Public female romance has no place in the modernist moral totality. There is, however, another story in Eliot's novels, as our reading of *The Mill on the Floss* has already suggested – the surreptitious story of the female *reader* of romance. To offer a rather premature characterization, anything that we might want to call feminism owes less to Eliot's moral realism than to the frustrated public aspirations of the romance reader. Romance becomes subversive as it allows female desire to become public. Crucially, this "becoming public" is an effect of *reading*, the private activity of women that always tends to become public (the same novels that give Mary Garth a notion of private female experience are realized as theater by her siblings).

We can go a little further than this, to contrast two kinds of feminism in George Eliot: a modernist realism of universal morality in action and a postmodern romance of intertextual desire. The latter is a minoritarian story, one that we have had to exhume, but it is nonetheless present to the modernist narrative: after all, the reading of romance is the only ground of female experience in the novels. Within the modernist tale, George Eliot would be a feminist only negatively, by virtue of her novels' depiction of the entrapment of women. It would be possible to read her account of the moral seriousness of self-sacrifice as a step on the way to our own discovery of self-assertion. Yet in doing so, we praise ourselves only for having achieved the capacity to desire like men.

Telling another kind of story, however, would mean activating that intertextual play of romance in order to explore the specificity of a female desire that might, perhaps, make up in postmodern imaginings what it lacks in modernist moral seriousness. What would it mean for women not to desire like men as the only possibility when confronted with failure or anonymity as alternatives? What would it mean for women's desires not to overcome the privations of purely private space only by entering the public sphere as if they were male desires? Can women enter the public sphere only by either becoming like men or enacting a separatist epic parallel to Deronda's Zionism? Within these questions lie many of the issues by which feminism today seems divided – yet each question is primarily a question directed at modernism. One might sum them up by asking whether feminism can be anything other than a modernist movement.

That it can, that in some sense it already is, is evident in the peculiar practice of reading romance that links Eliot's heroines despite the resolute philosophical modernism of her cultural project. The reading of romance occupies an uneasy space within her novels because it questions the female subjectivity of which it is, apparently, both the ground and the curse. If Eliot tries to liberate her heroines from romance, to make "real [realist] people" of them, that project consistently fails because they either vanish like Dorothea, Maggie, and Gwendolen or turn into surrogate men, like Romola. What I want to suggest is that the problem lies not with these women's failings, nor solely with the repressive external conditions of society, but with the notion of subjective identity in terms of which the project of liberation is framed. The surreptitious reading of romance binds these women into a community of desire. However, that desire remains unrepresentable in these novels, not because it is simply unreal or fantastical, but because it is not the simple property of a subject. I might rather say, it is curiously intertextual; it opens a space that is beyond the authority of the unified authorial subject, an interplay of signifying elements that do not reflect a pre-existing female experience, but out of which the possibility of female experience has to be constructed, as Mary Garth knows (but forgets). Romance is not merely the space of Rosamond Vincy, the conventional figuration of a female desire by means of which society controls women, since the "unreality" of that desire is only realized as matrimony. To put this another way, in conventional romance, society controls female desire by acknowledging it as a fantasy for which a woman must "really" sacrifice herself. The reading of romance opens another kind of space, an intertextual play in which no absolute self-sacrifice is possible because there is no absolute self.

But this is not George Eliot. In order to trace the destabilization of modernity's masculinism by the surreptitious reading of romance I will have to look elsewhere, at some explicitly "postmodern" romances. Yet it is George Eliot, and Walter Scott too, and I shouldn't delude ourselves into thinking that postmodern romance is the romance of the contemporary, is a new liberation from modernist superstitions. For Kathy Acker and Jacques Derrida, the postmodern romancers of my next chapter, are nothing if not readers: readers of romance, readers of modernism, subversive readers of the romance within modernism that overthrows the binary opposition of private to public space upon which the metanarrative of liberation is built.

5

A POSTSCRIPT WHICH
SHOULD HAVE BEEN
A PREFACE:
THEORY'S ROMANCE

"Everything seems finished when it begins."

So far this book has offered what we might call a "theory" of postmodern romance. It has found romance as a signature of the necessary and disturbing postmodernity of the history of the modern novel. Were it to stop here, then for all its playfulness, for all its anachronisms, this would remain in a strong sense a modernist work: offering reading subjects a liberating awareness of their own freedom from ignorance. The fragmentation and dispersion of historical knowledge, the upsetting of the epistemological assurance of realism, would have been noted only so as to be overcome at the level of theory. We would know for sure, thanks to theory, that we are uncertain; we would all agree about our theories of fragmentation.

In the paradox of these phrases, we find the essential modernism of the theoretical mastery of objects, however much our institution of literary studies may want to think of literary theory as something "postmodern." In this final chapter, I want to think about the intersection of postmodernism with the epistemological claims of theoretical knowledge. It will by now come as no surprise that I propose romance as the genre within which theory becomes postmodern; this has the advantage of forcing us to recognize that postmodernism is not so much a rejection of the modern as the recognition that we have always been, in a very troubling sense, in love with modernism. I propose to trace in the writings of Kathy Acker and Jacques Derrida an encounter with theory in the field of romance rather than "real knowledge," a brief and somewhat slippery encounter that will help us to understand what is at stake in recent recognitions of the importance of the term "seduction," as we move from a theory of seduction to an attempt to think theory as seduction.

I want to begin by claiming that postmodern theory is not a matter of defining or refining our metalanguage; such would indeed be a modernist project along the lines of the work of Gadamer or Habermas. This book will not have been a tool kit of conceptual abstractions that designates a place for everything and puts everything in its place. Rather than reflecting on texts in order to tell the truth about them, postmodern theory reflects on texts – and reflects upon our reflections upon texts, and so on and so on – *without forgetting* that our reflections are also texts, that they are caught up in an economy of textuality. I want to suggest, then, that it's only a certain kind of *textual* marker that indicates whether a text is a text (literature) or a text about a text (criticism) or a text about textuality (theory).

It is worth pointing out that this is *not* an argument which proposes that everything is just a text – that there is nothing but books. This would be simply yet another misunderstanding of Derrida's infamous sentence from *Of Grammatology*: "*There is nothing outside of the text* [there is no outside-text, *il n'y a pas de hors-texte*]."[1] Instead, what I am arguing here is that there is no escape, in language, from effects of textuality, even for texts that claim to be about textuality. Modernist theory does a lot of damage when it forgets this, and it tends to become either reductive or megalomanic. The text simply becomes an example of general laws, such as those of structure. Thus Genette or Propp can delineate the morphology of narrative form with great precision, but they do so in a way that is hard put to explain why we might need more than one example of any particular morphological unit or series, or even why we might want to read them in the first place.[2] On the other hand, theory may become domineering. As Foucault has shown us, knowledge is not neutral, rather it is always bound up with systems and effects of power. That is to say, the theoretical claim to totalizing knowledge is also a seizing of despotic power.

In this chapter, then, I will explore what it might mean to be a theoretician but not a modernist, a theoretician who is without a project for universal understanding or pure knowledge. To put this another way, the postmodern theorist will have been one who does not think that self-knowledge is freedom (as Kant and other modernists have claimed), and who doesn't believe that awareness of textuality is enough to escape the condition of textuality.

Coming to know: theory and pleasure

"Pure pleasure and pure reality are ideal limits, which is as much as to say fictions. The one is as destructive and mortal as the other."

Theory has one kind of textuality that upsets its claims to objectivity: an element of romance. Theory, as we all know but are afraid to admit, is sexy. Postmodernism is in part an admission of this fact, which I shall illustrate by focusing on two very disparate kinds of texts: Jacques Derrida's *The Post Card*, in which the acknowledged master of deconstruction finds his theory sexy and likes it, and the novels of Kathy Acker, in which the queen of postmodern S/M discovers that she likes her sex theoretical.

First, a brief word about Derrida. Derrida speaks of a friend presented with an "apparently rigorously theoretical text . . . written such that it gave him an erection whenever he read it."[3] Derrida links the demand of theoretical rigor, so often heard on the Left with the masculinist discourse of penile tumescence. The very rigidity that would lend theoretical discourse its systematic objectivity is identified with a far from neutral machismo. And the persistent pun on *se bander*, meaning to get a hard on, and the *double bande* or double bind, which deconstruction tends to isolate in any theoretical discourse, marks this as a no-win situation for theoretical rigidity.

Kathy Acker's *In Memoriam to Identity*, on the other hand, marks the inseparability of sexual desire from its theorization. The story of Airplane intermingles a discussion of sexuality between a female patient and a psychiatrist with a description of a live sex show. It is impossible to determine whether she is recounting the sex show as part of her therapy or whether a mock therapy session is part of the live sex show. After all, as Airplane muses, "perhaps *come* equals *know*."[4] Theoretical knowledge about sexual desire proves as erotic, if not more erotic, than the supposedly actual sexuality that is the object of knowledge. For Acker, sexual activity is pre-eminently fictional, in that pleasure is produced from the interplay of desire and fantasy, in a way that renders the fictions of the sex trade indistinguishable from those of the psychiatric theorist. This turns out to be inseparable from the concerns of feminism: it is a rape that causes Airplane to ask whether to come means to know, a phrase beneath which the question is posed of whether we can "know" whether "no" means no.

These postmodern texts fail to preserve a decent distance between theory and sexuality, confronting the theory of sexuality with the sexuality of theory. Modernist theory seeks to put an end to desire by offering instruction, the satisfaction of enlightenment: so that Marxism, for example, substitutes the determinate knowledge of social processes for the desire for social justice, a theory of historical materialism for utopian socialism. By contrast, Acker's *In Memoriam to Identity* asks us to remain suspicious of the role of enlightenment reason; as Acker puts it: "What the fuck is *reason* in this life, a life of disease and sex show?" (*IMI*, 133). Postmodernism, that is, reminds us that the one desire that knowledge cannot replace with a truth is the desire for knowledge itself: the seductions of theory.

Others have brought the question of seduction to our attention in relation to theory: most notably with regard to ideology.[5] Althusser's replacement of ideological falsification by the interpellation of an ideological subject is a step on this road, not least because in a sense what postmodernism refuses is the epistemological anonymity of the knowing subject. That particular situation of the subject, one which I would argue is modernist, is perhaps best typified by the work of Georg Lukács. Lukács identified Marx's notion of ideology as a system of lies, "false consciousness" that needed only to be dispelled by correct analysis of the forces of material production at work under the cloudy veils of priestcraft.[6] Thus, if we were to apply Lukács's methods to the tradition of the British novel, we could accuse Jane Austen of suggesting that wealth and privilege proceed from birth rather than from the exploitation of workers. Her argument that merit rather than birth should be rewarded can thus be dismissed as a classical piece of bourgeois ideology. Since her novels tend to imply that aristocratic and middle-class prosperity is deserved and earned rather than stolen, injustice is merely the product of biological degeneracy. This notion of ideology has its appeals; I've always been tempted by the rallying cry, "People on Wall Street don't make money, they steal it from the workers who really make it." However, this statement implies that the subject is capable of breaking finally from ideological illusion, rendering itself anonymous as it passes an objective judgment on the real state of affairs. Althusser's contribution was to point out that no conspiracy theory of priestly drug dealers, offering the opium of the people at street prices, orchestrated the function of ideology. Rather, ideology consisted in the "hailing" or "interpellation" of the subject as a free and autonomous individual when s/he was, in fact, the product of determining material constrictions. Althusser thus introduces a double reserve. On the one hand, there is no simple true state of affairs which may be revealed by theoretical analysis. On the other hand, individuals' relation to their world is not simply determined as true or false; rather these relationships become a process and a performance to be measured in terms of their effectivity.[7]

Unfortunately, Althusser gives up on both these insights. In the first place, he introduces the notion of the epistemological break, which replays the old modernist paradigm through which knowledge of the system is freedom from it.[8] On the second count, the determinate goal of political revolution (or at least the program of the French communist party in its latest manifesto) turns the analysis of effects back into a question of revealed truth, since effects are measured in terms of proximity to defined goals. So the subject is returned to objective anonymity, with its epistemological assurance, by means of an anthropomorphization of the party.

Cultural studies has drawn many of its hermeneutic instruments from the notion of a subject constituted by the receipt of ideologically loaded messages: Laura Mulvey's account of visual pleasure and narrative cinema is a powerful text in this tradition.[9] However, the limitation of such an approach is that, if it speaks of falsification, hegemony, or violence as somehow "bad things," it tends either to imply that a nonideological, natural subjectivity can be located, or to invoke a notion of "strategy" which still requires a teleological justification, an end. Either way, an attack on ideology *as such* is a problem, because it must imply a non-ideological origin or goal in opposition to which ideology can be justified. For the Marxist tradition this was no problem: we can understand the Althusserian paradigm shift as the refusal of any nonideological origin in favor of an ultimately nonideological goal of revolution, however long the lonely hour of the last instance might be in coming. Althusser's proclamation that there is no

145

history to ideology is always underscored by the proviso that there must be a space outside ideology, even though it would be as yet unthinkable except as critical science.

For theory to think, or think in, its postmodernity, it would have to dispense with the notion of ideology, *if* ideology is in any way linked to falsification. For all his rejection of the notion of ideology as "false consciousness," Althusser does have a teleological account of truth to oppose to ideology. In place of falsification, I want to think about seduction: which is to return ideology to its status as a kind of persuasion, as a *rhetorical* activity. The term seduction gets away from the truth/falsehood opposition in a way that has a double valency for our juxtaposition of Acker and Derrida. With regard to deconstruction, the rhetorical overtones of "seduction" allow us to recognize that the study of the problematic rhetorical status of textuality has a significant cultural and political import precisely in that it forces us to rethink culture and politics. With regard to feminism, the sexual overtones of "seduction" introduce differences of gender and sexuality (which are also, but not "ultimately," differences of power) to the supposed anonymity of cultural knowledge.

The addition of the term "seduction" to our understanding of the situation of the knowing subject confronts knowledge with a sense of its own processes that it cannot finally know. That is to say, seduction does not imply the simple statement of a truth: there is always some rhetorical, persuasive play. On the other hand, seduction is not simply falsification and lying, ideological deceit. Thus, we might talk about the experience of watching TV or going to the movies as not simply one of being deceived, but of one of being seduced; for the analysis and correction of the many deceptions that we encounter in visual culture has proved singularly ineffective in dissuading its subjects. To take a hypothetical example, people flock out of eastern Europe to a land with 197 different kinds of shampoo, even if scientific analysis can tell us that they are all the same, in effect, and no more or less beneficial than, say, the one East German state brand. That ideology critique can unravel the web of deceit which causes us to buy these products (the cultural construction of femininity by which they are advertised, for instance) has little purchase on us. All of this is to say: knowledge will not put an end to desire.[10]

In speaking, then, of the seductions of theory, one is not simply concerned to issue a warning against sirens so much as to recognize, as Derrida does, that:

> I do nothing that does not have some interest in seducing you [*à te séduire*], in setting you astray from yourself in order to set you on the way toward me, uniquely – nevertheless you do not know who you are nor to whom precisely I am addressing myself. But there is only you in the world. (*PC*, 69)

This peculiar love letter, this anonymous, impersonal, and yet absolutely singular seduction, rewrites the notion of ideological interpellation outside of any simple process of falsification. The play of desire that grounds any exchange cannot be regulated in terms of an opposition of truth to falsehood. Knowledge cannot put an end to desire, since knowledge will always be set astray by the wandering of the desire for the pleasure of certainty. A *caveat* here is that desire will not put an end to knowledge either: I am not advocating an indifferent and general jouissance – as it is sometimes claimed that Barthes or Baudrillard do – a grand orgasm that will liberate us from a constricting rationality. To do so would be simply a parodic inversion of the modernist theoretical separation of knowledge from desire. To put it bluntly, we are not just lost in the funhouse. After all, I wouldn't vote for any man whose view of rape was simply "relax and enjoy it."[11]

Thus we can see that a concern with seduction is not merely a sign of either playful Parisian chic or an undifferentiated welcoming of late-capitalist commodity culture. Rather, it allows us a certain suspicion of the pretension of theory to survey objects from an indifferent point of view. In discussing the dislocation of metalinguistic mastery, I want to turn to the encounter between theoretical discourse and the generic concerns of romance. A peculiar rewriting of the romance genre is the most obvious affinity between Acker's novels and Derrida's *The Post Card*. And this is not coincidental, since it relates both to Acker's attempt to imagine a feminine sexuality and Derrida's stated aim in *Spurs* of philosophizing from the position of a woman.[12] Romance is, after all, in some sense a "women's genre." In each of these cases, I shall focus on the way in which the seduction of theory by romance brings with it a dispersal of unified subjectivity. It will bear repeating that this dispersal is not merely a recent historical function – that the postmodern is not simply the contemporaneous. Rather, Derrida's concern with the economy of telecommunication in relation to the

147

question of writing, and Acker's concern with a sexual economy
in its relation to violence and pleasure, intersect with the romance
genre in order to evoke the problematic subjectivity of the female:
what both might call the "non-name of woman." My wider claim
will be that postmodernism can in this sense be of vital importance
to the feminist movement, in thinking around the modernist project
of liberation through identity politics.

In suggesting the limitations of identity politics, it is necessary
to proceed with a great deal of caution and respect for the efforts
of those who pioneered feminist activism and the academic study
of feminism under the banner of either "women's experience" or
"women's identity." It is all too easy to suggest that the sophistication of our notion of gender by psychoanalysis or the recognition
of its dispersal in the postmodern reduce those struggles merely to
past errors now superseded. If we have moved from the "female
imagination" to an exploration of "*écriture féminine*" it is because of
rather than despite the efforts of scholars such as Sandra Gilbert,
Susan Gubar, Kate Millet, Ellen Moers, and Elaine Showalter.[13]
However, it would lack respect for our "mothers" to remain merely
slavish. In the space opened up by a series of modernist inquiries
aimed at securing an identity and a proper place for women,
difference between women (race, sexuality, and age perhaps are
the most obvious examples here), the very differences that the
patriarchal economy of exchange sought to level, have become
apparent, most notably in the rise of a lesbian criticism which
introduces a play of desire and danger as well as an atmosphere
of nurture and support to relations among women. This example
should suffice to make it clear that a suspicion of the notions of
"proper place" and "identity" evident in attacks on feminism as a
modernist project is not simply a question of revising "theoretical"
insufficiencies but necessary if our solidarity is to avoid being just
as normalizing as the stereotyped "femininity" of "The Donna
Reed Show." Romance allows each of these postmodern writers to
imagine, invent, or experiment with the question of female gender
and sexuality (which are not always the same thing, as anyone who
has ever taught at a woman's college knows) in a way that may
liberate women from the modernist account of women's liberation,
which thinks freedom as a gain in identity and property.

Interpretation and gender

"A correspondence: this is still to say too much, or too little."

In light of these concerns, I want to begin by tracing more precisely the ways in which Derrida and Acker turn to romance as a privileged genre in postmodern prose writing. The effect of romance, with its insistence on the problems that gender creates for realist assumptions, is to pose a difficulty for the interpretative tradition of western thought. While Acker insists upon the interpretative problems raised by gender, what counts in Derrida's text is a relation between hermeneutics and the love letter. *The Post Card* returns Derrida's abiding concern with the system of communication and the supplementary relation of writing to that system (what we might summarize as the circuit of the letter) to the condition of epistolary novel. By far the largest part of this apparently theoretical book (*"Envois"*) is taken up by a series of missives that detail a romance, which is both larded with philosophical allusions and with explicitly clichéd sentimentality in a manner not unlike *The Name of the Rose*. In calling attention to this, I want to argue that something more than either an inflated sense of the significance of his own personal life or an unavowable desire on Derrida's part to make himself a laughing stock seems to be at stake here.

Perhaps the best place to begin to understand the significance of Derrida's project is with the word *"envois."* Derrida's title is a complex allusion to Heidegger's interpretation of Being as "sent," of the *es gibt*. Derrida's text thinks this sending in the context of a series of love letters written on post cards.[14] The hermeneutic thought of Being is placed within a historical and cultural context that emphasizes the conditions of a praxis. Explicitly the one interruption in the series of "sendings" is the refusal by Derrida of a collect call purporting to come from Martin or "martini" Heidegger.[15] What is important for this discussion of postmodern romance is the way in which Derrida's encounter with the system of sending (in the attempt to think Being) insistently raises an indeterminate question of gender. As Derrida puts it:

> I am always addressing myself to someone else (no, to someone else still!), but to whom? I absolve myself by remarking that this is due, before me, to the power, of no

149

matter what sign, the "first" trait, the "first" mark, to be remarked, precisely, to be repeated, and therefore divided, turned away from whatever singular destination, and this by virtue of its very possibility, its very address. It is its address that makes it into a post card that multiplies, to the point of a crowd, my addressee, female. And by the same token, of course, my addressee, male." (*PC*, 112)

Through ambiguous pronouns ("I," "you," and "me," not "he" or "she") mindful of Benveniste, Derrida refers the subject to an instance of discourse whose gender is always in question, because it cannot be determined outside that pragmatic instance. The addressee is multiple, previously marked and even re-marked. We could say, then, that Being is sent; the world and language are inextricably given. But that givenness cannot be dissociated from the question of gender, a question that will not go away, that always remains to be answered.

It is with regard to this question of gender that Derrida's (and Acker's) postmodern romance takes its greatest distance from hermeneutics. Derrida's own *envois* show the limitations of Gadamer's modernist critique of modernity, and thus the limitations of hermeneutics for feminism. To understand this point more clearly, I want to look at the way in which Gadamer takes up romance. At the end of his essay, "The Universality of the Problem," Gadamer makes a few remarks about the relationship between the modern industrial world and language in such a way as to call attention to romance. He concludes this discussion with the following narrative:

When we hear modern lovers talking to each other, we often wonder if they are communicating with words or with advertising labels and technical terms from the sign language of the modern industrial world. It is inevitable that the leveled life-forms of the industrial age also affect language, and in fact the impoverishment of the vocabulary of language is making enormous progress, thus bringing about an approximation of language to a technical sign-system. Leveling tendencies of this kind are irresistible. Yet in spite of them the simultaneous building up of our own world in language still persists whenever we want to say something to each other. The result is the actual relationship of men to each other. Each one is at first a kind of linguistic circle, and these linguistic circles come into contact with each other, merging more and more. Language occurs once again, in vocabulary and grammar as always, and never without the inner infinity of the dialogue that is in progress between every speaker and his partner. That is the fundamental dimension of hermeneutics.[16]

At first glance, Gadamer's "parable" of the modern lovers seems only like a restatement of Heidegger's position that technology is a menace and modernity a threat to human existence. I would not want to deny this Heideggerian echo. However, what is significant for us about Gadamer's remarks is that he has to take up the case of *modern lovers* in order to make his point. In so many words, Gadamer asks us to consider romance in the name of hermeneutics.

This romance is important to Gadamer because it illustrates how the "industrial age" (modernity) reduces or impoverishes language by turning it into a mere "technical sign-system" – so many advertising labels and technical terms. Modern lovers speak in bits and give each other love-bytes, know things go better with Coke, and experience Absolut Joy. This is not genuine speaking, claims Gadamer. However, in spite of the dilemma of modern romance, there still remains the actual relationship of men to each other where once again our horizon fuses into a single linguistic circle of pure historical understanding.

That romance might concern questions of gender, that language itself might found or be founded upon gender, does not occur to or does not concern Gadamer. Only one gender or sex here: men. We write: meneutics. Allowing that when Gadamer says "men" he means "human beings" of both genders, the single reference to "men" draws our attention to the real problem in *his* romance: the inability of hermeneutics to acknowledge gender as a category of or within existence. Modern lovers, with all their linguistic problems, are not explicitly gendered lovers, and good hermeneutes, engaged in genuine speaking, are always implicitly men.

At no time does Gadamer acknowledge that genuine speaking might actually have prearranged signals of its own – signals which might include, among others, those which indicate gender difference. In some miraculous way, at the snap of the hermeneutical fingers, we are transported to a linguistic horizon that has done away with gender differences, has never even considered it. What, we may wonder, has become of gender? Has it been relegated to the same rubbish heap as the jargon of advertising labels and technical terms? Simply put, the way in which "philosophical hermeneutics" theorizes language makes it impossible to speak of gender differences. Just as Greek roadsides were littered with phallic tributes to the god Hermes, hermeneutics contains within it the litter of a phallocentric tradition that refuses point-blank to acknowledge the significance of gender differentiation.[17]

If Gadamer develops Heidegger's work so as to create a noticeable silence, Derrida develops it so as to open up the possibility for questioning the grounds and terms of gender. If for postmodern theory gender remains uncertain, that is not to say that gender remains unthought as it does in Gadamer's hermeneutics. If we cannot answer the question of gender, in postmodern romance we can still pose the question that is gender, even if no communicative horizon can fuse the insistent eruption of gender difference. As Derrida argues when he follows the word "post":

> Of course, if I am following the word *post*, as you [*tu*] say, if I am reciting it to myself and sucking it all the time, if I always have it in my mouth, to the point of fusing and confusing myself with it, it is that it is hermaphroditic or androgynous, *mannweibliche*, the neuter or third or first sex (initially taken up by Freud from the mouth of Aristophanes after Plato, he dares to say, had "let him develop it.") *La poste, le poste*, the two love each other [*s'aiment*] and send back to themselves the other (what a couple!), this is the law of the genre/gender [*genre*] . . . . And it is the *postal*, the Postal Principle as differantial relay, that regularly prevents, delays, endispatches the depositing of the thesis, forbidding rest and ceaselessly causing to run, deposing or deporting the movement of speculation. (*PC*, 54)

The Postal Principle is, in principle, the staging of an erotic romance between *la poste* and *le poste* – that which is sent and the sending station.[18] This romance, however, is not a determinable, heterosexual affair, as the division of gendered nouns might suggest. Gender is not given (or sent) to Being in any simple sense. Rather, gender difference is, from the moment of its confused origin, divided from itself like Plato's hermaphrodite. The differential relay of the sending and receiving of gender, the confusion of sender and receiver, endlessly defers the end of both speculation and seduction. An endless romance of/in the post, as it were.

152

Romance introduces gender, which is never given in advance, to the givenness of Being. And Derrida gives the object of interpretation on a postcard, reminding us that the given is necessarily, even if only minimally, inscribed within a postal system so that the hermeneutic circle is exposed to the uncertain circuit of sending and delivery, a circuit that will not form a stable horizon. Thus, Derrida performs multiple interpretations of the "one" postcard of Plato and Socrates, upon which his missives are inscribed. In this postmodern romance, depicted on a postcard found in the Bodleian library shop and printed in *The Post Card*, Socrates comes before Plato, writing at his desk while Plato looks over his shoulder. But for Derrida, Socrates comes before Plato in another sense, for Derrida also sees the story of a rather explicit romance between the two philosophers:

> For the moment, myself, I tell you that I see *Plato* getting an erection in *Socrates'* back and see the insane hubris of his prick, an interminable, disproportionate erection traversing Paris's head like a single idea and then the copyist's chair, before slowly sliding, still warm, under *Socrates'* right leg, in harmony or symphony with the movement of this phallus sheaf, the points, plumes, pens, fingers, nails and *grattoirs*, the very pencil boxes which address themselves in the same direction. (*PC*, 18)

An irreverent romance, carried out in the scene of writing, upsets the tradition of philosophical influence. No postscript will insure that Plato comes before Socrates. Postmodern romance fails to send a message that would assure any one relationship – between Socrates and Plato, between sender and receiver. Plato and Socrates could even be "two robed transvestites" carrying "the name of the other above his head" (*PC*, 121). The figure underneath the word "Socrates" could be Plato, while the figure beneath "Plato" could be Socrates. To put it grammatically, S is P. The identities of the figures are as uncertain as their genders in the endless seduction of the interpretation of their philosophical relationship of endless romance.

From sexy theory (the romance of Plato and Socrates) to theoretical sex: Acker's work combines allusions to popular romance and philosophical discourse. For instance, at the beginning of *My Death, My Life by Pier Paolo Pasolini*, we learn of Sally Gernhart's romance: "Sally had her first boyfriend."[19] Yet if this narrative detail, like the boyfriend's nickname "Gype," would not be out of place in popular romance, we may find ourselves surprised to learn in the following paragraph that Gype's full name is Jack Lewis Habermas. Hermeneutics meets *First Love*.

Yet what is this reference doing here? What might Jürgen Habermas (staunch supporter of the incomplete project of modernity) have to do with Jack Habermas ("ex or H-addict"; consistently insubordinate, member of an LA gang called "The Skulls")? And do we really need to care if "the whole problem revolves around who Sally Gernhart really is" (*MDML*, 180)? Acker lets us dangle – a hermeneutic activity as incomplete as modernity itself.

If interpretation does not come full circle, that the emphasis is on the female character and not on the philosophical allusion seems significant. Whereas Acker's incomplete interpretative problem implicitly raises the question of gender relations and focuses our attention on the female character, Habermas's own incomplete project – modernity – only includes women as they figure as translators of his prose.[20] Seen in this way the situation is rather simple: Acker raises the question of gender for postmodernism; Habermas, like his fellow hermeneute Gadamer, doesn't find gender even a philosophical question.

Acker's engagement with romance, however, extends even further than this single passage from *My Death, My Life* can reveal. In *Don Quixote*, Acker's plagiarizing of Borges's idea of the plagiarizing of Cervantes ("Pierre Menard") twists Cervantes' own parody of courtly romance overtaken by modernity. Acker's romance is not Don Quixote's: her Don is a woman, her Sancho Panza a dog of indeterminate and multiple sexual identity. Here repressed romance returns in the guise of women's supermarket fiction and the uncomfortable slippage of gender identity in order to haunt modernist assumptions of authorial identity and propriety. As the dog narrates to Don Quixote:

> "I want you." I drew her(him) out of her(his) fantasy. "I don't want just another affair, fantasy. All that romance, cause the mind always changes its thoughts, is peripheral. I want something beyond. I want you."
>
> She(He) nodded her(his) head, slightly.
>
> "But you're much younger than me. You probably don't want something like this: To settle down."
>
> She(He) said as usual that she(he) wasn't worth anything.[21]

Acker makes clear from the beginning of this passage that "genders were complex those days," to borrow her phrase from *Empire of the Senseless*.[22] And if one were to risk a plot summary of this section of *Don Quixote* it would perhaps read: He/She was the man/woman of his/her dreams.

Yet such disturbing gender slippage occurs only in the context of the persistence of romance clichés, which is also the work of seduction or drawing out (Lat. *seducere*), even as the drawing of him/her *out* of fantasy. Reality would be the product of a seduction away from fantasy, always already invested by desire. This multiply gendered dog/human recounts a scene that could be a modified passage from a Barbara Cartland novel, to use Umberto Eco's nemesis as an example. She/he utters the clichéd phrases of romantic encounters – "I want you," "I don't want just another affair" – and is concerned about whether his/her potential partner wants "to settle down."

Similarly, after a particularly graphic description of four women (or dogs) having sex with multiple dildos and discussing the relative merits of anal and vaginal penetration, we are told that Don Quixote "felt sad because no man loved her" (*DQ*, 178). The structure of allusion has become indeterminate, as with Eco's intertwining of Barbara Cartland and the Song of Songs. Acker's texts differ, however, in that they contain an added effect of destabilization: the dispersal of any possibility of psychological realism. Private emotion proves to be the product of a citation of uncertain origin. As Don Quixote puts it to St Simeon early in the novel, "Of course I'm not interested in personal identity" (*DQ*, 29). Don Quixote's more pressing question is: "what is it to be female?" (*DQ*, 29). Acker's point, whose importance cannot be overestimated, is that this question is *not* also a question of identity. Explorations of identity through the use of psychological realism prove insufficient to address what it is to be female.

It is at this moment, then, that we can begin to understand the important role that romance plays in Acker's work. If Cervantes' Don believes foolishly in ideas of justice and chivalry long since discarded by a world of hypocrites, Acker evokes romance as a means of calling attention to the difficulty of making sense of feminine experience when "being born into and part of a male world, she had no speech of her own. All she could do was read male texts which weren't hers" (*DQ*, 40). Romance, that is, evokes a peculiar relation to the possibility of psychological, narrative realism. Rather than simply being opposed to realism (which is, after all, still fiction), romance writes a reality that is *invested by desire* – desire that cannot itself be given "realist" expression, that remains alien to realism, since it is not simply the property of a speaking subject. As Acker says of realism: "This is *realism*: the unification of my perceiving and what I perceive or a making of a mirror relation between my world and the world of the painting."[23] For Acker, realism is ready-made reality: representation given to the viewer as unproblematically real. And she knows enough of Duchamp's "ready-mades" to problematize this immediacy. The mirror relation, which characterizes realism, only gives rise to an instantaneous, uncritical, reception, or as Acker puts it, "I see what I see immediately; I don't rethink it."[24]

That we are so unable to rethink the perception of representation is a result of education, an education that teaches children not to think. Such is one of the lessons that the dog dreams:

> In my dream, my teacher said to me: "All the accepted forms of education in this country, rather than teaching the child to know who she is or to know, dictate to the child who she is. Thus obfuscate any act of knowledge. Since these educators train the mind rather than the body, we can start with the physical body, the place of shitting, eating, etc., to break through our opinions or false education." (*DQ*, 165–6)

Yet lest we are led to believe that we can come to understand the truth of the falsity of education (this would be Althusser's lesson about ideology), Acker turns the dog's dream into a combination of repetitious realism and raunchy romance, which undercuts any such claim. The realistic dialogue of the Socratic method takes on the repetitious quality of a scratched record:

> Delbène said: "We must do what we consider crimes in order to break down our destructive education."
> "But *crimes* are evil because they're human acts by which humans hurt other humans."
> "But *crimes* are evil because they're human acts by which humans hurt other humans."
> "But *crimes* are evil because they're human acts by which humans hurt other humans."
> "A good reply," answered my teacher, "according to the world."

156

"A good reply," answered my teacher, "according to the world."

"A good reply," answered my teacher, "according to the world."

"Wrong," my teacher thundered, "for any answer that seems to be the correct answer denies this world whose nature is chance and relativity. There is no correct answer."

"Wrong," my teacher thundered, "for any answer that seems to be the correct answer denies this world whose nature is chance and relativity. There is no correct answer."

"Wrong," my teacher thundered, "for any answer that seems to be the correct answer denies this world whose nature is chance and relativity. There is no correct answer."

"Wrong," my teacher thundered, "for any answer that seems to be the correct answer denies this world whose nature is chance and relativity. There is no correct answer."
(*DQ*, 166–7)

The point of this scene is probably best summed up by the dog's observation that "you still don't know anything" (*DQ*, 167). Certainty is never certain in Acker's dream of pedagogy.

Nor can we be certain of the place or role of romance, for within the scene of education, seduction moves past the point of "common decency." As the dog explains:

Since the body is the first ground of knowledge, my teacher made me take off my clothes. A mouth touched and licked my ass. A finger stuck into my asshole. A dildo thrust into my asshole and a dildo thrust into my cunt. Both dildoes squirted liquid into me which I saw was white. I was so over-the-top excited, I came. The main thing for me was my body's uncontrolled reactions. (*DQ*, 168)

The teacher tells the dog in the dog's dream that the physical body is the site of resistance to established education, opening an exploration of possibilities ("who she might be") against the hegemonic discourse of identity ("what she is"). The play of violence and eroticism in this passage, which as we have seen leads to the clichés of romance, seems immediately threatening and antifeminist in its implications. Given Acker's insistence on rape as a topos for female sexuality, one is disinclined to put this down to an effect of ignorance, accident, or ideological subjugation.

Although I will return later to a consideration of the juxtaposition of violence and eroticism in Acker's work, for now it is sufficient to understand that Acker refuses realism's conventions of decorum on the grounds that the "good writing" taught in schools is "a way of keeping you from writing what you want to" (*MDML*, 246).

"I always get my sexual genders confused."

I would like to continue exploring the implications of Acker's statement and argue that, within both Acker's and Derrida's work, romance – which would be another name for "bad writing" – stands to realism as postmodernism to modernism, as a counter-discourse on history and the real. Romance, that is to say, is not simply the negation of realism, postmodernism the negation of modernism; rather romance and postmodernism are not present in simple or stable states that might allow their apprehension by a knowing subject. Therefore, a feature of romance is that it is never "pure fantasy." Always impure, romance refuses the modern rationality that constructs reality by means of the exclusion of desire by a knowing subject. Thus, my use of the term romance as linked to the postmodern differs from "Romanticism" in that this irrepressible desire cannot even be contained as the property of an individual subjective will, as in Nietzsche's assault on rationalism. That is to say, in its displacement of even an irrational subjective mastery, postmodern romance will not have been Romantic.

Indeed, the most obvious formal feature shared by Acker's and Derrida's romances is a persistent disruption of the identity of the speaking subject. Acker's novel *In Memoriam to Identity* foregrounds a process common to her entire oeuvre, by which "each person has the possibilities of being simultaneously several beings, having several lives" (*IMI*, 92). Multiple voices speak schizophrenically from a single pronominal position, a single voice appears identified with a multiplicity of apparently different "characters," in a heteroglossia that lacks even the coherence of the dialogic.

Derrida's interest in the multiple and contradictory nature of linguistic identity appears in the "polylogue" for "n+1 female voices" entitled "Restitutions" in *The Truth in Painting*, where the nonfinite series of n+1 refuses even the wholeness of an *infinite* dispersion.[25] "Envois" in *The Post Card* explores this dissemination of subjective identity, not simply by formal insistence on the status of pronominal markers of identity as precisely that, as shifters by which gender, number, and position can be shuffled and multiplied:

Although since the gender and number remain inaccessible for me I can always play on the plural. . . . You understand that whoever writes must indeed ask himself what it is asked of him to write, and then he writes under the dictation of some addressee, this is trivial. But "some addressee," I always leave the gender or number indeterminate, must indeed be the object of a choice of object, and chosen and seduced. (*PC*, 143)[26]

Here Derrida is not simply mirroring a "postmodern condition" in which identities have become divided and multiple. Derrida's postmodernity is not, as Fredric Jameson would claim, an accidental schizophrenia resulting from the effects of late-capitalist commodity relations, a historical moment of crisis. Identity is not something that we have recently lost, or might recover. Rather, Derrida is concerned to insist upon the dispersion of subjectivity as a structural necessity that both constitutes and confounds communication:

Who *will prove* that the sender is the same man, or woman? And the male or female addressee? Or that they are *not* identical? To themselves, male or female, first of all? That they do or do not form a couple? Or several couples? Or a crowd? Where would the principle of identification be? In the name? No, and then whoever wants to make a proof becomes a participant in our corpus. They would not prevent us from loving each other. And they would love us as one loves counterfeiters, impostors, *contrefacteurs* (this word has been looking for me for years). (*PC*, 234)

The postal system (Derrida's name for the circuit of communication) insists upon a structural deferral or *post*ponement inhabiting the very heart of the dream of telecommunications. The message that might fix the identity of the sender or addressee of a previous message is precisely that, another message, which the sender and addressee would require in turn to be established, and so on in nonfinite series. And the *facteur* or postman goes on looking for the right person to whom to deliver a message. The *facteur* can only do so by entering the circuit of the letter, or post card (to give the material support of written communication its most etiolated form), by becoming him/herself a *contrefacteur*. In entering the circuit of the letter, the letter-carrier becomes an exchanger of letters, a *contre facteur*. But this is no gain in identity, since a *contrefacteur* is precisely a forger or counterfeiter. The postman keeps on looking, for years, postponed in the very attempt to overcome delay.

Far from being the accidental product of material circumstances, delay – and the hole that it opens in the identity both of and between sender and receiver – is structural to the postal system, even for its smallest imaginable unit, the postcard marked only by a date and a signature. The postcard hides nothing, enfolds nothing. The medium is the message, as it were. Here Derrida's interest is in showing how, even at the apex of telecommunicational efficiency, a deconstructive logic of differance splits and defers the possibility of identity. As Derrida puts it, "letters are always post cards: neither legible nor illegible, open and radically unintelligible" (*PC*, 79).

This disruption of identity is also carried out in relation to the status of the author/signature. In the writings of both Derrida and Acker, it is the very insistence of apparently direct interpolated autobiographical material that most marks the inability of the writer to "be herself" (or himself or both, as the case may be), to achieve an identity. For instance, Acker writes of the travels and travails of "Kathy" and even puts her photograph on the Grove editions of her novels. And in *The Post Card* Derrida drops a series of proper names (Hillis, Cynthia, Jonathan, and Paul, to name only a few) that invite the reader to read Derrida's text as if it were some kind of autobiographical *roman à clef*. But this is not all. To add to the referential confusion, Derrida signs and re-signs in his text, continually punning on his name. Gregory Ulmer describes this condition well when he points out that "what Derrida wishes to expose is the truth effect of the signature, of the 'I' who appears to speak, by displacing the opposition between pre-text and text, life and art."[27] The effect is one of dispersion, as the proper name falls into the very linguistic dissemination to which the common noun is prey. The name, which should mark an autonomous integrity for which language is a tool, instead becomes itself part of an anonymous work of language quite independent of any subjective presence.

Derrida summarizes and enacts this problematic – one which he analyzed earlier in "Signature Event Context" and *Signéponge* – when he remarks that: "The name is made to do without the life of the bearer, and is therefore always somewhat the name of someone dead" (*PC*, 39). This disruption of the modernist logic of identity opens a space within knowledge analogous to the space that romance opens within the real. That space cannot itself be named, unless with the non-name of woman. As Acker puts it:

> Men told me they remembered whom they fucked: they brought out memories for display, notches cut into a belt, to name identity. Being female I didn't and don't have to prove that I don't exist. (*IMI*, 203–4)

In Acker's novel the male sexual trophy parallels the effect of the signature in Derrida's analysis – the "proof" of identity that marks its capacity to exist in the absence of the sender. Here, I would want to go so far as to say that as a postmodernist Acker asks what happens when desire is no longer the property of an individual subject. The importance of her work for feminism is that in some sense this has always been the situation of women, unable to call a desire their own, unable to have property in their own desire. Oversimplifying, I could say that Acker finds in the non-name of woman the kind of deconstructive trace effect that Derrida has tended to call "writing."

Plagiarism and author-ity

"Everything has been said. These lines are not my writing."

This connection is perhaps most clearly seen in Acker's own interest in writing as the illicit reproductive work of a signifier always in supplementary excess over the message it should convey. For Acker, the strong example of the trace-effect of writing is plagiarism, a concern which I raised earlier in the context of Acker's interrogation of gender. What was not evident in this earlier discussion, however, is the extent to which Acker's work persistently thematizes plagiarism in order to call attention to a postmodern understanding of "reproductive rights" (certainly a feminist concern). The disruption of the authoritative original in an insistence upon its preoriginary marking by reproduction is not simply a theoretical account of the sign, nor a critique of creativity (although it is both those things).[28] In the very widest sense, a sense that stretches from questions of philosophical influence to surrogate motherhood, it is an assault upon western culture's privileging of abstraction, of the signifier over the signified, an assault on the legal fiction of paternity.

The obvious cases are two of Acker's titles: *Don Quixote* and *Great Expectations*.[29] Such overt plagiarism is enough to give any book-store clerk a moment's pause. But Acker "borrows" more than titles. To name only a few examples: characters from Shakespeare's *Macbeth* and *Romeo and Juliet* and a section of Dickens's *Great Expectations* appear in *My Death, My Life*; *Florida* is an unacknowledged rewrite of the film *Key Largo*;[30] and Acker even repeats her own material in *Empire of the Senseless*. The significance of these multiple acts of plagiarism is best summed up in a letter Emily writes to Charlotte Brontë in Brussels in *My Death, My Life*: "I can talk by plagiarizing other people's words that is real language, and then . . . then I make something" (*MDML*, 289–90). To say something different is not necessarily to say something original: it may be to plagiarize. Thus, for Acker, intertextual relations work to split apart the fusion of originality and identity that grounds the modernist notion of creative authority, or authorial subjectivity.[31]

Plagiarism is also, of course, a persistent concern of Derrida in *The Post Card*; as he puts it, "I am citing, but as always rearranging a little. Guess the number of false citations in my publications" (*PC*, 89). Every "original" statement is doubly unauthentic, an inaccurate quotation in words that are only recognizable if they have already been used by others. And the reader, in the face of Derrida's taunts, can't with certainty sort out "authentic" from "false" citations – a condition reminiscent of the role anachronism plays in Eco's and Scott's romance. To put this another way, postmodern romance contains purloined letters – letters stolen and forged from the past – which may or may not reach their historical destinations. Redirected, these letters may end up as the anachronisms and false citations of postmodern romance.

What is important about the stolen and counterfeited letters of postmodern romance is that they provide for a freedom from tradition, including the restrictions of realism which so concerned Acker. Tradition could be said to exert its influence in much the same way as that of the stamp: in order to send a message via the post, the sender must purchase a stamp, must pay her/his debt to the post. Likewise, "a master thinker emits postage stamps or post cards, he constructs highways with tolls" (*PC*, 200). The bottom line is that one cannot send a message without attempting to pay one's debt to the past, and thus, "the anxiety of influence is born" in the form of the postage stamp. Yet the possibility of purloined letters ensures that "contrary to appearances, no one perceives or receives a thing" (*PC*, 200); the message is delayed, misdirected, lost.

In this postal context, postmodern romance is a way to loosen the tyranny of tradition, which exerts its control in the form of preoccupations as mundane as chronological and alphabetical order – in texts as common or uncommon as phone books, street directories, and histories of philosophy. By contrast, the order of romance is not self-evident. For instance, in "Envois" Derrida arranges his letters chronologically, and yet there is the single "misplaced" letter on the back cover. Dated November 17, 1979, it begins by telling the reader that:

> You [*Tu*] were reading a somewhat retro loveletter, the last in history. But you have not yet received it. Yes, its lack or excess of address prepares it to fall into all hands: a post card, an open letter in which the secret appears, but indecipherably. You can take it or pass it off, for example, as a message from Socrates to Freud.

Does this letter come "first," in that the reader will read the back cover of the book first? Or do we hold dear the tyranny of chronological order and know to place it as the last in the series of letters – the concluding love letter of "Envois," the end of romance? As the contents of the letter suggest, however, no simple relationship between sender/receiver, origin/destination exists here. The last love letter in history has not yet been received; it is, one assumes, still purloined in the post. That romance does not provide an order for love letters, that it does not attempt to assure the receipt of its messages, would thus be the point that Derrida stresses when he provides us with his multiple versions of the romance between Plato and Socrates.

All of this is to say that postmodern romance should not be considered a genre that dictates aesthetic or historical order. In a sense, postmodern romance is a genreless genre because it is, impossibly, all genres. As Derrida puts it, "I will have . . . loved according to every genre/gender [*genre*]" (*PC*, 109). The future anterior of romance's love story invades all genres/genders and is limited by none.

That postmodern romance is not preceded by rules is a point that Acker's fiction stresses even more directly. The unanswerable question that she poses is: What might romance be? In *Great Expectations* this question takes shape in the second section, entitled "The

Beginnings of Romance," where the origin of romance is anything but clear. If the opening of the section could resemble a sordid version of Freud's family romance, in which the mother admits to not wanting her daughter and the father dies before ever appearing on the narrative scene, the remainder of the section strays further from any conventional understanding of romance. The narrator, for instance, understands her life in such a way that has nothing to do either with romance or with beginnings: "I realize that all my life is endings," she claims (*GE*, 64); a subsequent subsection purports to cover "Seattle Art Society," while going on to discuss "historical examples"; and the concluding pages relate in dialogue format the complex relationship between Sarah, Clifford, She, and Portrait in Red. In each of these instances, no pattern emerges that would underscore the structure of postmodern romance. Propp or Genette would have a difficult time here.

This is not to suggest, however, that there is necessarily anything purely original about postmodern romance either. That the preceding section of *Great Expectations* is called "Plagiarism" is significant. In some sense, we've heard it all before; "everything has been said," as Acker puts it (*GE*, 123). The connection between plagiarism and the formlessness of postmodern romance becomes even clearer in *My Death, My Life*. Here Acker begins the section entitled "Narrative Breakdown for Carla Harriman" (*MDML*, 234) with what are effectively unacknowledged plot summaries of scenes from Pasolini's *The Decameron*. And after this gesture of plagiarism, Acker later adds a section that links the question of form with romance:

> Accent her. Hand armors on wonder. Orphan forces war or instance of ovary. The manor of stove.
> An instance of romance. Or form. Or form. Or form. Or form. Or form. Or form. Or form. Or form. Or form. Or form. Or form.
> An land. An land. An land. An land. An land. An land. An land. An land. An land. An land. An land. An land. An land. An
> And scape escape romance. And scape escape romance. And scape escape romance. And scape escape romance. And scape escape romance. And. . . .
> 2. *Language breakdown.* (*MDML*, 244)

This then would be the message to Carla Harriman, that "Ack" sent her ("Accent her"), with a signature that absents the sender even as it emphasizes her. Without a present signatory, this "orphan" sounds only like "or form." Just as "instance of ovary" is reshuffled as "manor of stove," the "or" reverses to the "ro" of "romance." The "land" of "An land" seems unable to join up with the "scape" of "And scape" to provide a recognizable landscape; instead we have merely the near homonym "and scape." In a strong sense, of course, this doesn't mean anything. Rather, the letters of romance and landscape are shuffled and hypogrammatized. The message plagiarizes itself, consumes itself, from its apparent "origin" in the words "One. One and one . . ." repeated thirty-six times before it reaches "one and two." Language is generated almost mathematically in this missive, but it occurs as autocannibalism:

> Language is more important than meaning. Don't make anything out of broken-up syntax cause you're looking to make meaning where nonsense will. Of course nonsense isn't only nonsense. I'll say again that writing isn't just writing, it's a meeting of writing and living the way existence is the meeting of mental and material or language of idea and sign. It is how we live. We must take how we live. (*MDML*, 246)

Like Derrida, Acker seems to be calling for a certain exhaustion of language, not a theory of romance in the modernist sense.[32] The broken syntax that brings together romance, form, and escape cannot be made to have "meaning" in the sense that these words or signs do not correspond to previously understood significations.

Derrida confronts the problem of language by way of the postcard. If for Heidegger language is the house of Being, for Derrida language is a house of postcards. As Derrida puts it: "Our entire library, our entire encyclopedia, our words, our pictures, our figures, our secrets, all an immense house of post cards" (*PC*, 53). The fragility of a house of cards exposed to the postal system. In this way Derrida dissociates language from a Heideggerian notion of Being, stressing that "Envois" will not have been a modernist theory of language, just as it will not have been a metahistory of the postal system, not outside the system but a postcard among postcards:

> By no longer treating the posts as a metaphor of the *envoi* of Being, one can account for what essentially and decisively

occurs, everywhere, and including language, thought, science, and everything that conditions them, when the postal structure shifts, *Satz* if you will, and posits or posts itself otherwise. This is why this history of the posts, which I would like to write and to dedicate to you, cannot be a history of the posts: primarily because it concerns the very possibility of history, of all the concepts, too, of history, of tradition, of the transmission or interruptions, goings astray, etc. And then because such a "history of the posts" would be but a minuscule *envoi* in a network that it allegedly would analyze (there is no metapostal), only a card lost in a bag, that a strike, or even a sorting accident, can always delay indefinitely, lose without return. This is why I will not write it, but I dedicate to you what remains of this impossible project. (*PC*, 66–7)

Herein lies the theoretical modesty of deconstruction, something which our critical academy has been inclined to miss. This theory will not claim to stand outside, to master, the textuality of which it speaks. As I remarked at the beginning of this chapter, this is theory in its postmodernity, whose "post" marks a dependency upon the very modernity of the system that it deconstructs. This "post" does not surpass; it "remains." "Remains," not "persists" or "endures," with all the undertones of the incomplete, the "left-over", the less-than-heroic. An original wound in modernism, a scar that remains, from the "battle" declared in *Of Grammatology* between writing and logocentrism.[33]

Sex and violence

"This text is violence."

With the Derridean language of wound and scar, we confront perhaps the most shocking, not to say flagrant, aspect of both Derrida's and Acker's writing. An insistence on violence in Derrida's thought, on the force of "pathbreaking" analysis, is perhaps the aspect that most strongly militates against deconstruction's being reduced to a moment of formal experimentation in the history of philosophy. What then, can become of our modernist dream of perpetual peace? Likewise, Acker's refusal to disentangle pleasure from sexual violence not only courts the charge of perversion, it strikes against the political tenets of a feminism that has sought to oppose sexual violence as a crime perpetrated by men against women. Will we no longer be able to oppose rape, to insist that "no means no"?

To which Acker's answer would be "yes," if we think that "no means no" rests upon an assumption that sex is accidental, that the female body, at rest, is devoid of sexual desire. This is the ground on which feminism has been able to form strategic if improbable alliances with Christian churches, for whom "only yes means yes" might prove more problematic. Acker's account of sexuality insists that sex is not something inherently male, which just "happens" to women. To focus our attention to rape on the slogan "no means no" locates sexual violence as a form of literal communication between two self-conscious subjects: altogether too rational a process.

Derrida's long-standing insistence on the violence of the letter, upon the way in which writing necessarily ruptures the self-presence of any being that it might be held to represent, recurs in "Envois":

> Understand me, when I write, right here, on these innumerable post cards, I annihilate not only what I am saying but also the unique addressee that I constitute, and therefore every possible addressee, and every destination. (*PC*, 33)

Since "a letter can always not arrive at its destination" and therefore "it never arrives" (*PC*, 33), the letter murders its potential addressees, functions in their absence even as it indicates the possibility of their presence. "The Violence of the Letter" in *Of Grammatology* has already insisted on the fact that writing does not happen as an accidental violation of the proper being of meaning. Instead, the violence that writing does to the possibility of pure language grounds that very possibility.

In a sense, this recognition, as it marks the origin and telos of an account of Being as self-presence so as to render the modernist project of the revelation of that Being impossible, holds fewer terrors for us now perhaps than Acker's interest in sado-masochism. We have less trouble being suspicious of the likely success of UN initiatives, however little we may welcome war, than we do in relinquishing a univocal opposition to the sexual violence that haunts our streets. Put another way, liberals can tolerate sado-masochism provided it is the activity of knowing subjects (consenting adults) taking place within the sphere of private property and domestic propriety – which is to say, as long as it does no violence to notions of identity and proper meaning.

The subheadings for the "Nominalism" section of *My Death, My Life* could be called Acker's trinity in her guerrilla struggle against identity and property: Sex, Language, Violence. The conversations in this section, whether carried forward by a "Situationalist With Italian Accent" or a member of the Lesbian Guerrilla Army interested in castration, consistently refuse to disentangle these three terms. Sexuality, language, and violence are as inseparable as life and death for Acker. As she puts it in *In Memoriam to Identity*: "since life and death are inextricably mixed, you can't condemn abortion. Maybe that's why I had so many abortions" (*IMI*, 250). Acker takes the argument that all men are potential rapists seriously enough to name the male character in Airplane's story as simply "The Rapist." No originary incident marks a violence that might supervene for Airplane. Indeed, the medical examination that will prove rape proves only to be another rape:

> The big man, the feeb, and a skinny guy who looked slimy as a ghost walked into my room. The big man ripped the bedsheet I had wrapped around part of my body off. The men looked at me.
>
> I wanted my body to be mine. Deep in me I didn't want it to be theirs. Something in me was revolting. Something in me was screaming, "No. No. No."
>
> So just as I was learning about my own body, I learned this kind of revolt. (*IMI*, 107)

Knowledge of the body is a gendered process so that the investigation into rape is itself a kind of rape. This scene, like many others throughout Acker's work, illustrates that, in some strong sense, for Acker female self-knowledge is not a simple process of accumulating self-presence. Rather, it is a process of rape and resistance, which is not simply a negative. As Airplane puts it: "I'm scared of the unknown and I love it. This is my sexuality" (*IMI*, 106). For a woman who, whatever happens, is "still bleeding between [her] legs," the language of violence cannot be distinguished from sexuality.

In putting it this way, I am not suggesting, however, that Acker is simply half in love with rape. I would argue that Acker does know about the risk that "she could be sick because she was letting men hurt her instead of feeling pleasure' (*IMI*, 144). Acker is concerned to insist that sexuality is *not* something natural or human. As R (Rimbaud) remarks:

> Our sexuality isn't human. This is the deepest secret. Being allied to wisdom, it's torn from the material bowels of the flesh. V put his hand into me and tore me. I learned that I didn't know how to handle pain. I turned to V to help me, but he turned away from me. I felt nothing but rancor and contempt for V. (*IMI*, 36)

Sexuality and pain arise as a tearing away from nature that is parallel to the condition of language: given with the world and yet not the same as it. An originary deviation with no way back. The material bowels of the flesh are bowels, nothing more. At the heart of the flesh lies the disappointment and inadequacy of metaphors that turn literal. And with the figural turn of paranomasia comes the tearing of violence and sexual awakening, which occurs like Derrida's writing as an originary violence to that nature which it seems to constitute.[34] This is not a defense, on Acker's part, of rape or violence as somehow natural; rather, it is an insistence that sex, violence, and language share the condition of being necessary yet inhuman constituents of the human in a way that detaches humanity from notions of identity or propriety. The violence of rape is oppressive precisely because it makes a claim to naturalize violence as an accident of nature. Acker's insistence that rape and violence constitute sexuality, and that sexuality is not to be renounced, marks out the challenge of feminism: the ethical difficulty of dealing with men when they are all potential rapists.

It is important to recognize that Acker's staging of this challenge is not in any way an attempt to glamorize violence. Acker is not the Rambo of the S/M scene. Her persistent concern with violence – or more precisely her concern with the relationship among sex, language, and violence – makes her work at times tediously repetitive. Instead of simply tossing this off as a writing that "lack[s] even the skill to shock," as Peter Bricklebank does in his review of *Blood and Guts in High School*, I want to argue that in every instance Acker refuses to glorify violence, to accord it special status or shock value.[35] Violence is *not* an event; it constitutes sexuality. As Acker's screenplay for Bette Gordon's film *Variety* repeatedly forces us to recognize, the price you pay in Acker's analysis is that sex and violence lose their "specialness."

In light of my earlier remarks about seduction, this might

seem to pose a real problem. If violence is endemic, does this mean that we can no longer distinguish seduction from rape? Were this the case, then Acker would seem to be playing into the hands of the patriarchy: the dispersal of subjectivity would leave women no position from which to denounce rape, which would then become one more instance of the violence constituting all sexuality. This problem is not merely specifically postmodern; it is crucial to feminism's simultaneous claims that "all men are potential rapists" and that rape is a specific act which should be opposed. The problem here is how to oppose a social structure that tends to treat women indifferently while at the same time insisting upon the difference of specific acts within that system. For example, if the visual regime of narrative cinema violates and exploits women, how are we to make this claim without cheapening the physical violence done to women in rape? One way would be to give priority to the physical act of rape and claim that more general manifestations, such as the structure of looking, merely shadow it. However, to sketch the problem in this way is to undermine the extent to which the potentiality of rape is inscribed in gender relations in western culture, to suggest that rape is a merely incidental happening, an error which could in principle be avoided. That has been the argument of the patriarchy to prevent the restructuring of gender relations, and it is something that Acker's writings directly oppose.

Nor is Acker's argument politically disenabling: one of the things that we know about rape is that it is far more frequent than reports would indicate. That is to say, something about rape makes it very hard to report, to talk about. I do not think that this means that women are merely weak and frightened, that they need simply to be made more conscious of themselves. Precisely what makes rape so difficult to report is the assumption that women are conscious of themselves – should have known better than to lead him/her on, should have resisted. In a sense, then, the assumption that rape is an exemplary act of violence which one knowing subject (male or female) does to another knowing subject (female or male) is what props up the endemic repression of our system of gender relations. Because within it rape just cannot be proved. No woman can ever finally free herself of the suspicion that as a knowing subject she must have consented to her victimization. My argument would be, and I have only the briefest space to sketch it here, that rape is the prolongation of sexual activity after the question of consent has been raised and answered negatively (even if the victim has not been given time to speak). Seduction is sexual activity where the question of consent has not arisen or has been postponed. Thus, although both are "sex without consent" there is no causal link between seduction and rape. Since rape is determined by a refusal of consent that has been ignored, it is not the case that women are "asking for it" by engaging in seduction practices. Rape, that is, is never simple, and the presupposition that it is is what makes it so hard to prove in court. Furthermore, the sufferings of victims during the "detection" and prosecution of rape cases should indicate to us that such legal actions are not directed primarily at the eradication of gender violence so much as at purifying masculinity once more by the eradication of the accidental smear of violence from the essential nature of the male gender.

Thus, what constitutes "a rape" is the product of an act of interpretation, something that has to be argued over (including in court), which doesn't make it any less violent or horrible. However, this does tend to invert our understanding of what it means for "a rape" to occur. Rather than a momentary lapse of gender relations into violence, "a rape" marks the point at which the underlying violence of gender relations has crystalized into an action which can be represented as the assault of one knowing subject on another. A suspicion of the term "knowing subject" doesn't mean that we should give up on prosecutions, merely that we should recognize that a prosecution means merely that an endemic violence has become or may become *representable* within the system for a moment.

By the same argument, we should not think that a series of successful prosecutions within our legal system means (or might ever mean, in principle) that the question of rape has been in any sense *solved*, either for the victims identified or for women in general. In this sense, it is only by relinquishing the assumption that sexual activity is always engaged in by individual knowing subjects, and that what constitutes sexual activity can be known by such subjects, that we can begin to approach the problem of rape.[36] Rape names a structure of violence that extends from the streets through the medical examination rooms and law courts into the psychic activity of individual women tormented by guilt and fear. And it is this entire system of rape, not merely against individual rapists, against which Rape Crisis Centers have to struggle. Rape, that is, names the double bind by which the very means of attesting

171

to the violence done to women by a system of gender relations repeat that violence; the full violence of the rape system (which distinguishes rape from simple assault) lies in the way it works to suggest that in fact violence is not part of the system but an accidental lapse which victims might have resisted.

"Eros in the age of technical reproducibility. You know the old story of reproduction, with the dream of a ciphered language."

The consideration of rape has begun to direct our attention toward the political stakes in the undermining of the notion of subjective identity that takes place in Acker's and Derrida's work. If the general effect of the textual operations that both Acker and Derrida perform is a deconstruction of the notions of coherent identity and individual subjectivity, then the risk I take in putting it this way is leaving myself open to the charge that I'm doing away with the subject and therefore making impossible any kind of politics. For feminism, this is a serious charge indeed. However, if the charge is serious, the verdict is not necessarily "guilty."

I would like to say right away that such a deconstructive interrogation of the subject and of identity is precisely what make a different, although not necessarily new, kind of politics possible. As Judith Butler points out:

> to deconstruct the subject is not to negate or throw away the concept; on the contrary, deconstruction implies only that we suspend all commitments to what the term, "the subject", refers, and that we consider the linguistic functions it serves in the consolidation and concealment of authority. To deconstruct is not to negate or to dismiss, but to call into question and, perhaps, most importantly, to open up a term, like the subject, to a reusage or redeployment that previously has not been authorized.[37]

Butler here summarizes an issue on which Derrida and a number of his commentators have repeatedly insisted. However, it bears repeating, given the enormous currency in cultural studies of the notion that deconstruction, as the vanguard theory of the postmodern, wants to do away with the subject and thus put an end to agency: a charge leveled by figures such as Edward Said, Terry Eagleton, and Seyla Benhabib, among others.[38] The persistence of this error suggests the nature of the stakes: the very intense difficulty of imagining what a politics would be that challenged modernism's account of the nature of political struggle – the goal of liberating an empowered subject into a new sense of its identity and historical destiny. Marxism has offered to liberate the proletariat as subject of history, feminism has adopted this paradigm for woman, liberal humanism has claimed that enlightenment will give a supposedly class, race and gender neutral human subject a mastery of himself and his world. And a certain kind of psychoanalysis has followed the same paradigm, suggesting that ego-psychology could strengthen identity through either a recognition or a "studied ignorance" of a subject's weaknesses, by which the individual might be restored to normality.

Just as ego-psychology is not the only kind of psychoanalysis, identity politics are not the only kind of feminism. Indeed, the value of both psychoanalysis and feminism is, in a sense, the way neither has been able to rest within the paradigm of their modernity, the way in which their modernity was always already troubled. And it is in the intersection of the two that the stakes of their postmodernity have been most apparent. Feminism's interest in psychoanalysis has been abiding. In these terms, I can perhaps produce a slightly extended account of their exchange. Despite Juliet Mitchell, feminism doesn't simply learn from psychoanalysis that gender is culturally constructed so as to reverse the normalizing drive of Freud the patriarch and "cure" all women into a liberated sense of their own identity.[39] Jane Gallop has drawn from Irigaray a double reserve: that identity may be part of the problem rather than the solution; that the scene of the production and transmission of knowledge about sexuality and gender is itself gendered and sexualized.[40] The ambiguous title of Gallop's *The Daughter's Seduction* calls attention to the same problematic as we found in Derrida and Acker: the confusion of sender and receiver, or "who's seducing whom?" We might want to go even further and pose this question as simply "seduction?", since seduction does not simply confuse the question of who occupies which pole (an issue that is in principle answerable) but confounds the poles: since the sender can only be confirmed as sender by virtue of his/her receipt of another message, and vice versa, as the receiver says, "I hear you."

That rather Derridean-sounding, "theoretical," point plays out in Acker's work as the confusion of the very family romance to which Gallop's title alludes. Psychoanalysis loses its normalizing tendency when it takes romance seriously, when it recognizes that

173

the paradigmatic message of desire, the message scrawled illegibly everywhere on Derrida's postcards, is as Kathy Acker points out, "I love you." Or as she puts it in *In Memoriam to Identity*: "But this world is decaying because nothing, like the words *I love you*, means anything and anything means nothing". (*IMI*, 112).

A nothing that can mean anything, and a mark that nothing means anything: this phrase reproduces the structure of Derrida's postcard, "neither legible nor illegible." The romance of the analyst's couch, in a series of feminist readings, reintroduces the play of desire into the very site where a theoretical knowledge offers to analyze the workings of desire itself and so put an end to it. Both deconstruction and feminism have found, in the magnificent failure (which has not been without its costs for many lives) of scientific psychoanalysis, a confrontation of the theory of desire with the desire for theory. Deconstruction has become suspicious of theoretical purity, feminism of theoretical rigidity, the supposed gender-neutrality of knowledge. Our response should not be to promote alternatives, be they irrationalism or "women's science." There is no new identity for a knowing subject on the other side of the deconstruction or the feminist critique of theoretical metalanguages.

This long story about the seductions of theory and the dispersion of identities certainly tends to cast doubt on traditional claims about the goals of intellectual and political endeavor. I have said something about a suspicion of theory that is common to deconstruction and to feminism, though our institutional practices tend to cast both as kinds of theory. And in some sense, each can be said to have invited this description. Deconstruction has at times been thought of as merely a method of literary analysis, and feminist accounts of liberation have rested on notions of identity which, as necessarily normative, have functioned in exclusionary and oppressive ways. In ceasing to think about subjectivity in terms of identity, ideology in terms of falsification, we do not abandon critical discourse; rather, we shift away from a merely negative or reactive understanding of resistance as inherently oppositional. The interaction of feminism and deconstruction begins here(after), when attention to difference replaces oppositional identity, when solidarity displaces critical isolation. Their postmodern romance, however, is the matter of another book than this one. For romance's dispersion of identities includes that of the theorist, which perhaps precludes any conclusion. You can never have too much romance.

174

NOTES

Introduction:
a preface which should have been a postscript

1 Barbara Cartland, *Love for Sale* (New York: 1980); Barbara Kruger and Kate Linker, *Love for Sale* (New York: Abrams, 1990).
2 A few of the texts that would illustrate this "trend" are: *Postmodernism and Its Discontents*, ed. E. Ann Kaplan (London and New York: Verso, 1988); Meaghan Morris, *The Pirate's Fiancée: Feminism, Reading, Postmodernism* (London and New York: Verso, 1988); *Universal Abandon: The Politics of Postmodernism*, ed. Andrew Ross (Minneapolis: University of Minnesota Press, 1988); *Feminism/Postmodernism*, ed. Linda J. Nicholson (New York and London: Routledge, 1990).
3 The materials for expanding a concern with romance into postcolonial literatures are beginning to be assembled, in texts such as Barbara Harlow's *Resistance Literature* (New York and London: Methuen, 1987); *Recasting Women*, ed. Kumkum Sagari and Suclesh Vaid (New Brunswick: Rutgers University Press, 1990); and Sarah Suleri's *Heatless Days* (Chicago: The University of Chicago Press).
4 M. H. Abrams offers this as one of the definitions of romance in his reference work, *A Glossary of Literary Terms*, third edition (New York: Holt, Rinehart and Winston, 1971), 22.
5 As Patricia Parker puts it in her valuable *Inescapable Romance: Studies in the Poetics of a Mode* (Princeton: Princeton University Press, 1979):

> The term "romance" is . . . neither [a] fixed generic prescription nor [an] abstract transhistorical category. The former is rendered impossible by the poets' own extension of the term beyond its strictly generic meaning . . . . The latter is invalidated by the changing connotations of the word "romance" in the centuries after Chrétien and his Renaissance successors.(5)

My own concern with nineteenth- and twentieth-century prose leads me to have slightly less confidence than Parker that romance's excess over formalism can be recuperated by "what Jameson calls a 'genuinely *historical* account' of the form" (7). One thing that becomes clear in the

175

prose texts to which I turn is that history is as subject to the categorical disruptions of romance as are the prescriptions of literary formalism.

Daniel O'Hara also begins to articulate the relationship between romance and literary theory in *The Romance of Interpretation* (New York: Columbia University Press, 1985). O'Hara quickly equates romance with the romantic and, *a fortiori*, with the internalization of the quest narrative as visionary perspective. As Parker points out and as I hope to illustrate, "romance" is a more troubled term than O'Hara is willing to concede. I also want to insist on the necessary relationship between romance and gender as a feminist issue. While O'Hara does acknowledge an interest in feminism – his book jacket reminds us that *The Romance of Interpretation* is "in the author's words 'the first full-scale feminist critique of modern theory written by a man'" – his references to feminism in the course of his argument are so brief that neither "feminism" nor "feminist" warrant an entry in his book's index (where the authors listed are exclusively male). Perhaps Mr O'Hara is imitating the desire he ascribes to Paul de Man: that of becoming "the perfect ironist" (235).

6 Janice Radway uses this opposition in *Reading the Romance: Women, Patriarchy, and Popular Literature* (Chapel Hill: University of North Carolina Press, 1984), 152. Radway outlines these two approaches to generic concerns when she argues that female readers of romances have an "ability to see that the romance is an alterable set of generic conventions rather than a natural and immutable organic form."

7 Jacques Derrida, "The Law of Genre," *Glyph* 7 (1980), 206, 210, 211.

8 Or as Derrida would have it, "There is no natural or symbolic law, universal law of a genre/gender here" ("Law of Genre," 223).

9 Richard Chase, *The American Novel and Its Tradition* (1957) (Baltimore: Johns Hopkins University Press, 1983). As Chase summarizes it:

> since the earliest days the American novel, in its most original and characteristic form, has worked out its destiny and defined itself by incorporating an element of romance. This purpose has led me to propose a native tradition of the novel. I understand this tradition, inevitably, as springing from England, but as differing from the English tradition by its perpetual reassessment and reconstitution of romance within the novel form. (viii)

10 Henry James, "Preface to *The American*," *The Art of the Novel* (New York: Charles Scribner's Sons, 1962), 33.

11 Richard Chase, *The American Novel and Its Tradition*, 28.

12 This is not the same thing as Radway's reference to the "alterable conventions" of romance. What I am suggesting is that romance's self-commentary, the ability of romance texts to act upon the genre of which they are said to be a part, occurs in such a way as to defy the very notion of generic conventions. Put another way, the texts of romance have a plastic action upon the genre, which necessitates a rethinking of genre itself.

13 F. R. Leavis, *The Great Tradition* (New York: New York University Press, 1960), 122, 123.

14 Even John Prebble's attempted "unromantic" portrayal of the common man's "real" experience of the campaign of Bonnie Prince Charlie reads as if it were historical romance: *Culloden* (Harmondsworth: Penguin Books, 1967).

15 Ihab Hassan, *The Postmodern Turn: Essays in Postmodern Theory and Culture* (Columbus: Ohio State University Press, 1987); *Postmodern Culture*, ed. Hal Foster (London and Sydney: Pluto Press, 1985), first published and subsequently cited here as *The Anti-Aesthetic* (Port Townsend, WA: Bay Press, 1983); Linda Hutcheon, *A Poetics of Postmodernism: History, Theory, Fiction* (New York and London: Routledge, 1988); Jean-François Lyotard, *The Postmodern Condition: A Report on Knowledge*, tr. Geoff Bennington and Brian Massumi (Minneapolis: University of Minnesota Press, 1984); *The Cultural Politics of "Postmodernism"*, ed. John Tagg, *Current Debates in Art History*, 1989; Brian McHale, *Postmodernist Fiction* (New York and London: Methuen, 1987); *Postmodernism and Its Discontents*, ed. E. Ann Kaplan; Herman Rapaport, *Milton and the Postmodern* (Lincoln and London: University of Nebraska Press, 1983).

16 Charles Jencks, *What Is Postmodernism?* (New York: St Martin's Press, 1987), 22.

17 Jean-François Lyotard, *The Postmodern Condition*, 79.

18 See Lyotard, "Re-writing Modernity," *SubStance* 54 (1987), 8–9.

19 Griselda Pollock, *Vision and Difference: Femininity, Feminism and Histories of Art* (London and New York: Routledge, 1988), 158.

20 Lyotard, "Re-writing Modernity," 3. Although in this section I am focusing on the ways in which postmodernism calls into question the chronological master narratives of history, significantly Lyotard's claim for postmodernism is that it calls into question all master narratives.

21 Lyotard, "Re-writing Modernity," 3.

22 See Lyotard, *The Postmodern Condition*, esp. 27–41.

23 In mentioning anachronism, I do not mean to suggest something along the lines of the Freudian atemporal unconscious, which brings together material without regard for historical periods or temporal order. Postmodern romance is not like a mystic writing pad, with a wax record unable to record the times of its inscriptions. For Freud's discussion of the unconscious as atemporal see, for instance, *The Interpretation of Dreams*, *The Standard Edition of the Complete Works of Sigmund Freud*, vols IV, V (London: The Hogarth Press and The Institute for Psycho-Analysis, 1958); and "A Note Upon The 'Mystic Writing-Pad,'" *Standard Edition*, vol. XIX.

24 See Hayden White, *Metahistory* (Baltimore: Johns Hopkins University Press, 1973) and *The Tropics of Discourse: Essays in Cultural Criticism* (Baltimore: Johns Hopkins University Press, 1978).

25 Cf. Lyotard, "Re-writing Modernity," 6.

26 Lyotard, *The Postmodern Condition*, 74.

27 Theodor Adorno, "What Does Coming to Terms with the Past Mean?" tr. Timothy Bahti and Geoffrey Hartman, *Bitburg in Moral and Political Perspective*, ed. Geoffrey Hartman (Bloomington: Indiana University Press, 1986), 115.

28 George Meredith, *Diana of the Crossways* (London: Virago, 1985), 231. For a more extended discussion of the relationship among romance, realism, and the figure of woman, see my "We Pray To Be Defended From Her Cleverness: Conjugating Romance in George Meredith's *Diana of the Crossways*," *Genre* 21 (Summer 1988), 179–201.

29 Italo Calvino, *If on a winter's night a traveler*, tr. William Weaver (New York: HBJ, 1981); *Se una notte d'inverno un viaggiatore* (Torino: Giulio Einaudi, 1979).

30 Meaghan Morris, *The Pirate's Fiancée*, 16. In calling attention to positions like Morris's, I do not want to suggest that this represents all critical thinking on the relationship between feminism and postmodernism. Patricia Waugh's *Feminine Fictions: Revisiting the Postmodern* (London and New York: Routledge, 1989) would be a good example of a counter-position. Waugh contends that "feminism and postmodernism clearly *do* share many concerns as they each develop from the 60's onward" (6). Waugh then goes on to develop this argument, explaining that feminism *and* postmodernism share a commitment "to the project of deconstructing both the subject and the 'master narratives' of history." Yet in acknowledging this common ground, Waugh also reminds us that "any account of the relation between feminism and postmodernism must . . . acknowledge their historical differences" (16).

31 Linda Hutcheon, *The Politics of Postmodernism* (London and New York: Routledge, 1989), 168. For an example of a defence of feminism as a modernist enterprise, see Sabina Lovibond, "Feminism and Postmodernism," *Postmodernism and Society*, ed. Roy Boyne and Ali Rattansi (New York: St Martin's Press, 1990), 154–86. Lovibond argues that the feminist movement "should persist in seeing itself as a component or offshoot of Enlightenment modernism, rather than as one more 'exciting' feature (or cluster of features) in a postmodern social landscape" (179). For less enthusiastic defenses of feminism's commitment to modernity, see Christine Di Stefano, "Dilemmas of Difference: Feminism, Modernity, and Postmodernism" and Sandra Harding, "Feminism, Science, and Anti-Enlightenment Critiques," *Feminism/Postmodernism*, ed. Linda Nicholson (New York and London: Routledge, 1990). It is also worth noting that for Alice Jardine the relationship between feminism and modernity is a crucial one (*Gynesis: Configurations of Woman and Modernity*, Ithaca: Cornell University Press, 1985). In her extended discussion, Jardine asks us to consider the notion of *gynesis*, a "putting into discourse of 'woman' as that *process* diagnosed in France as intrinsic to the condition of modernity" (25). Jardine's argument is somewhat curious in that it fails to address at any length what is at stake in the debate over the distinction between modernity and postmodernity. That she avoids considering the rather heated debate between Lyotard and Habermas contributes to the problem.

32 Fredric Jameson, *The Political Unconscious* (Ithaca: Cornell University Press, 1981), 104.

33 Northrop Frye, *The Secular Scripture* (Cambridge, MA: Harvard University Press, 1982), 57.

NOTES

34 Pierre Macherey, *A Theory of Literary Production*, tr. Geoffrey Wall (London: Routledge and Kegan Paul, 1985), 60.
35 See Northrop Frye, *The Secular Scripture*, 164 and *The Anatomy of Criticism* (Princeton: Princeton University Press, 1973), 186.
36 Rosalind Coward, *Female Desires: How They Are Sought, Bought and Packaged* (New York: Grove Press, 1985), 189–96. Coward concludes her discussion by stating that "women do acquire power in these fantasies . . . this power, however, is always familial, always regressive" (196).
37 Janice A. Radway, *Reading the Romance*.
38 In *Loving With a Vengeance*, Tania Modleski captures the gist of Radway's argument when she reminds us that "contemporary mass-produced narratives for women contain elements of protest and resistance underneath highly 'orthodox' plots," even though these solutions would not be likely to please modern feminists (Hamden, CN: Archon Books, 1982, 25). In singling out Modleski, Radway, and Coward as I have done, I do not want to suggest that theirs is the only work which calls attention to the politics of romance. Other noteworthy studies include: *Rewriting English: Cultural Politics of Gender and Class*, ed. Janet Batsleer, Tony Davies, Rebecca O'Rourke, and Chris Weedon (London: Methuen, 1985); *The Progress of Romance: The Politics of Popular Fiction*, ed. Jean Radford (London and New York: Routledge and Kegan Paul, 1986); CCCS (Center for Contemporary Cultural Studies), *Women Take Issue: Aspects of Women's Subordination* (London: Hutchinson, 1978); Dana Heller, *The Feminization of Quest-Romances: Radical Departures* (Austin: University of Texas Press, 1990); Carol Thurston, *The Romance Revolution: Erotic Novels for Women and the Quest for a New Sexual Identity* (Urbana and Chicago: University of Illinois Press, 1987).
39 Ihab Hassan, "Joyce, Beckett, and the Postmodern Imagination," *Tri Quarterly*, 34 (Fall 1975), 200. See also *The Postmodern Turn*.
40 Zevi quoted in Jencks, *What is Postmodernism?*, p. 13; Fredric Jameson, "Postmodernism and Consumer Society," *Postmodernism and Its Discontents* ed. E. Ann Kaplan, 29. I quote here the "latest" version of Jameson's essay (there are two others). It is important, I think, that Jameson keeps rewriting the same essay on postmodernism. Why this might be, will be a topic I will consider in chapter 1.
41 Hal Foster, *Recodings: Art, Spectacle, Cultural Politics* (Port Townsend, WA: Bay Press, 1985). Foster's work is probably the most useful analysis of postmodern art to date. A less sophisticated version of Foster's analysis can be found in Linda Hutcheon's *A Poetics of Postmodernism*. She argues that postmodernism is "doubly encoded," is politically contradictory (205).
42 Fredric Jameson also argues for the inevitable connection between postmodernism and politics, although his position leans in a slightly different direction from mine ("Postmodernism, or The Cultural Logic of Late Capitalism," *New Left Review*, July/August 1984, 35).
43 Tiresias was blinded by Hera for having used his ability to change sex in order to inform Zeus whether women or men had more pleasure in sex.

179

1 P.S. "I Love you": Umberto Eco and the romance of the reader

1 Umberto Eco, *The Name of the Rose*, tr. William Weaver (New York: HBJ, 1983), xiii; Umberto Eco, *Il nome della rosa* (Milan: Bompiani, 1980). Unless indicated, all further references are to the English edition.

2 If my argument were to stop here, it would have a striking resemblance to Georg Lukács's *The Theory of the Novel* (tr. Anya Bostock, Cambridge, MA: MIT Press, 1983). However, the postmodernity of Eco's text does not lie in its ability to console. This is a point which will be made clearer in my discussion of irony when I again return to Lukács.

3 In light of the fact that literate Italians are more likely to be able to read Latin than their English-speaking counterparts, Weaver's "fidelity" to Eco's "original" text is all the more curious. His editorial decision, in my view, calls attention to the way in which most readers read: they do not read or remember every word on the page; they cannot be completely faithful readers. There is always a certain unread, blank space. The Latin passages, like the other untranslated bits of Provençal or German, function for many English-speaking readers like these blank spaces. In a novel as full of hermeneutic puzzles as *The Name of the Rose*, the blank, unreadable spaces hold out the possibility that the reason the reader can't "get it" – can't understand what Eco's novel is all about – is because s/he can't actually read all of the text. This seems a particularly compelling explanation, since the final lines of the novel are in Latin. However, as Eco's text is willing to underscore, no passage holds the "truth" of the text, the hermeneutic key. Understanding the "foreign language" passages does not necessarily make for a "fuller" or better reading; we might be fooling ourselves even more if we think we are reading all the words on the page.

4 To say that this unnamed female character is completely mute is not quite fair. We are told by Adso that:

> for all her shouting, she was as if mute. There are words that give power, others that make us all the more derelict, and to this latter category belong the vulgar words of the simple, to whom the Lord had not granted the boon of self-expression in the universal tongue of knowledge and power. (398)

For a detailed discussion of the role of women in *The Name of the Rose*, see Teresa de Lauretis, "Gaudy Rose," *SubStance*, 47 (1985).

5 For an extensive discussion of the relationship between the medieval and the modern in Eco's novel, see Theresa Coletti, *Naming the Rose: Eco, Medieval Signs, and Modern Theory* (Ithaca: Cornell University Press, 1988). It is significant that Coletti insists on the modernity of Eco's novel. Although my discussion of *The Name of the Rose* focuses on the ways in which that text is postmodern, for reasons that will become apparent later in this chapter, I would argue that in some

NOTES

respects Coletti is correct to point out the ways in which the novel can be considered modern.

6 Walter Scott, *Old Mortality* (Boston: Fields, Osgood, 1869), 38.

7 Umberto Eco, *Postscript to The Name of the Rose*, tr. William Weaver (New York: HBJ, 1984). All further references to this text will be indicated parenthetically within the text as *PS*.

8 More precisely, I mean that the construction of the Eiffel Tower can be viewed as an event which inaugurates, which marks the beginning of, modernism. And this marking is complacent in that it does not make any pretension to be a self-conscious critique of that event. As far as Marx's *Capital* is concerned, it produces the time of capitalism by defining the time of capitalism as the ground of its analysis. Accordingly, the time of capitalism that is produced and defined by *Capital* is also the time in which a Marxist analysis of capital will have its usefulness.

9 In a series of articles to which I will refer at length later in this chapter, Fredric Jameson argues that pastiche *is* a defining characteristic of postmodernism. As Jameson sees it, pastiche is a sort of blank parody, which occurs when "the producers of culture have nowhere to turn but to the past" and when there is no "normalicity" to which parody refers. Put another way, "the disappearance of the individual subject, along with its formal consequences, the increasing unavailability of the personal *style*, engender the well-nigh universal practice today of what may be called pastiche." ("Postmodernism, or The Cultural Logic of Late Capitalism," *The New Left Review* (July/August, 1984), 64–5). In a break with Jameson's conceptualization of postmodernism, I will argue that pastiche is a formal property of the avant-garde, not a defining property of postmodernism.

10 For a perceptive discussion of this issue, see Hal Foster, "The 'Primitive Unconscious of Modern Art,' or White Skin Black Masks," *Recodings*. Foster also reproduces the Philip Morris ad. to which I refer (189).

11 Cleanth Brooks, *The Well Wrought Urn* (New York: HBJ, 1947), 257, 258.

12 Brooks, *The Well Wrought Urn*, 102.

13 That irony can synthesize conflicting attitudes and interpretations is a point that Georg Lukács underscores with a Hegelian inflection in *The Theory of the Novel*. For Lukács, it is because of irony that an interior subjectivity "sees through the abstract and, therefore, limited nature of the mutually alien worlds of subject and object," that "the creative subjectivity glimpses a unified world in the mutual relativity of elements essentially alien to one another, and gives form to this world" (74–5).

14 Roland Barthes raises a similar issue in *The Empire of Signs*: "The text does not 'gloss' the images, which do not 'illustrate' the text. For me, each has been no more than the onset of a kind of visual uncertainty, analogous perhaps to that *loss of meaning* Zen calls a *satori*" (*The Empire of Signs*, tr. Richard Howard, New York: Hill and Wang, 1982, xi).

15 Edgar Allan Poe, "The Case of M. Valdemar," *The Complete Tales and Poems of Edgar Allan Poe* (New York: Vintage Books), 103.

181

16 Jacques Derrida, "Discussion, 'To Write: Intransitive Verb?'" *The Structuralist Controversy*, ed. Richard Macksey and Eugenio Donato (Baltimore: Johns Hopkins Press, 1972), 156.

17 In this respect, our author's use of "irony" is closer to Paul de Man's than Cleanth Brooks's. De Man contends that:

> Irony divides the flow of temporal experience into a past that is pure mystification and a future that remains harassed forever by a relapse within the inauthentic. It can know this inauthenticity but can never overcome it. It can only restate and repeat it on an increasingly conscious level, but it remains endlessly caught in the impossibility of making this knowledge applicable to the empirical world. ("The Rhetoric of Temporality," *Blindness and Insight: Essays in the Rhetoric of Contemporary Criticism*, second edition, revised Minneapolis: University of Minnesota Press, 1983, 222)

De Man does not stop his argument here, however. Significantly he points out that this is a "dangerously satisfying and highly vulnerable" conclusion, for it does not take into consideration the "predicament of the conscious subject" – which, as our author has shown, is what Derrida discussed at length. In so many words, de Man seems to be suggesting that his incomplete formulation of irony, as it appears above, can easily turn into just another version of the modernist myth of supreme self-consciousness – even if that consciousness is of inauthenticity.

The problem with Ihab Hassan's conception of postmodern irony is the failure to understand just that point. According to Hassan, "irony, perspectivism, reflexiveness: these express the ineluctable recreations of mind in search of a truth that continually eludes it, leaving it with only an ironic access or excess of self-consciousness" ("Pluralism in Postmodern Perspective," *The Postmodern Turn: Essays in Postmodern Theory and Culture*, Columbus: Ohio State University Press, 1987, 170). Hassan's postmodern irony is what our author would call a modernist ironic attitude. Ironically, Hassan lists de Man as an example of a postmodern ironist.

18 In this regard, the way in which our author is using the notion of ironic temporality sounds closer to what Richard Rorty, rather than Brooks, means by the term "irony." As Rorty begins to explain it, "irony is, if not intrinsically resentful, at least reactive. Ironists have to have something to have doubts about, something from which to be alienated" (Richard Rorty, *Contingency, Irony, and Solidarity*, Cambridge: Cambridge University Press, 1989, 88). The problem with Rorty's formulation of irony, however, is a confusion of irony with ironist – yet another instance of the privileging of the human subject who is always in control of his/her language. Rorty, as our author will show, is right to say that the ironist is "the typical modern intellectual," because Rorty (or Rorty's ironist) fails to confront the postmodern possibility that taking irony seriously is not always a move which aims only at resisting "redescription" (89).

19 In light of these remarks, it is perhaps ironical that the book around

which the mystery plot of *The Name of the Rose* turns is Aristotle's lost book on comedy.

20 Alex Callinicos also criticizes Eco's account of postmodernism, but he does so only in order to return us to the progressive radicalism of the Enlightenment ("Reactionary Postmodernism?" *Postmodernism and Society*, ed. Roy Boyne and Ali Rattansi, 112).

21 Robert Caserio's excellent consideration of Eco's theory of language, ("The Name of the Horse: *Hard Times*, Semiotics, and the Supernatural" *Novel*, 20, Fall 1986, 5–23) points to the homophobic aspects of Eco's novel. Although I agree with Caserio's reading, I would argue that *The Name of the Rose* is more conflicted in that it plays through a narrative that is both homosocial and homophobic.

22 Craig Owens, "Feminists and Postmodernism," *The Anti-Aesthetic*, ed. Hal Foster (Port Townsend, WA: Bay Press, 1983), 61.

23 Hal Foster, *Recodings: Art, Spectacle, Cultural Politics*, Port Townsend, WA: Bay Press, 1985, 149.

24 Whether postmodernism is really a form of resistance is the question that Fredric Jameson keeps struggling with, as he continually reworks his essay on postmodernism. The running problem for Jameson is that postmodernism may only mirror and not critique the logic of late-western capitalism. On this count, I am more convinced than Jameson of postmodernism's resistance to capitalism. Jameson's argument about postmodernism appears in three essays, which read like two versions of a hit single alongside the extended play release: "Postmodernism and Consumer Society," *Postmodernism and Its Discontents*, ed. E. Ann Kaplan (London and New York: Verso, 1988); "Postmodernism and Consumer Society," *The Anti-Aesthetic*, ed. Hal Foster; "Postmodernism, or the Cultural Logic of Late Capitalism", *New Left Review* 146 (1984). Most recently, Jameson has further expanded his argument in his lengthy book, *Postmodernism, or The Logic of Late Capitalism* (London: Verso, 1991).

25 "Resistance," as I use the term here, would be radically different from Linda Hutcheon's notion of "critique from within," a phrase she is fond of employing in connection with postmodernism (*A Poetics of Postmodernism: History, Theory, Fiction*, London and New York: Routledge, 1988.)

26 For a consideration of the impossibility of exhaustively defining context, see Jacques Derrida, "Signature Event Context," *Margins of Philosophy*, tr. Alan Bass (Chicago: University of Chicago Press, 1982).

27 Lyotard, "Re-writing Modernity," *SubStance* 54 (1987), 3.

2 Delayed in the post: Walter Scott and the progress of romance

1 F. R. Leavis, *The Great Tradition* (New York: New York University Press, 1960); Raymond Williams, *Culture and Society 1780–1950* (Harmondsworth: Penguin Books, 1963).

2 Georg Lukács, *The Historical Novel*, tr. Hannah and Stanley Mitchell (Lincoln and London: University of Nebraska Press, 1983), 33.

3 Walter Scott, *Ivanhoe* (Harmondsworth: Penguin Books, 1986), 533. Hereafter cited parenthetically within my text as *I*.

4 The political is simultaneously the history of romance and the necessity for romance to provide a concomitant account of the history of romance. Edward Waverley's *Bildungsroman* is also the history of the development of historical romance from the wistful attractions of folklore (Rachel's tales) or the Renaissance reinvention of chivalry (Ariosto), to the attempt at the political realization of romance on the world-historical stage in the rebellion of Charles Edward Stuart.

5 Walter Scott, *The Monastery, The Waverley Novels* (Boston: Fields, Osgood, 1869), 40. Hereafter cited parenthetically within my text as *M*.

6 Walter Scott, *Waverley* (New York: Penguin Books, 1983), p. 389. Hereafter cited parenthetically within my text as *W*.

7 Scott continues to criticize his own romance (*The Monastery*) on these very "grounds." He explains that his romance fails because it is *inartificial* and therefore *not* perfectly intelligible (*M*, 22).

8 In terms of historiography and poetics, the distinction Michel de Certeau uses, we could say that: "The project of historiography is the inverse of the poetic one. It consists of furnishing discourse with referentiality, to make it function as 'expressive,' to legitimize it by means of the 'real,' in short, to initiate discourse as that which is supposed to have knowledge" ("The Freudian Novel," *Heterologies: Discourse on the Other*, tr. Brian Massumi, Minneapolis: University of Minnesota Press, 31).

9 Walter Scott, "An Essay On Romance," *The Miscellaneous Prose Works of Sir Walter Scott*, vol. IV (Paris: Baudry's European Library, 1837), 267. First published in the supplement to the *Encyclopedia Britannica*, 1824. Hereafter cited parenthetically within my text as *ER*.

10 It is this uncanny return of the past as romance that Fredric Jameson fails to distinguish within Scott's work. Jameson's own nostalgia for "real" history makes him blind to Scott's postmodernity. For Jameson, E. L. Doctorow's novels do indeed provide "an extraordinary sense of déjà-vu and a peculiar familiarity [which] one is tempted to associate with Freud's 'return of the repressed' in 'The Uncanny'"; however, Scott's novels only institute "a narrative dialectic between what we already 'know' about The Pretender, say, and what he is then seen to be concretely in the pages of the novel." ("Postmodernism, or The Cultural Logic of Late Capitalism," *New Left Review*, July/August 1984, 69–70).

11 Walter Scott, *Rob Roy* (London and Melbourne: J. M. Dent, 1986), 386, 5. Hereafter cited parenthetically within my text as *RR*.

12 In *The Historical Novel* Lukács makes a relevant observation about Ranke, although not in relation to Scott. According to Lukács, for historians like Ranke, "history is a collection and reproduction of interesting facts about the past" (176). As we shall go on to see, what that might mean is not entirely clear.

184

13 A. O. Cockshut, *The Achievement of Walter Scott* (New York: New York University Press, 1969), p. 159 n. 2.

14 Along this line, Richard Waswo argues that "[t]he social nexus of interpretation that confers the writer's identity becomes the arbiter of the destinies of his characters. It is in this sense that fiction *becomes* fact, as in the novels history becomes the fictions that individuals and groups tell about each other and themselves" ("Story as Historiography in the Waverley Novels," *English Literary History*, 47 (1980), 310).

15 In making these claims for the way in which Scott articulates the distinction between romance and history I am departing from arguments like those proposed by George Levine or James Kerr. For Kerr, Scott employs romance "as a way of excluding history from his fiction, of keeping the past at a distance and thereby reducing its disruptive force" (*Fiction Against History: Scott as Storyteller*, Cambridge: Cambridge University Press, 1989, 19). Levine takes his argument about Scott in the direction of realism and argues that Scott's novels established "a pattern for the tradition of realism as it displaces romance" (*The Realistic Imagination: English Fiction from Frankenstein to Lady Chatterley*, Chicago and London: University of Chicago Press, 84).

16 Judith Wilt is right to suggest that "what really concerns Scott and his character-historians is the destruction, the disappearances, the crucial and personal losses which make up the fabric of history, the wiped-out voids which the persistence of ruins, or even the sudden discovery of hidden fragments, only emphasizes" (*Secret Leaves: The Novels of Walter Scott*, Chicago and London: University of Chicago Press, 1985, 166).

17 The full title of Selkirk's work, revealing in itself, is: *Observations on the Present State of the Highlands of Scotland, with a View of the Causes and Probable Consequences of Emigration* (1805).

18 Walter Scott, *The Fair Maid of Perth* (Boston: Fields, Osgood, 1871), 22.

19 A young peasant remarks of Athelstane: "Dead, however, he was, or else translated" (*I*, 496). Here, of course, translation is religious possibility. The bardic text must view translation as a threat rather than a promise of eternal life, a displacement in quite the opposite direction to heavenward.

20 In suggesting that translation takes place in the scene of romance, I do not wish to argue, as Wolfgang Iser does, that Scott "draws attention to an inevitable individualization of reality," that "reality is something that is constantly individualized and diversified" (Wolfgang Iser, *The Implied Reader*, Baltimore and London: Johns Hopkins University Press, 1983, 90). Translation is not a question of subjectivity or individualization, in the traditional sense of the terms. I will leave a more in-depth explanation of this point for the last chapter.

21 In the Dedicatory Epistle to *Ivanhoe*, Scott goes on to explain that he translates the past into modern manners and language so that they will hold our interest, so that we will see what it is we have in common with the past. This could be read as just another bourgeois ploy, co-opting the past, erasing its difference from the present. But I don't think that is the case. Rather romance shows how difficult it is to think the past

as past, to think of the past as that which is *not* modern (*I*, 526–7). The understanding of the past that romance provides must in some way, as Scott repeatedly tells his readers, also rely on the representation of the uncommon. It is as if romance has to show that which is also common in the uncommon, a paradox not unlike recognizing difference as not the same difference to which we are accustomed.

22 De Certeau makes a similar point when he argues that "the ground of our certainty is shaken when we can no longer think a thought from the past." It is interesting to note that de Certeau's statement is itself an example of not being able to think the past. He makes this remark in conjunction with an analysis of Michel Foucault's work; however, in the context of the article it is impossible to tell whether the statement is meant to be a paraphrase of Foucault or an additional comment on de Certeau's part ("The Black Sun of Language," *Heterologies*, 177).

23 Walter Scott, *Peveril of the Peak* (Boston: Fields, Osgood, 1869), 53. Hereafter cited parenthetically within my text as *PP*.

24 Scott's "factual errors" are so egregious that they recently have led Penguin Books to apologize for them on the back cover of their edition of *Ivanhoe*. "Despite the many glaring historical inaccuracies," Penguin remind us, Scott's novel "unfailingly spellbinds the modern reader." Apparently Penguin realize that Scott is of interest for reasons other than his faithful reproduction of modernist history.

25 Walter Scott, *Anne of Geierstein* (Boston: Fields, Osgood, 1869), 5. Hereafter cited parenthetically within my text as *AG*.

26 See Jean-François Lyotard, *The Postmodern Condition: A Report on Knowledge*, tr. Geoff Bennington and Brian Massumi (Minneapolis: University of Minnesota Press, 1984), 79.

27 It is interesting to note the length to which Scott goes in order to call attention to the fictional status of the Author of *Waverley*. When Dr Dryasdust inquiries about the abrupt departure of his literary guest, his servant denies having seen any one at all. In the servant's mind, the empty liquor decanters that the doctor submits as evidence of the presence of a visitor mean nothing because Dryasdust is wont to empty them on his own accord. The strong suggestion is that Dr Dryasdust has been visited by a literary ghost of his imagination (*PP*, 65–6).

28 In the final sentences of *The Postmodern Condition*, Lyotard approaches this same issue, although from a somewhat different direction: "For the stakes would be knowledge (or information, if you will), and the reserve of knowledge – language's reserve of possible utterances – is inexhaustible. This sketches the outline of a politics that would respect both the desire for justice and the desire for the unknown" (67).

29 A similar passage occurs at the end of *The Bride of Lammermoor*, except this time there is an excess of truth:

> By many readers this may be deemed overstrained, romantic, and composed by the wild imagination of an author, desirous of gratifying the popular appetite for the horrible; but those who are read in the private family history of Scotland during the period in which the scene is laid, will readily discover, through the disguise

of borrowed names and added incidents, the leading particulars of
AN OWER TRUE TALE." (*The Bride of Lammermoor*, Edinburgh:
Adam and Charles Black, 1886, 313)

3 Romantic letters and postmodern envelopes: Joseph Conrad and the imperialism of historical representation

1 Joseph Conrad, *Nostromo* (Harmondsworth: Penguin Books, 1983), 97. Hereafter cited parenthetically within my text as *N*.
2 This focus on history in *Nostromo* takes further the implications of observations such as Avrom Fleishman's that in "Conrad's treatment of Costaguana, history, either as legend or fact, colors every feature of the country's face" (*The English Historical Novel: Walter Scott to Virginia Woolf*, Baltimore and London: Johns Hopkins University Press, 1971, 227).
3 Robert Caserio recently has called our attention to Conrad's complex use of romance in *The Rescue*: "*The Rescue* and the Ring of Meaning," *Conrad Revisited: Essays for the Eighties*, ed. Ross C. Murfin (Tuscaloosa: University of Alabama Press, 1985).
4 Numerous critics have commented, with varying degrees of sympathy and detail, on Conrad's employment of the romance/adventure story. Suresh Ravel (*The Art of Failure: Conrad's Fiction*, Boston: Allen and Unwin, 1986) notes that "*Nostromo* is part of Conrad's rethinking of the genre of romance" (91); he also argues that "Conrad's is a framework of 'monumental history,' to borrow a phrase from Nietzsche" (97). Jacques Darras (*Joseph Conrad and the West: Signs of Empire*, tr. Anne Luyat and Jacques Darras, Totowa, NJ: Barnes and Noble, 1982) draws a parallel between *Heart of Darkness* and the medieval quest/romance, although he does not extend the comparison to *Nostromo*. Walter F. Wright (*Romance and Tragedy in Joseph Conrad*, 1949, New York: Russell and Russell, 1966) discusses romance in Conrad's work but treats *Nostromo* as a tragedy, as does John Barbour (*Tragedy as a Critique of Virtue: The Novel and Ethical Reflection*, Chico, CA: Scholars Press, 1984) and Claire Rosenfield (*Paradise of Snakes*, Chicago and London: University of Chicago Press, 1967). Martin Green (*Dreams of Adventure, Deeds of Empire*, New York: Basic Books, 1979) draws a parallel between romance and adventure stories in Conrad's work, although he argues that Conrad's transformation of the adventure story through the use of romance only results in ambiguity which could be mistaken for "a subtly profound strategy" (298). Finally, Jefferson Hunter contextualizes the adventure/romance relationship within Edwardian fiction (*Edwardian Fiction*, Cambridge, MA: Harvard University Press, 1982).
5 See, for instance, Jocelyn Baines, *Joseph Conrad: A Critical Biography* (Harmondsworth: Penguin Books, 1971); Claire Rosenfield, *Paradise of Snakes*; Juliet McLaughlan, *Conrad: Nostromo* (London: Arnold, 1969); J. I. M. Stewart, *Joseph Conrad* (London: Longman, 1968).
6 This is the progress brought about by a shift from a society dominated

by religion to one dominated by the state. As Hegel explains in *The Phenomenology of Spirit*, tr. A. V. Miller, Oxford: Oxford University Press, 1977, 348 (#572): "Enlightenment, then, holds an irresistible authority over faith because in the believer's own consciousness are found the very moments which Enlightenment has established as valid."

7 As Gould explains, "I shall write to Holroyd that the San Tomé mine is big enough to take in hand the making of a new State" (*N*, 323).

8 For Hegel world history entails "events in time through which spirit manifests itself in a people or a state." The whole process of history as the "realization of the Idea of Spirit" is "directed to rendering this unconscious impulse a conscious one" (*The Philosophy of History*, tr. J. Sibree, New York: Dover Publications, 1956, 25–57). And as such, there is an inevitable progress of history. Hegel also clarifies what he means by progress when he states that "progress appears as an advancing from the imperfect to the more perfect; but the former must not be understood abstractly as *only* the imperfect, but as something which involves the very opposite of itself – the so-called perfect – as a *germ* or impulse" (57).

9 For a discussion of the relationship between Hegelian thought and imperialism, see Alan Sandison, *The Wheel of Empire* (New York: St Martin's Press, 1967, p. 62). Sandison argues that:

> political imperialism serves expressly as the translation of the Hegelian system's "boundless expansion on the plan of thought." The need to secure their own identity dictated an incessant war against an alien and chaotic nature with the elusive end in the subjugation of the latter . . . The embarkation of the self on its rapacious cognitive conquest to overcome the world's "otherness" thus finds an equivalent physical expression in the imperial idea.

Sandison also devotes a chapter to Conrad; however, he does not treat *Nostromo* at length.

10 Friedrich Nietzsche, *The Use and Abuse of History*, tr. Adrian Collins (New York: Macmillan 1985), 14. In his essay, "Conrad and Nietzsche," Edward Said also discusses the complex relationship between Conrad's and Nietzsche's work: *Joseph Conrad: A Commemoration*, ed. Norman Sherry (New York: Barnes and Noble, 1976), 65–76.

11 Nietzsche, *The Use and Abuse of History*, 16.

12 Notably, in *Nostromo* there are no monumental histories featuring great women. Tales of imperialist romance reduce female characters either to objects of desire or to powerless good fairies. Antonia exemplifies the first case, in that she figures in the text primarily as the object of desire, motivating Decoud's political actions. As he explains it: "I cannot part with Antonia, therefore the one and indivisible Republic of Costaguana must be made to part with its western province. Fortunately it happens to be also a sound policy" (*N*, 200). Mrs Gould illustrates the second option, for she "resembled a good fairy, weary with a long career of well-doing, touched by the withering suspicion of the uselessness of her labours, the powerlessness of her magic" (*N*, 430).

13 Edward Said makes a similar observation: "For Mitchell, life in Costaguana has been a series of adventurous episodes, which he proudly dubs 'historical events'" (101). Said's analysis differs from mine in that he posits a need within the novel to reconcile action and record, with Mrs. Gould as the character who effects such a reconciliation (107). Said would also like to put less emphasis on the political and historical aspects of the novel and focus instead on "the real action" which he claims is "psychological and concerns man's overambitious intention to author his own world because the world as he finds it is somehow intolerable" (118) (*Beginnings: Intention and Method*, New York: Columbia University Press, 1985). In his later work, *The World, The Text, and The Critic* (Cambridge, MA: Harvard University Press, 1983), Said clarifies his position when he states: "The whole of *Nostromo* is built out of competing histories of Costaguana, each claiming to be a more perspicacious record of momentous events, each implicitly critical of other versions" (95).

14 Nietzsche, *The Use and Abuse of History*, 14.

15 Significantly, this juxtaposition of progress and correspondence is the opposite of what Hegel, as the speculative philosopher of difference, had in mind. For Hegel, history should celebrate absolute difference through dialectical thought. Yet, as we have seen, it is not difference but correspondence that Conrad reveals to be complicitous with such a philosophy of historical progress.

16 Nietzsche, *The Use and Abuse of History*, 16.

17 Conrad has this to say about Pedrito Montero:

> lodged in the garrets of the various Parisian hotels where the Costaguana Legation used to shelter its diplomatic dignity, [he] had been devouring the lighter sort of historical works in the French language . . . and had conceived the idea of an existence for himself where, like the Duc de Morny, he would associate the command of every pleasure with the conduct of political affairs and enjoy power supremely in every way. Nobody could have guessed that. And yet this was one of the immediate causes of the Monterist Revolution. (*N*, 328)

18 Nietzsche makes this point when he reminds us that "monumental history [the transcription of events] lives by false analogy" (*The Use and Abuse of History*, 16).

19 Nietzsche, *The Use and Abuse of History*, 19.

20 Nietzsche, *The Use and Abuse of History*, 24.

21 Nietzsche, *The Use and Abuse of History*, 21.

22 Roland Barthes argues the case for myth somewhat differently. According to him, "statistically, myth is on the right," by which Barthes means on the side of bourgeois oppression. As the "right" attempts to silence the oppressed by calling their narratives myths, so too does it use myth to obscure the undecidable criteria on which its own "authorised" histories are founded. Myth, then, also functions as a way to obscure the historical by obscuring memory and motive. Barthes explains how this mechanism operates when he says that "in

passing from history to nature, myth acts economically: it abolishes
the complexity of human acts, it gives them the simplicity of essences
. . . it establishes a blissful clarity: things appear to mean something
by themselves" (*Mythologies*, tr. Annette Lavers, NY: Farrar, Straus,
and Giroux, 1972, 143). The way in which the colonizers make
Nostromo into a mythical figure would certainly support Barthes's
argument.

23 For an extended discussion of the ways in which colonial discourse
   forms authorized versions of otherness, see Homi Bhabha, "Of
   Mimicry and Man: The Ambivalence of Colonial Discourse," *October
   28* (Spring 1984), 125–33.

24 Nietzsche, *The Use and Abuse of History*, 7. Nietzsche rephrases this
   point in a number of places in his text. It seems that he does not
   want the reader to forget that "forgetfulness is a property of all
   action" (6).

25 Some of Nietzsche's critics argue that he rejects history altogether. Paul
   de Man, for instance, in "Literary History and Literary Modernity,"
   insists that Nietzsche ruthlessly forgets about history, and Hayden
   White goes so far as to claim that "Nietzsche hated history more than he
   hated religion" (de Man, *Blindness and Insight*, second edition, revised,
   Minneapolis: University of Minnesota Press, 1983, 147); White, "The
   Burden of History," *Tropics of Discourse: Essays in Cultural Criticism*,
   Baltimore and London: Johns Hopkins University Press, 1978, 32).
   To be fair to Nietzsche, however, we must remember that although
   he stresses the importance of the unhistorical and notes with some
   derision that "the value we put on the historical may be merely a
   Western prejudice," he also concludes that history is indispensable:
   "History is necessary to the living man . . . in relation to his action and
   struggle, his conservatism and reverence, his suffering and his desire for
   deliverance," functions which correspond to monumental, antiquarian,
   and critical history (*The Use and Abuse of History*, 11–12).

26 Michel de Certeau, *The Practice of Everyday Life*, tr. Steven Rendall
   (Berkeley: University of California Press, 1988), 135.

27 Nietzsche, *The Use and Abuse of History*, 15.

28 Nietzsche, *The Use and Abuse of History*, 6.

29 Joseph Conrad in collaboration with Ford Madox Ford, *Romance*
   (London: J. M. Dent, 1968), 5.

30 Jean-François Lyotard, *The Postmodern Condition: A Report on Knowledge*
   tr. Geoff Bennington and Brian Massumi (Minneapolis: University of
   Minnesota Press, 1988), 81.

31 Jacques Derrida, "Outwork," *Dissemination*, tr. Barbara Johnson
   (Chicago: University of Chicago Press, 1981), 3. "*Ceci (donc) n'aura
   pas été un livre.*" ("*Hors livre,*" *La Dissémination*, Paris: Editions du
   Seuil, 1972, 9).

32 Lyotard, *The Postmodern Condition*, 81.

33 Placing terms in quotation marks, that deconstructive tic, is thus not
   a relativist insistence that things mean only as they are spoken. Rather
   it is a recognition that meaning is suspended in time, influenced by a
   context that can only be identified at a later date, afterwards.

34 Georg Lukács, *The Historical Novel*, tr. Hannah and Stanley Mitchell (Lincoln and London: University of Nebraska Press, 1983), 19.

35 Norman Sherry, *Conrad's Western World* (Cambridge: Cambridge University Press, 1971).

36 The fiction in fact displaces the status of history. The ruse here is the one Francis Barker points out in *The Tremulous Private Body* when he states that history's "greatest achievement has been to conceal its own fictionality" (London and New York: Methuen, 1984, 68).

37 See Hayden White, *Metahistory* (Baltimore: Johns Hopkins University Press, 1973); *Tropics of Discourse* and *The Content of Form: Narrative Discourse and Historical Representation* (Baltimore: Johns Hopkins University Press, 1987).

38 Jacques Derrida, "From Restricted to General Economy: A Hegelianism without Reserve," *Writing and Difference*, tr. Alan Bass (Chicago: University of Chicago Press, 1978).

39 Hegel, *The Philosophy of History*, 73. *"Der Geist, die Hülle seiner Existenz verzehrend, wandert nicht bloss in eine andere Hülle über, noch steht er nur verjüngt aus der Asche seiner Gestaltung aus, sondern er geht erhoben, verklärt ein reinerer Geist aus der selben hervor."* (*Philosophie der Geschichte, Werke*, ed. Eduard Gans, Berlin: Verlag von Dunder und Humbolt, 1840, 90–1.)

40 Fredric Jameson continues, in the modernist tradition, to deny the textuality of history; however, he reintroduces the question of textuality when he negotiates the way in which we have access to history. According to Jameson, while the *reality* of history is something outside its textual representation, our knowledge of history is not:

> history is *not* a text, not a narrative, master or otherwise, but that as an absent cause, it is inaccessible to us except in textual form, and . . . our approach to it and to the Real itself necessarily passes through its prior textualization, its narrativization in the political unconscious.

As Jameson understands it, history makes its presence known as an absence best understood not in the "realistic" texts of realism but rather in the texts that seem to miss the boat altogether – in romances like Conrad's (*The Political Unconscious*, Ithaca: Cornell University Press, 1981, 35).

41 The modernist philosophy of history, of course, thought it had answered this question. Hegel, for instance, could claim that history was the dialectical development of consciousness and that this development had come to an end by the nineteenth century (hence Hegel's belief that it was possible for him to survey all history). Later positivist historians would claim that history was the facts of the past. However, in each case, the modernist philosophy of history can only explain what history is by avoiding textuality. This may indeed show the extent to which Heidegger is a postmodernist thinker in that he claimed that the question "What is history?" could not be answered.

42 See *Of Grammatology*, tr. Gayatri Chakravorty Spivak (Chicago: University of Chicago Press, 1976), 158, and Derrida's subsequent

comment, "Afterward: Toward an Ethic of Discussion," *Limited Inc.* (Evanston, IL: Northwestern University Press, 1988), 136–8.
43 Conrad, *The Rescue* (Harmondsworth: Penguin Books, 1985), 352–3.
44 Nietzsche, *The Use and Abuse of History*, 40.

4 Heroines and hero worship: Walter Scott's uncertain women and George Eliot's uncertain romance

1 An example of the straightforward gendering of genres is Elaine Showalter's argument in *Sexual Anarchy: Gender and Culture at the Fin de Siècle* (New York: Viking Penguin, 1990). She claims that romance was originally a female genre, but that in the late nineteenth century a generic crossover took place, with boys turning to imperial romances such as Rider Haggard's or Robert Louis Stevenson's and girls seeking comfort in Eliotian realism. As Showalter puts it:

> Finally, male writers needed to find a place for themselves in Eliot's wake, to remake the high Victorian novel in masculine terms, to lead a revolt of man against Queen George. The revival of "romance" in the 1880's was a men's literary revolution intended to reclaim the kingdom of the English novel for male writers, male readers, and men's stories. (78–9)

2 For an extended discussion of the weaknesses of Scott's heros, see Alexander Welsh's *The Hero of the Waverley Novels* (New Haven: Yale University Press, 1963).
3 Examples of similar treatments of female characters are numerous throughout Scott's novels. Since there is not space to go through all of the examples here, let me just say that Scott's novels frequently conclude with the central female characters either killed (Die Vernon in *Rob Roy*, Lucy in *The Bride of Lammermoor*), confined to a convent (Flora in *Waverley*, Rebecca in *Ivanhoe*), or imprisoned in the oblivion of marriage (Rose in *Waverley*, Lilias in *Redgauntlet*, Rowena in *Ivanhoe*).
4 In phrasing it this way, I am in danger of falling back into the same binary opposition that I am trying to argue against. I want to emphasize that I am not suggesting that there is anything real or true about the equation of female/passive and male/active, merely that this mythological convention of patriarchy is at play within Scott's novels and upset by an excess of romance.
5 Jacques Lacan, "Guiding Remarks for a Congress on Feminine Sexuality," *Feminine Sexuality: Jacques Lacan and the école freudienne*, tr. Jacqueline Rose (New York: W. W. Norton, 1985), 97. I would also like to stress the ways in which Lacan's remark is highly problematic. First, he conceives of homosexuality as the assumption of "putting on" the opposite sex: lesbians are women masquerading as men, while gay men are masquerading as women. Second, in the context of the remark, Lacan opposes all feminine homosexuality ("such women") to "transsexual men." In so doing, Lacan avoids any discussion of the

NOTES

various forms of homosexuality (distinctions between transsexual and transvestite, for example) and instead prefers to collapse all possibilities into two convenient categories. Thus, in referring to Lacan's remark in this context, I am not trying to suggest that Lacan articulated the truth about homosexuality. Rather, my juxtaposition of Scott and Lacan is intended to reveal the ways in which each embrace patriarchal assumptions about gender and sexuality.

6 This is much the same point Luce Irigaray makes when she discusses femininity. According to Irigaray, "'femininity' is a role, an image, a value, imposed upon women by male systems of representation. In this masquerade of femininity, the woman loses herself, and loses herself by playing on her femininity" ("The Power of Discourse," *This Sex Which Is Not One*, tr. Catherine Porter, Ithaca: Cornell University Press, 1985, 84). The masquerade of femininity can, however, be used by women in order to subvert the patriarchal system of gender roles. Irigaray suggests a subversive strategy of *mimicry*, where "one must assume the feminine role deliberately," for "to play with mimesis is thus, for a woman, to try to recover the place of her exploitation by discourse, without allowing herself to be simply reduced to it" (76). My argument continues Irigaray's in that it also suggests the way in which all gender roles combine masquerade and mimicry, even if these combinations do not assume symmetrical shapes. The opposition of masculine and feminine is brought into question through the possibility of a plurality of genders which cannot be named as such. For other illuminating discussions of the relationship between masquerade and gender identity, see: Joan Riviere, "Womanliness as Masquerade," *Formations of Fantasy*, ed. Victor Burgin, James Donald, Cora Kaplan (London: Methuen, 1986), first published in *International Journal of Psychoanalysis*, vol. 10 (1929); Jacques Lacan, "The Meaning of the Phallus," *Feminine Sexuality*; and Judith Butler, *Gender Trouble* (London and New York: Routledge, 1990).

7 The distinction I am elaborating here could be understood in the terms that Irigaray proposes when she speaks of the way in which a mechanics of solids has been elaborated in favour of an extended exploration of the complications of the "mechanics" of fluids: "The 'Mechanics' of Fluids," *This Sex Which Is Not One*, 106–18.

8 Flora's role is postmodern here not so much because she is unable to act, as because action takes place as the shifting of a signifier between relay stations.

9 Deirdre David, *Intellectual Women and Victorian Patriarchy: Harriet Martineau, Elizabeth Barrett Browning, George Eliot* (Ithaca: Cornell University Press, 1987), 165.

10 Deirdre David, *Intellectual Women and Victorian Patriarchy*, 177.

11 The discussion to which I refer is the often cited chapter 17 of Eliot's *Adam Bede*.

12 As Cottom puts it, for Eliot "romance is the falsity of individual conflict which must be recognized so that realism may be recognized as [the] social truth." For all the recognizing that is going on in this passage, the way in which Eliot valued romance is not one of the

things that Cottom sees (*Social Figures: George Eliot, Social History, and Literary Representation*, Minneapolis: University of Minnesota Press, 1987, 138).

13 George Eliot, "Silly Novels by Lady Novelists," *Essays of George Eliot*, ed. Thomas Pinney (New York: Columbia University Press, 1963), 315.
14 George Eliot, "Silly Novels by Lady Novelists," 321, 316.
15 Catherine Gallagher persuasively argues the case for Eliot's support of an Arnoldian notion of culture. Her strong example is the case of *Felix Holt*. As Gallagher points out, "Felix, as a representative of the Arnoldian best self, signifies a culture and a politics that exist on a single plane of differentiation, a plane on which . . . politics and culture represent only one another" (*The Industrial Reformation of English Fiction: Social Discourse and Narrative Form, 1832–1867*, Chicago: University of Chicago Press, 1985, 248).
16 George Eliot, "*Westward Ho!* and Constance Herbert," *Essays of George Eliot*, 128.
17 Gordon Haight, *George Eliot: A Biography* (1968) (New York: Penguin Books, 1986), 7.
18 *The George Eliot Letters* vol. VII, ed. Gordon S. Haight (New Haven and London: Yale University Press, 1978), 65. Hereafter referred to as *Letters*.
19 For Lewes's comment see *Letters*, III, 295
20 *Letters*, III, 339. Felicia Bonaparte somewhat curiously argues that it is because Eliot was moving toward *epic* that she called *Romola* a "historical romance" (*The Triptych and the Cross: The Central Myths of George Eliot's Poetic Imagination*, New York: New York University Press, 1979, 14).
21 Haight, *George Eliot*. Haight is referring to material from George Eliot's journals (4, Aug. 21, 17 Nov. 1861).
22 *Letters*, III, 340.
23 *Letters*, III, 474.
24 In calling Eliot a modernist, I mean specifically a philosophical modernist, someone who is concerned with enlightenment. Literary modernism, though explicitly post-Victorian in the formulations of Ezra Pound, is a formal shift within the modernist project (as T. S. Eliot's relation to Arnold hints). Literary modernism is the point at which the striving for liberation becomes an explicitly *formal* activity in literature. Liberation is not a matter of adjusting content so much as of breaking forms.

   George Eliot's modernism lies in her understanding of the task of literary representation as a social project. Perhaps the most coherent argument for such a social rationality of the public sphere in our own day is Jurgen Habermas's account of communicative rationality, summarized in "Modernity: An Incomplete Project" in *The Anti-Aesthetic*, ed. Hal Foster (Seattle: Bay Press, 1983), 3–15.
25 *Letters*, V, 174–5. Eliot refers here to the Florentine joke in chapter 16 of *Romola*. The reference Eliot makes to Shakespeare and musical glasses is actually from William Goldsmith's *The Vicar of Wakefield*

194

(*Collected Works of Oliver Goldsmith*, vol. IV, ed. Arthur Friedman, Oxford: Oxford University Press, 1966, 54): "They would talk of nothing but high life, and high lived company; and other fashionable topics, such as pictures, taste, Shakespear [sic], and the musical glasses" ("musical glasses" refers to a water harp or glass harmonica).

26 George Eliot, *Romola* (Harmondsworth: Penguin Books, 1981), 90. Hereafter cited parenthetically within my text as *R*. It is important to note that from the very beginning of the novel, Eliot calls our attention to the problems of historical perception and the degree to which inaccuracies inevitably establish themselves in the historical "scene." Speaking of the fourteenth-century "Shade" who "has been permitted to revisit" Florence, Eliot notes that:

> For though he misses the seventy or more towers that once surmounted the walls, and encircled the city as with a regal diadem, his eyes will not dwell on that blank; they are drawn irresistibly to the unique tower springing, like a tall flower-stem drawn toward the sun, from the square turreted mass of the Old Palace in the very heart of the city – the tower that looks none the worse for the four centuries that have passed since he used to walk under it. (*R*, 44–5)

27 Neil Hertz, "Recognizing Casaubon", *The End of the Line: Essays on Psychoanalysis and the Sublime* (New York: Columbia University Press, 1985), 87.

28 George Eliot, *Daniel Deronda* (Harmondsworth: Penguin Books, 1983), 469. Hereafter cited parenthetically within my text as *DD*.

29 The culture of fellow-feeling is explained thus by Romola in one of her tutorials with the young Lillo:

> It is only a poor sort of happiness that could ever come by caring very much about our own narrow pleasures. We can only have the highest happiness, such as goes along with being a great man, by having wide thoughts, and much feeling for the rest of the world as well as ourselves. (*R*, 674)

30 Deirdre David makes a similar point when she argues that "in *Romola*, Eliot replaces female desire for autonomy with a coercive discourse of fidelity to community" (*Intellectual Women and Victorian Patriarchy*, 192).

31 Deirdre David, *Intellectual Women and Victorian Patriarchy*, 253.

32 *Letters*, V, p. 170. Haight relates Eliot's activities on this day and provides a brief explanation of Eliot's involvement with the centenary festival (*George Eliot*, 439). With regard to her health, Eliot also remarked to John Blackwood, that the journey might cause her to "break down and die without finishing [*Middlemarch*]" (*Letters*, V, 164).

33 *Letters*, V, 175.

34 *Letters*, I, 24.

35 Laurie Langbauer makes a similar point when she argues that in *Adam Bede* "Eliot may need to shatter Hetty's romance building in order to

preserve the very legend of George Eliot, a self carefully constructed through her novels and other writings" (*Women and Romance: The Consolations of Gender in the English Novel*, Ithaca: Cornell University Press, 1990, 210). Langbauer makes this observation as part of a longer argument that draws connections between Eliot's use of detail and her employment of romance.

36 Quoted in Haight, *George Eliot*, 319. See also *Letters*, III, 240.

37 Haight, *George Eliot*, p. 39. Haight is quoting J. W. Cross's *George Eliot's Life as Related in Her Letters and Journals* (new edition Edinburgh and London, 1887, 48).

38 Eliot provides a literary treatment of this biographical element in the figure of the Princess Halm-Eberstein in *Daniel Deronda*. When women have unorthodox ambitions, they become not quite human, like the Princess Halm-Eberstein, Deronda's mother (*DD*, 687–8). In their brief meeting, she explains to him that:

> Every woman is supposed to have the same set of motives, or else to be a monster. I am not a monster, but I have not felt exactly what other women feel – or say they feel, for fear of being thought unlike others. When you reproach me in your heart for sending you away from me, you mean that I ought to say I felt about you as other women say they feel about their children. I did *not* feel that. I was glad to be freed from you. But I did well for you, and I gave you your father's fortune. (*DD*, 691)

The Princess "wanted to live a large life" (*DD*, 693), and tried to realise this desire through an acting career, relinquishing motherhood, and turning away from Judaism. She is the figure in the novel who most overtly seems to fit romance codes, yet her aspirations deviate from romance closure. In a sense, her surreptitious romance exposes and rebels against the myth of motherhood in exploring the possibilities of female desire. As she puts it, "Had I not a rightful claim to be something more than a mere daughter and mother?" (*DD*, 728).

39 George Eliot, *Middlemarch* (Harmondsworth: Penguin Books, 1983), 167. Hereafter cited parenthetically within my text as *M*.

40 Lydgate "used to know Scott's poems by heart" (*M*, 304). Trumbull reads from Mary's copy of *Anne of Geierstein* and comments on *Ivanhoe* (*M*, 346–7). He also makes general claims for Scott's merits earlier in the novel.

41 My argument suggests that we should pay close attention to Barbara Hardy's remarks about the formal problems in *Middlemarch*. According to Hardy, "*Middlemarch* has often been praised as a great realistic novel, and, more latterly, as a triumph of unified organisation, but both its realism and its unity are flawed" ("Implication and Incompleteness in George Eliot's *Middlemarch*," *The Victorian Novel: Modern Essays in Criticism*, ed. Ian Watt, Oxford and New York: Oxford University Press, 1971, 292).

42 George Eliot, *The Mill on the Floss* (Harmondsworth: Penguin Books, 1982), 362, emphasis added. Hereafter cited parenthetically within my text as *MF*.

43 It is possible to extend the parallel with Scott to include Eliot's tendency to feminise male characters in *The Mill on the Floss*. While Tom attends school he "became more like a girl" (*MF*, 210); Philip Wakem has hair that "waved and curled at the ends like a girl's" (*MF*, 234), is "by nature half feminine in sensitiveness" (*MF*, 431), and is also brought up "like a girl" (*MF*, 537).

44 It seems somewhat symptomatic of this that when Mary Jacobus discusses at length the significance of Maggie's reading she does not consider at all the fact that Maggie reads romances. Jacobus's focus is on the "serious" literature by men – the Eton Grammar, Thomas à Kempis. Romance, it would seem, is not the stuff of serious literary criticism either. See Mary Jacobus, *Reading Woman: Essays in Feminist Criticism* (London and New York: Methuen, 1986), 62–79.

45 In "Realism and the Ends of Feminism," Penny Boumelha makes a similar point when she argues that "the dammed-up energy created by the frustrated ambitions and desires, intellectual and sexual, of the woman is so powerful that it cannot be contained with the forms of mimesis." According to Boumelha, Eliot may refuse romance in her conclusion, but nonetheless, she tests "the potentialities and limits of the realist mode for the representation of the desires and aspirations of women" (*Grafts*, ed. Susan Sheridan, London and New York: Verso, 1988, 86–90).

46 Maggie bears some resemblance to Scott's famous reader of romances – Lucy Ashton in the *Bride of Lammermoor* (Edinburgh: Adam and Charles Black, 1886). Scott is careful to have us understand Lucy as a reader of romance, as the narrator reminds us:

> We have described her in the outset of our story as of a romantic disposition, delighting in tales of love and wonder, and readily identifying herself with the situation of those legendary heroines, with whose adventures, for want of better reading, her memory had become stocked. (284)

At first we are led to believe that the result of Lucy's extensive reading of romance is to mold her into a submissive and silly creature – the perfect bride. But as the novel progresses, Lucy proves anything but submissive, and on her wedding night she attempts to murder her less than perfect husband. Unfortunately for Lucy, it is her husband who lives and she who dies of convulsions. Like Maggie, Lucy must die before the transgressive force of her dark romance can be represented.

47 Dorothea has "dark-brown hair parted over her brow and coiled massively behind" (*M*, 114).

48 We may compare Gwendolen Harleth's self-seclusion at the conclusion of *Daniel Deronda*. Whereas Daniel sails into the sunset, on his voyage to Palestine, Gwendolen remains in England – her future more uncertain and more likely to end in cultural obscurity. Consider her final letter to Deronda:

> Do not think of me sorrowfully on your wedding-day. I have

remembered your words – that I may live to be one of the best of women, who make others glad that they were born. I do not yet see how that can be, but you know better than I. If it ever comes true, it will be because you helped me. I only thought of myself, and I made you grieve. It hurts me now to think of your grief. You must not grieve any more for me. It is better – it shall be better with me because I have known you. (*DD*, 882)

49 A minority, furthermore, concerning which Eliot elsewhere expressed frankly racist opinions, as in her letter to John Sibree, the translator of Hegel's *Philosophy of History*. In this letter Eliot's remarks are chilling. Speaking out against D'Israeli's theory of races, she argues that: "Extermination up to a certain point seems to be the law for the inferior races – for the rest, fusion both for physical and moral ends. . . . Everything *specifically* Jewish is of a low grade" (*Letters*, I, 246–7). I wish to thank Sabina Sawhney of Bryn Mawr College for calling my attention to this letter.

50 J. Hillis Miller also suggests that *Middlemarch* undermines its own claims for an organic community, but Miller's focus is on optics rather than epic. According to Miller, "the presence of several incompatible [optic] models brings into the open the arbitrary and partial character of each and so ruins the claim of the narrator to have a total, unified, and impartial vision." See "Optic and Semiotic in *Middlemarch*," *The Worlds of Victorian Fiction*, ed. Jerome Buckley (Cambridge, MA: Harvard University Press, 1975), 144. My reading, like Miller's, also challenges Sandra Gilbert's and Susan Gubar's argument about Eliot's work. For them "Eliot dramatizes the virtues of a uniquely female culture based on supportive camaraderie instead of masculine competition." See *The Madwoman in the Attic: The Woman Writer and the Nineteenth-Century Literary Imagination* (New Haven and London: Yale University Press, 1979), 498.

5 A postscript which should have been a preface: theory's romance

1 Jacques Derrida, *Of Grammatology*, tr. Gayatri Chakravorty Spivak (Baltimore: Johns Hopkins University Press, 1976), 158.

2 See especially: Gérard Genette, *Narrative Discourse: An Essay in Method*, tr. Jane E. Lewin (Ithaca: Cornell University Press, 1980); and Vladimir Propp, *Theory and History of Folklore*, tr. Ariadna Y. Martin and Richard P. Martin (Minneapolis: University of Minnesota Press, 1984).

3 Jacques Derrida, *The Post Card: From Socrates to Freud and Beyond*, tr. Alan Bass (Chicago: University of Chicago Press, 1987), 175; *La Carte postale: de Socrate à Freud et au-delà* (Paris: Flammarion, 1980). Hereafter cited parenthetically within my text as *PC*. Page numbers refer to the English edition.

4 Kathy Acker, *In Memoriam to Identity* (New York: Grove Weidenfeld, 1990), 141. Hereafter cited parenthetically within my text as *IMI*.

5 Other considerations of the relationship between theory and seduction

include: Jean Baudrillard, *De la séduction* (Paris: Editions galilée, 1979); Jane Gallop, "French Theory and the Seduction of Feminism," *Men in Feminism*, ed. Alice Jardine and Paul Smith (New York and London: Methuen, 1987); Ellen Rooney, *Seductive Reasoning: Pluralism as the Problematic of Contemporary Literary Theory* (Ithaca: Cornell University Press, 1989).

6 See especially Georg Lukács, *History and Class Consciousness: Studies in Marxist Dialectics*, tr. Rodney Livingstone (Cambridge, MA: MIT Press, 1985); and *The Historical Novel*, tr. Hannah and Stanley Mitchell (Lincoln and London: University of Nebraska Press, 1983).

7 See Louis Althusser, "Ideology and the State Apparatuses (Notes Towards an Investigation)," *Lenin and Philosophy*, tr. Ben Brewster (New York and London: Monthly Review Press, 1971); and Louis Althusser and Etienne Balibar, *Reading Capital*, tr. Ben Brewster (London: New Left Books, 1977).

8 An ideological break occurs when ideology reaches critical self-knowledge, so that ideological subjects become scientists capable of symptomatic readings. The prime example for Althusser is the later Marx, the Marx of *Capital*, who provides a theory of historical materialism that allows the critical reader to overcome the limitations of Marx's own historically determined perspective with the aid of principles drawn from *Capital* itself. Thus, the empirical inadequacies of *Capital* are transcended by the theoretical second or symptomatic reading which the text proposes for itself.

9 The impact of Mulvey's "Visual Pleasure and Narrative Cinema" is perhaps best attested to by the frequency with which it has been anthologized since its first appearance in *Screen* 16, no. 3 (Autumn 1975).

10 The resistance of haircare to revolutionary Marxist analysis appears also in the apocryphal story of Lenin in Geneva prior to the Russian Revolution, when he supposedly spent as much time chasing a cure for baldness around the pharmacies as in the library studying Marx.

11 My reference here is to the 1990 Texas gubernatorial candidate, Clayton Williams, who in a press conference remarked that Texas weather is like rape: "If it's inevitable, just relax and enjoy it." That Williams lost the election to Ann Richards bears remembering. Her victory slogan read: "A woman's place is in the Dome." For a fuller account of the incident, see Jan Jarboe, "Clayton Williams: Onward to the Past," *Texas Monthly*, October 1990.

12 See Jacques Derrida, *Spurs: Nietzsche's Styles/Eperons: Les Styles de Nietzsche*, tr. Barbara Harlow (Chicago: University of Chicago Press, 1979). Along these lines, John Caputo also claims that for Derrida "woman spells the end of hermeneutics" (*Radical Hermeneutics*, Bloomington: Indiana University Press, 1987, 157).

13 See for instance: Sandra M. Gilbert and Susan Gubar, *The Madwoman in the Attic: The Woman Writer and the Nineteenth-Century Literary Imagination* (New Haven: Yale University Press, 1979); Kate Millet, *Sexual Politics* (London: Virago, 1977); Ellen Moers, *Literary Women: The Great Writers* (New York: Doubleday, 1977); Elaine Showalter, *A Literature*

of Their Own: British Women Novelists from Brontë to Lessing (Princeton: Princeton University Press, 1977). For an extended discussion of the relationships between Anglo-American feminist criticism and French feminist theory, see Toril Moi, *Sexual/Textual Politics: Feminist Literary Theory* (New York and London: Methuen, 1985).

14 In his translation of *The Post Card*, Alan Bass includes an excellent explanation of the various meanings of "envoi" on which Derrida plays: "Glossary," *The Post Card*, xx–xxi.

15 Jacques Derrida, "Envois," *The Post Card*, 21.

16 Hans-Georg Gadamer, "The Universality of the Hermeneutical Problem," *Philosophical Hermeneutics*, tr. David E. Linge (Berkeley: University of California Press, 1976), 16–17.

17 In this context, it seems significant that Derrida reconsiders the union of Hermes + Aphrodite (*PC*, 145).

18 *La poste* refers to the postal system (the mail is female), while *le poste* refers to a position, be it a military post or a professional appointment.

19 Kathy Acker, *My Death, My Life By Pier Paolo Pasolini, Literal Madness* (1984) (New York: Grove Press, 1989), 180. Hereafter cited parenthetically within my text as *MDML*.

20 I am referring here, of course, to Habermas's essay "Modernity – An Incomplete Project," *The Anti-Aesthetic*, ed. Hal Foster (Seattle, WA: Bay Press, 1983), 3–15. In the course of this extended discussion of modernity and its relationship to postmodernism, Habermas never mentions a single female author, nor does he consider gender an issue for either modernity or postmodernism. The question of gender is left to the signature of the female translator (Seyla Ben-Habib), which appears at the end of the essay.

21 Kathy Acker, *Don Quixote* (New York: Grove Press, 1986), 134. Hereafter cited parenthetically within my text as *DQ*.

22 Kathy Acker, *Empire of the Senseless* (New York: Grove Press, 1988), 179–80. Hereafter cited parenthetically within my text as *ES*.

23 Kathy Acker, "Realism for the Cause of Future Revolution," *Art After Modernism: Rethinking Representation*, ed. Brian Wallis (New York: Godine, 1984), 33.

24 Kathy Acker, "Realism for the Cause of Future Revolution," 33.

25 Jacques Derrida, "Restitutions of the truth in pointing [*pointure*]", *The Truth in Painting* (1978), tr. Geoff Bennington and Ian McLeod (Chicago: University of Chicago Press, 1987), 256.

26 Another example of Derrida's insistence on the multiplicity of gendered positions would be his remarks to Christie V. McDonald in what is now a widely cited interview ("Choreographies," *Diacritics*, Vol. 12, no. 2, (Summer 1982). This rather brief attempt to explain the complexity of the effect of "polysexual signatures" has been dismissed by some critics as simply utopian. I would argue that Derrida's more extended discussion in "Envois" makes such a dismissal much more difficult.

27 Gregory L. Ulmer, *Applied Grammatology: Post(e)-Pedagogy from Jacques Derrida to Joseph Beuys* (Baltimore and London: Johns Hopkins University Press, 1985), 131–2.

28 For a general account of the philosophical problems of reproducibility for the thought of original creation, see Rosalind Krauss, "The Originality of the Avant-Garde: A Postmodern Repetition," *Art after Modernism*, ed. Brian Wallis (Boston: Godine, 1984). On surrogate motherhood, see Katha Pollitt, "When Is A Mother Not a Mother?", *The Nation*, vol. 252, no. 23 (December 23, 1990).

29 Kathy Acker, *Great Expectations* (New York: Grove Press, 1982). Hereafter cited parenthetically within my text as *GE*.

30 Kathy Acker, *Florida, Literal Madness* (New York: Grove Press, 1989).

31 Glenn A. Harper makes a similar point when he argues that the result of Acker's plagiarism is "the breakup of the illusory self-centeredness of language and, as in feminist appropriation, the refusal of the rules of art-as-commodity" ("The Subversive Power of Sexual Difference in the Work of Kathy Acker," *SubStance*, 54, no. 3, 1987, 47). Larry McCaffery takes a somewhat different line on Acker's style, comparing it to punk music ("Kathy Acker and 'Punk' Aesthetics," *Breaking the Sequence: Women's Experimental Fiction*, ed. Ellen Friedman and Miriam Fuchs, Princeton: Princeton University Press, 1989, 215–30).

32 In making this connection between Acker and Derrida, here I think particularly of Derrida's remark in "Envois": "What counts then is that it is still up to us to exhaust language" (*PC*, 56).

33 Derrida argues for eighteenth-century modernity as the moment in the history of metaphysics when the defence of logocentrism is most explicitly carried forward against the threat of an awareness of the materiality of writing:

> What threatens indeed is writing. It is not an accidental and haphazard threat; it reconciles within a single historical system the projects of *pasigraphy*, the discovery of non-European scripts, or at any rate the massive progress of techniques of *deciphering*, and finally the idea of a *general science of language and writing*. Against all these pressures a battle is then declared. "Hegelianism" will be its finest scar. (*Of Grammatology*, 99)

34 For Derrida's discussion of the relationship between writing and violence, see "The Violence of the Letter" in *Of Grammatology*, especially pp. 112–13.

35 Peter Bricklebank, "Blood and Guts in High School," *Library Journal* 109 (September 23, 1983), 1769. The extent to which Bricklebank fails to understand Acker's work is perhaps most evident when he criticizes the illustrations in *Blood and Guts* for not being "well drawn." Unbeknownst to Bricklebank, the crudeness of the drawings is precisely the point.

36 For a detailed treatment of the way in which the interpretative practices of the rape system, in situating woman as a subject, mark her as guilty participant in any rape to which she is subjected, see Judith Butler "Feminism and the Question of Postmodernism," unpublished paper, Proceedings of the Greater Philadelphia Philosophy Consortium, September 22, 1990.

37 Judith Butler, "Feminism and the Question of Postmodernism," 17–18. Butler earlier called attention to the problem of the subject when she pointed out that "Foucault's critique of the discourse on desire, on the figure of the 'subject of desire,' does well to remind us that desire is a name that not only accounts for an experience, but determines that experience as well, that the subject of desire may well be a fiction useful to a variety of regulative strategies" (*Subjects of Desire: Hegelian Reflections in Twentieth-Century France*, New York: Columbia University Press, 1987, 238).

38 See especially: Edward Said, "Criticism Between Culture and System," *The World, the Text, and the Critic* (Cambridge, MA: Harvard University Press, 1983); Terry Eagleton, "Frère Jacques: The Politics of Deconstruction," *Against the Grain* (London: Verso, 1986); Seyla Benhabib, "Epistemologies of Postmodernism: A Rejoinder to Jean-François Lyotard," *New German Critique*, no. 33, 1984.

39 See Juliet Mitchell, *Psychoanalysis and Feminism* (New York: Pantheon Books, 1974).

40 See Jane Gallop, *The Daughter's Seduction: Feminism and Psychoanalysis* (Ithaca: Cornell University Press, 1982).

INDEX

Abrams, M.H.: *A Glossary of Literary Terms* 4, 175 n4
Acker, Kathy 4, 13, 140, 141, 143, 146, 149, 160, 161, 167, 173; and destabilization 154–5; and plagiarism 162, 163–4; and rape 144, 157, 167, 168–72; and realism 156, 158; and sexual desire as pre-eminently fictional 143–4; and sexual economy 148; *Blood and Guts in High School* 169; *Don Quixote* 154–5, 156–7, 162; *Empire of the Senseless* 155; *Florida* 162; *Great Expectations* 18, 103, 162, 163–4; *In Memoriam to Identity* 143–4, 158, 161, 168–9, 173; *My Death, My Life by Pier Paolo Pasolini* 153–4, 158, 162, 164–5, 168; *Variety* 169
Adorno, Theodor 15, 50, 177 n27
Althusser, Louis 144, 145–6; and critical self-knowledge 199 n8
anachronism 12, 13, 35–6, 141, 162; and Eco 31–2, 35, 119; and Eliot 118–21; and Scott 35, 69–71, 119
Arnold, Matthew: and George Eliot 116
Austen, Jane 144

Barthes, Roland 147, 182–3 n19, 189–90 n22
Baudrillard, Jean 147

Benhabib, Seyla 172
Blackwood, John: and *Romola* 117, 118
Borges, Jorge Luis 1; and magical realism 30
Bricklebank, Peter: and failure to understand 169, 201 n35
Brooks, Cleanth 37, 44; and irony in New Criticism 38–40; and "The Well Wrought Urn" 37
Butler Judith 172, 193 n6; "Feminism and the Question of Postmodernism" 201 n36

Calvino, Italo: *If on a winter's night a traveler* 17–18
Cartland, Barbara 1, 5, 47; and Acker 155; and Eco 46, 48; and Kruger 175 n1
Caserio, Robert 187 n3
Chase, Richard 6–7, 176 n9
Cixous, Hélène 103
Cockshut, A. O. 59
Conrad, Joseph 4, 13; *Nostromo* 15, 18, 50, 80–101, 103, 189, n17; and critical history 91–2; and the Hegelian notion of progress 85–6; and ironic temporality 84–5; and myth and legend 92, 189–90 n22; and temporal progress 83; and the use of monumental history 87–9, 188 n12; *The Rescue* 101
Cottom, Daniel 115;

203

150–1; "The Universality of the Problem" and hermeneutics 150–1
Gallop, Jane: *The Daughter's Seduction* 173
Genette, Gerard 142
Gilbert, Sandra 103, 148, 198 n50
Gilliam, Terry: and *Brazil* 95
Gubar, Susan 103, 148, 198 n50

Habermas, Jürgen 142; and communicative rationality 194–5 n24; and gender 200 n20; and Harlequins 154
Haight, Gordon 117
haircare and Lenin 199 n10; and shampoo-consumerism in East Germany 146
Hardy, Barbara: *The Victorian Novel* 196–7 n41
Harlequins: and Chrétien de Troyes 5; and Habermas 154; and love-making 5; and romance 1, 17; and Rosalind Coward 20; and Scott 106
Hassan, Ihab: and postmodern irony 182 n17; and postmodernism as anarchic 21, 177 n15
Hegel, Georg Wilhelm Friedrich 98; *The Philosophy of History* 85, 86, 89, 188 n8; and imperialism 85–6, 89, 188 n9
Heidegger, Martin 149, 152, 165
Hertz, Neil 120
historical correspondence 52–3; and imperialism 82; and modernist history 69, 80–1, 84–5; and *The Post Card* 149; and the postal services 53
Hutcheon, Linda 18–19, 178 n31

identity: as concept 150, 158–60, 163, 171–2; and gender 102–4, 111–12, 113–14; as politics 22–3, 148, 173–4
imperialism 22; and Conrad 80–2, 89–91; and Hegel 85–6, 89; and historical correspondence

82; and history 82–3, 92; and Nietzsche 87–9, 90; and Scott 67
Irigaray, Luce: and femininity as masquerade 193 n6
Iser, Wolfgang: *The Implied Reader* 185 n20

Jacobus, Mary: *Reading Woman: Essays in Feminist Criticism* 197 n44
James, Henry 6–7, 176 n11
Jameson, Fredric: and history 191 n41; and pastiche 181 n9; and politics of romance 19–20, 21, 98, 175 n5; and postmodernism and politics 179–80 n42, 183 n25;
Jencks, Charles 9; *What is Postmodernism?* 177 n16

Kruger, Barbara: *Love for Sale* 1, 175 n1

Lacan, Jacques 111; and homosexuality 192–3 n5
Leavis, F.R. 7, 51, 134
Lewes, George Henry 117, 118, 125
Lukács, Georg 51, 59, 96, 144; and irony 181 n13; and Ranke 184 n12
Lyotard, Jean-François: 50, 73, 95; and questioning of master narratives 177 n20; *The Postmodern Condition* 9–10, 12, 186 n28; "Rewriting Modernity" 11–12
Lytton, Bulwer: *Paul Clifford* 5; *Rienzi* 117

Meredith, George 8; *Diana of the Crossways* 17, 178 n28; and Diana as "Heroine of Reality" 8
Miller, J. Hillis: "Optic and Semiotic in *Middlemarch*" 198 n50
Millet, Kate 148
Mitchell, Juliet 173
Modleski, Tania: *Loving With a Vengeance* 179 n38
Moers, Ellen 148